DESPERATELY SEEKING SELF-IMPROVEMENT

DESPERATELY SEEKING SELF-IMPROVEMENT

A YEAR INSIDE THE OPTIMIZATION MOVEMENT

CARL CEDERSTRÖM AND ANDRÉ SPICER

OR Books

New York · London

Published for the book trade by OR Books in partnership with Counterpoint Press. Distributed to the trade by Publishers Group West.

All rights information: rights@orbooks.com

First printing 2017

Cataloging-in-Publication data is available from the Library of Congress. A catalog record for this book is available from the British Library.

ISBN 978-1-944869-39-7

Text design by Under|Over. Typeset by AarkMany Media, Chennai, India.

10 9 8 7 6 5 4 3 2 1

All the events described in this book are real. The names are real and so are the dates and the timeline, except in a few rare instances, where they have been changed to improve readability or preserve anonymity.

PREFACE

THE MODERATOR: *We have Carl Cederström and André Spicer below the line with us for the next hour. I encourage readers to post their questions now.*

It was the second day of January 2017, and readers were responding to an article we had just published in *The Guardian* about our yearlong experiment.

EMMI26: *Please tell me this is a spoof.*

André was at home in London, in front of his laptop, his newborn son sleeping next to his desk. *No, this is a very serious research project,* he wrote back in the comments field. Carl, sitting in his kitchen in Stockholm, tried to make the same point.

Almost exactly one year earlier, on January 1, 2016, we embarked on something that many *Guardian* readers clearly regarded as insane. We spent one year testing everything that the self-improvement industry had to offer with the plan to write it up in a book: a book which you now hold in your hands. In pursuit of a coherent structure for the project, we agreed on twelve areas of self-improvement, one for each month of the year. We began, in January, with productivity. Then, in successive months, we dealt with the body, the brain, relationships, and spirituality. During the summer months we focused on sex, pleasure, and creativity. In the fall, we optimized money, morality, and attention. The final month was dedicated to meaning, in the hope that we could come to understand the deeper motivations behind this project.

LITTLE_RED: *Oh dear, it all sounds like lots of hard work.*

Over the year, we spent thousands of hours and tens of thousands of dollars test-driving self-improvement techniques. We hacked our brains, used smart drugs, experimented with sex toys, and underwent plastic surgery. We talked to psychics and life-coaches, danced naked with unknown men, attended motivational seminars, participated in professional weight-lifting competitions, and submitted ourselves to therapy.

MRFLABBYBUM: *I am struck by the lack of an underlying and unifying principle to all this.*

Which was a fair point. But then what, beyond the elusive claim to make yourself better, is the "underlying principle" of self-improvement? A glance at the endless stream of advice pouring out each year reveals that this $10 billion industry is by no means unified. If anything, it is confusing and conflicted. We decided this was something we were happy to mirror in our own book. For each month, we set new goals. These could either be concrete and measurable, like memorizing 1,000 digits of pi, or abstract and elusive, like having a spiritual experience. To achieve our goals, we tried out a dizzying array of methods, from mindfulness apps to the "Master Cleanse." We selected these methods because they were popular, not because they were scientifically credible.

It was the Stoic philosopher Epictetus, more than two millennia ago, who first insisted that opinions matter more than real events. Since then, advice on how to live our lives has poured out in a steady torrent. And why not? Who doesn't want a better life? In some ways self-improvement is like drinking: it is a perfect consolation in bad times. And a great companion to good times.

Take the commercial boom of self-improvement in the 1930s. It is no coincidence that it emerged in the wake of the Great Depression in the United States. In *Think and Grow Rich*, from 1937, Napoleon Hill offered a calming theory, saying the Depression was merely an effect of people's fears and opinions. Dale Carnegie's *How to Win Friends and Influence People*, from the year before, offered similarly hopeful advice: smile. It would seem that, in a time of economic and social depression, when people had nothing to rely on except themselves, self-improvement was an attractive proposition.

But self-improvement was no less popular in the more prosperous 1970s. After three decades of economic growth, large portions of the American population had been liberated from poverty. Never before had so many enjoyed so much money and so much freedom. But instead of using these riches to improve society, as Tom Wolfe observed in a classic essay from 1976, they spent it on improving themselves, plunging "straight toward what has become the alchemical dream of the Me Decade." Millions flocked to self-improvement seminars. Between 1971 and 1984, 700,000 people underwent three days of EST (Erhard Seminar Training), where they learned to put themselves first, recognize that they were fully responsible for their own fates, understand that there were no victims in the world, and realize that they created their own reality.

Self-improvement today is so integrated into our society that it is hard to know where it begins and ends. Yoga is taught at elementary schools. Mindfulness is used in prisons. Life-coaching is promoted as a way of combating poverty. And self-help has now moved into the White House: Donald Trump's first marriage was officiated by Norman Vincent Peale, the father of positive thinking.

Times change, and self-improvement trends change along with them. The old gurus have been replaced by new ones like Tony

Robbins and Tim Ferriss. Old trends like aerobics and faking it until you make it have been replaced by CrossFit and life-logging. The only constant is the promise that you can change your life. All we need to do is to stop worrying and start believing in ourselves, without being concerned too much about modesty. As true now as it was then, stories of transformation require no subtlety. While Napoleon Hill bragged about miraculously curing his son's muteness through thought-power, today's self-help gurus boast about their achievements, whether they're learning new languages, warding off disease by taking ice baths, mastering new martial arts techniques, or making a fortune investing in Silicon Valley start-ups.

Meanwhile, comments kept pouring in from *Guardian* readers.

LORDBADGER: *It seems to me you tried a bunch of things for at most a month, when any one of these are things that people can spend a lifetime trying to master.*

We received this comment more than once. Some people might spend a lifetime mastering one thing, whether it's becoming more productive or getting the perfect body, but most people spend their lives hopping from one technique to the next, failing to master anything. The only reasonable explanation for why self-improvement continues to grow year after year is that people restlessly keep trying new advice, irrespective of whether their previous attempts have worked. If you browse through the self-help section in a bookshop, you will find guidance on everything from improving your relationship and sex life to becoming smarter and more muscular. And they often promise quick results, whether in two weeks or twenty-four hours.

In a consumerist society, we are not meant to buy one pair of jeans and then be satisfied. The same goes for self-improvement. We are not expected to improve only one area of our lives. We are encouraged to upgrade *all* parts of our life, all at once. We should be fitter, happier, healthier, wealthier, smarter, calmer, and more productive—all at once, all today. And we are under pressure to show that we know how to lead the perfect life.

This book does not advance its own theory about how to become a better person, but rather reflects the desperation and frustration, the drama and humor, intrinsic to the search for self-improvement—the same search that millions of people engage in every day.

What about our influences? One reader said it all sounded like a voice-over from an early Woody Allen film. Which pleased us, because this book was never meant to be a heroic tale of two men overcoming themselves. When facing new challenges, whether it was learning weight lifting or the art of the pick-up, we probably looked more like the confused narcissists of Allen's movies than confident self-improvement experts.

Another reader said it reminded him of the Australian television comedy, *Review with Myles Barlow*. Which was no coincidence. While we had only watched one episode of the original series, we had seen the American remake, *Review with Forrest MacNeil*. In this mockumentary, Forrest MacNeil hosts a show-within-a-show where he reviews not books or films, but life itself. On behalf of the viewers, he tries out everything from being buried alive to marrying a stranger. He also reviews classic themes of self-improvement, such as happiness (three stars), having the perfect body (half a star), leading a cult (two stars), and getting rich quick (four stars). Although a fictive character, MacNeil's professional determination and blind commitment seemed like a good example to follow.

But unlike *Review*, nothing in this book is made up. It is a social scientific experiment in which we immersed our minds and bodies into extreme situations and then resurfaced to share our experiences. For years, we had studied the self-improvement industry from a safe academic distance. We had never attended self-improvement seminars, nor been regular gym goers, nor used wearable technologies or productivity apps. When the French ethnographer Loïc Wacquant complained that researchers too often remain physically and emotionally detached from their subjects, he could have been talking about us prior to the researching of this book. Living as he preached, Wacquant spent three years training with boxers, which, for him, was necessary to capture the "taste and the ache of the action."

Even though we were both skeptics when we started this project, we had no clear-cut hypothesis that we wanted to prove. Nor was there a moral message hidden beneath the surface of our research, of the sort you might find in a documentary like *Super Size Me*, where Morgan Spurlock, eager to show the harmfulness of the fast-food industry, binge-eats McDonald's food for one month. Unsurprisingly, he felt quite poorly afterwards, with doctors expressing concern about his health.

More relevant to our project were the great experiments of George Plimpton who, in one of his books, challenged Archie Moore, the world's light-heavyweight champion, to a three-round boxing match. His aim was to understand what happened when amateurs were thrown into the ring with professionals. When he was asked afterwards what he got out of it, he replied: "so far, a bloody nose."

The accusations we received were also levelled against Plimpton. Before entering the ring, someone said to Archie Moore that the match was just a spectacle, a freak show. Plimpton protested:

"No, no, no," he said. "It's all very serious."

UKREFUGEE: *Do you wish you could have your year back?*

CARL: *Too late for that now, I guess.*

JANUARY

PRODUCTIVITY

CARL, JANUARY 1

My wife Sally was still fast asleep when I snuck out of the bedroom and put on some coffee. Outside it was pitch dark. Snow on the ground. Freezing cold.

My daughter Esther was sleeping in her room, next to a stuffed panda. I went back to the kitchen and took out the two black wristbands from a drawer. They had cost me about $150 each. One of them, called Jawbone, was designed to track my sleep, movements, and heart rate. The other, Pavlok, was programmed to send out electric shocks. I wrapped them around my left and right wrists. For the rest of this month, they were going to be part of me. They would help bring the new and optimized version of me to life.

After breakfast, I Skyped André. He was in New Zealand on vacation and had just finished dinner. Unshaven, his long hair askew, he gave me a long lecture about productivity hacks. I found it hard to concentrate on him and tuned out after a while. Then I remembered my wearables. I took out my phone, opened the Pavlok app, and pressed zap. *One second; two seconds.* The shock arrived. I jumped out of my chair, letting out a scream. André burst into laughter.

Later in the afternoon, eager to rack up some steps on my Jawbone, I went for a walk along the frozen bay. The trail was snowy and slippery, and the light was already draining from the sky. By the time I got home, just after five p.m., it was completely dark. I checked my wristband. 7,423 steps. Still 2,577 steps short of the daily goal of 10,000. But I had no desire to head out again. Instead I started searching for productivity advice on YouTube.

I watched a toned man in his early thirties with a shaved head, talking about his battle with procrastination. Then more videos, and more men. All with shaved heads. All muscular. All tanned. Not a single woman. Was this my first insight into the world of self-improvement? Was it a world of only men? Anxious men in their thirties and forties, desperate to make themselves better? Was that us?

I returned to YouTube. Tim Ferriss showed up on the screen. His podcast had 80 million listeners and *Wired* called him the "Superman of Silicon Valley." I had flicked through his best-selling books in the past— *The 4-Hour Workweek*, *The 4-Hour Body*, *The 4-Hour Chef*—in which he shared his best tips to become super-optimized. Ferris was staring straight into the camera, explaining that, to get things done, I needed long blocks of uninterrupted time. Underneath his black V-neck T-shirt I could distinguish a lean, muscular body. Don't waste your days making phone calls or sending emails, he said. And learn to say "no."

Next, I watched a video of the biohacker Dave Asprey, another Silicon Valley icon, who had created his own beverage called Bulletproof Coffee, which promised to boost cognitive performance. The title of his talk was "How I Made My Mind My Bitch." He boasted about having written the better part of his new book in the course of six manic days. He had slept only two and a half hours each morning, keeping himself energized with his Bulletproof Coffee while sending electric currents through his brain. He used a standing desk, with his feet on a bed of nails. During short breaks, he did a one-minute handstand, his palms pressed against a vibration plate. He had been doing all of this for six days, and he was, he assured the audience, *kicking ass.*

Now another video. Robin Sharma. Another self-help guru with a shaved head. The key to success, he said, was to write down a "magnificent obsession statement"—a statement about who you would like to become in one year's time—and then repeat this statement to yourself, every morning and evening, for the rest of the year, until you had become that person.

As I was going to bed, I was thinking about what my "magnificent obsession statement" might be. Who did I want to become this year? Tim Ferris? Dave Asprey? Robin Sharma? Did I really want to transform myself from a tall and skinny academic into one of these muscular men who had optimized every aspect of their lives?

ANDRÉ, JANUARY 1

It was 7:00 a.m. when I eased out of the starched sheets. My partner Mel was still asleep. We had spent New Year's Eve at a designer hotel in central Auckland. I went into the bathroom and looked into the mirror. It wasn't a pleasant sight. My skin was sallow. My beard and hair were unkempt. I was overweight. I beat a retreat from the mirror and sat down at a dark wooden desk, still in my underwear. The leather chair was cold and sticky against my skin. My eyes fell on a small package next to my computer. It was the Jawbone that Carl had insisted I buy.

Carl and I were going to spend the first month trying to optimize our productivity. Which was a good thing. There were two books I had to finish writing. Both well overdue.

A few hours later, we arrived back at my parents' house, an hour's drive outside of Auckland. I headed for my computer and began searching for productivity tips. I wrote them down in my notebook:

Turn off alerts, ignore the news, exercise, drink lots of water, say no, hug pets, silence the inner perfectionist, get rid of to-do lists, declutter, use productivity tools, do unpleasant tasks first, eat breakfast, get enough sleep, make verbal commitments, make bad habits difficult, set realistic goals, and keep all meetings short—30 minutes max.

Putting my notebook aside, I returned to my laptop and began working on one of the unfinished books. Despite constant interruptions from my three-year-old daughter, I kept at it for eight hours.

At around 10:30 p.m., Carl Skyped from Stockholm. He asked about my goals for the month.

"Well, um, I'm not sure," I said. "But I've compiled a list of productivity tips."

As I neared the end of the list, I heard a piercing scream. Carl had electrocuted himself using a new device. An evil thought crossed my mind: *I wonder if I could get hold of the control for that thing?*

I finished the call within thirty minutes, then continued working until midnight. It seemed like a great day at the office: one chapter edited, a couple of thousand words in emails sent, meeting completed, domestic tasks done. And it was a public holiday!

CARL, JANUARY 2

My goal for the month: to finish writing an academic book. I had emailed the publisher saying they would receive the completed manuscript by the end of the month. There was only one minor issue. I had just started it.

The topic of the book was happiness, which seemed kind of ironic given the punishing routine I was about to follow. My plan was to start working at 5:00 a.m. each day, which would give me three hours of writing time before Sally and Esther woke up.

The journalist Mason Currey, in his book *Daily Rituals*, had described how Anthony Trollope, author of 47 novels, started at 5:30 a.m. and wrote for exactly three hours. If he finished the last sentence of one book, he would immediately take out another piece of paper and start on the next. Stephen King also wrote in the morning and wouldn't go anywhere until he had written 2,000 words. Kingsley Amis, when in his seventies, had a less ambitious goal. 500 words each day. After that he headed straight to the pub, arriving at about 12:30 p.m.

So my plan was to do what real writers had always done: make a schedule and follow it. But I would add a modern touch. I had purchased an app called Pomodoro, which structured your work time around rest periods. After working for twenty-five minutes it instructed you to take a five-minute break. After finishing four cycles, it gave you a longer break.

One more twist to the old-fashioned author's trick: I would remove the limits. Why stop after three hours if I could go on writing? And why stop after 2,000 words if I could do more?

ANDRÉ, JANUARY 2

Immediately after my alarm went off at 5:00 a.m., I sat up, made my bed, and started chanting an aphorism from the Roman Stoic Marcus Aurelius: "The people I deal with today will be ungrateful, arrogant, dishonest, and surly."

According to *Morning Makeover* by Damon Zahariades, mornings were the most precious time of the day. This wasn't the only book advocating an early wake-up followed by a precise morning ritual. Carl had suggested I read a book with the ominous-sounding title *The 5 AM Miracle: Dominate Your Day Before Breakfast*. Tim Ferriss recommended a five-part morning routine. The first step was to make my bed while repeating the words of Marcus Aurelius.

I sat on the floor, crossed my legs, and counted my breaths for a few minutes, trying to meditate. Opening my eyes, I stood up and did ten downward dogs, a standard yoga move I learned years ago. I was no Tony Robbins yet, so I skipped the cold shower and made a cup of tea. It was not the mixture of black tea, green tea, ginger, turmeric, and coconut oil that Ferriss suggested. Earl Grey would have to do. With the warm cup beside me, I began to write in my notebook. Following Ferriss's morning routine, I wrote down three things I was grateful for (my family, interesting work, my friendship with Carl), three things that would make the day great (making progress on a chapter, lunch with family, ignoring social media), and my personal aphorism for the day (*I am focused! I am productive! I am determined!*).

It was already 5:30 a.m., the sun was shining, and it was time to work. I opened my laptop and, ignoring my inbox, I jumped straight into my first task for the day. Once I had ticked that off, I rewarded myself with a cup of coffee and some muesli. It wasn't yet 8:00 a.m., but I was already feeling like a productivity god.

CARL, JANUARY 3

I had arranged to meet with a productivity expert. He often appeared in the newspaper and on TV, giving advice about how to take control of one's life. We were in Starbucks, drinking black coffee from oversized mugs. I explained my plan to write an academic book in one month, then showed him the apps I had downloaded.

"This is how much I've slept and moved around over the last few days," I said, pushing my phone over the table.

"You really need more sleep," he said.

I had slept five to six hours each night. "You also need more exercise," he said, checking my steps. "Without exercise, your brain stops working. Every morning, before sitting down to write, you should head out for a short walk. To wake up your brain."

He took a sip of coffee. "And you should reward yourself when you've reached your target."

"Oh, really?" So far I had only been thinking about punishment. I looked down at my Pavlok.

"Reward yourself with something you enjoy."

"A glass of wine?"

"Yeah, but make sure to drink only one glass, and don't drink it after 7:00 p.m. or it might mess with your sleep."

As we walked out on the freezing street, he said there was something else I could try to boost my productivity.

"What's that?"

"Modafinil."

ANDRÉ, JANUARY 4

I was surprised by how well the Pomodoro app worked. It was so simple, yet so effective.

The app was based on the Pomodoro technique, which was developed by an Italian named Francesco Cirillo during the late 1980s. He named it after the tomato-shaped kitchen timer he used to keep track of his twenty-five-minute intensive work stints. Since then, it had spread around the world and had become particularly popular with computer programmers.

During the day, I kept doing one Pomodoro after another. Time flew by, and by the end of the day, I had gotten through dozens of pages. At first, I struggled to find something meaningful to do during the five-minute breaks, but I had come up with a solution. Whenever the alarm went off, I left the kitchen table and headed into the backyard to beat the hell out of a punching bag.

CARL, JANUARY 6

Taking smart drugs like Modafinil seemed like an obvious choice. I had a mountain of work ahead of me and needed all the help I could get. But I didn't know much about these drugs.

To find out more, I made an appointment with a well-known psychiatrist who specialized in ADHD. We sat in his spacious office, facing each other across a shiny conference table. He listed the drugs usually labelled as "smart":

"Ritalin. Adderall. Attentin. Metamina. Concerta."

"So would these drugs work on me?"

"Yes."

"Even if I don't have ADHD?"

"They may not work as effectively as if you had ADHD, but they'd still work."

"How?"

"They'd help you concentrate."

"Like coffee?"

"Better than coffee! It's not without reason that 20 percent of Ivy League students use drugs like these."

"So you would recommend them?" I asked.

"No, I wouldn't recommend them, since you don't have a diagnosis," he said, clearing his throat. "But they would help you concentrate."

"Let's say that I use these drugs. Would anyone be able to notice that I'm under the influence?"

"No."

"Not even my mom?"

"Not unless you take very large doses. Then you could become a bit fidgety, like this," he said, illustrating the condition with his fingers.

"What are the main risks?"

"With a drug like Attentin, the risk is that you become addicted."

"But if I use them for, say, only three weeks, would there be a risk?"

"No. Not for that short a period."

Back home I did more reading about these drugs. First I came across a meta-analysis by researchers at Harvard Medical School and Oxford. They claimed that Modafinil had significant cognitive benefits, improving one's ability to plan and make decisions. They also claimed it had a positive effect on learning and creativity. Next I found a study by researchers at Imperial College London. They found that Modafinil helped sleep-deprived surgeons become better at planning, become better at redirecting their attention, and become less impulsive when making decisions. I also read some personal accounts saying that the drugs had made people short-tempered and generally unpleasant. That didn't pose much of a problem for me. I was going to spend most of my time this month alone, in front of a computer.

The risks surrounding ADHD drugs seemed more serious. I found a study in *Pediatrics* comparing the side effects of methylphenidate and dexamphetamine (two types of ADHD medication), and the study showed they could cause insomnia and appetite suppression, and, in some cases, "emotional symptoms, such as irritability, proneness to crying, anxiousness, sadness/ unhappiness, and nightmares."

ANDRÉ, JANUARY 7

We were in the car on our way to the supermarket when my mother-in-law told me that she wanted to write a book. I heard myself replying to her in the voice of a life coach:

"It's all about building the right habits," I explained.

"What do you mean?" she asked.

"Well, a few years ago this guy called Charles Duhigg published a book. *The Power of Habit*. He said a key part of building good habits is learning new routines."

"How can you do that?"

"Well one thing I've found useful is Pomodoros."

"Pomodoros?"

"Yeah. The idea is simple—work solidly for twenty-five minutes, then take a five-minute break."

"Okay."

"Think about a book in terms of Pomodoros. If you work two hours a day, then break it into four Pomodoros. Let's say you do that five or six days a week for a year, then that's enough. You'll have your book."

As we walked across the hot supermarket parking lot, my first fully formed productivity slogan rolled on out:

"You don't *think* your way out of things; you *do* your way out of them."

She stopped for a moment, looking at me with surprise.

"Yes, that makes a lot of sense," she said.

After one week, I was already thinking of myself as a productivity expert.

Today, I planned to use the drugs for the first time. I was still nervous about one thing: they were illegal. Which was why, a few weeks earlier, I had gone to see the head of my department. He was the kind of person who played by the book.

As I entered his office, he was standing at his ergonomic raised desk, typing away.

"Come in," he said. He brought over his Motörhead coffee cup and sat down by a conference table.

"I need your advice," I said, explaining my idea of using smart drugs as part of a research project. I asked if I could lose my job as a consequence.

He looked confused. "Generally speaking, in Sweden, it's hard to fire people on the basis of drug use. You have to prove they've been abusing drugs over a longer period of time and that their addiction has had negative consequences for their work."

He paused and scratched his beard. His voice grew stern: "Hang on. Are you saying that you plan to use illicit drugs at work?"

"Well, no, not really. It's just hypothetical," I said.

"If you say you're going to use the drugs," he continued, "I would have to report it straight away."

"What? To whom?"

"HR." He drew a long sigh and shook his head. "Why can't researchers just be like they were in the good old days?"

I started to think about human resources. What would they make of all this? I wasn't using drugs to escape work, but to immerse myself in it, to become better and more efficient. Wasn't that what HR was all about?

"Okay, so here's a scenario," I said. "Let's say, hypothetically of course, that I send you a diary describing my use of these drugs, and you get in touch with HR, and we meet, all of us."

"For fuck's sake, Carl," he said, burying his face in his hands. "Do you realize what position you're putting me in now?"

"Maybe I should talk to the lawyers at the school?"

"Look, I don't think you should do this at all."

I started to think about that hypothetical meeting with HR again.

"Would it be worse," I asked, "if I handed over that diary and then, halfway through the meeting, suddenly announced it was all a prank and that I never actually used these drugs, but only claimed to have taken them, to see how you and HR would react?"

He just shook his head.

ANDRÉ, JANUARY 9

It was a long flight back home to London. More than twenty-four hours. To prepare myself, I started looking around the Internet for productivity tips when traveling. There were dozens of articles with titles like "10 Tips for Being Super Productive on Your Next Flight." As I read through some of them, I took careful notes:

Keep gadgets charged, avoid WiFi, take regular breaks, use headphones to block out distracting sounds, do micro-exercises like walking up and down the aisles, and set productivity goals for each flight.

As we waited in the departure lounge, I entered my travel goals for this trip into my new Evernote app: *finish editing chapter, finish reading book, sleep 6 hours to avoid jet lag.*

My new life as a productive traveler started off perfectly. On the first flight, I was deeply immersed in my work, blocking out all disturbing sounds with my headphones. I took regular breaks to stretch in the aisle. As we were flying over Indonesia, I had worked for a good eight hours, and I could tick off the first item on my list.

But then, as we waited for our connecting flight in Brunei, everything started to fall apart. Mel was grumpy, my daughter Rita was unhappy, and my head was spinning. I checked my Jawbone and noticed that I had only walked a few hundred steps all day. I started walking around in circles. The airport proved to be the perfect place for this. It was a small hexagonal-shaped terminal, devoid of distractions. No shops, no bars. Just one duty-free store, a closed Burger King, and a mosque.

When we boarded again, I was feeling tired, and I zoned out shortly after take-off. For the next couple of hours, I drifted in and out of sleep. After a final transfer in Dubai, I returned to work. This time my task was to finish reading a book. As we flew over the English Channel, I read the last pages. I had achieved two out of my three goals. Sleep would have to wait.

CARL, JANUARY 10

Getting hold of smart drugs proved remarkably easy. After asking around among my friends, I was equipped with generous quantities of Modafinil and Attentin, and I got them all for free. Perhaps that said something about my friends.

When reading about Modafinil, it was described as the world's first safe smart drug. Still, I felt a twinge of nervousness when I popped the large white pill out of its aluminum strip. Shortly after swallowing it I thought I could feel something, but the effect was subtle, hard to describe. I was feeling alert and awake, as though I had downed five coffees.

I finished about 2,000 words that day. But the following day, after a bad night's sleep, things got worse. I was feeling fidgety and anxious. When trying to read a book, the words and sentences passed me by, like speeding cars on a highway, and whenever I tried to write something down, the words kept disappearing. During the five-minute Pomodoro breaks, I went into the bathroom and stared at my empty face in the mirror.

Was this experience common? Why was I so unfocused, when I was supposed to become sharp? Checking Reddit, I soon found a story that sounded like my own. It was from a guy who had swallowed 100mg of Modafinil. He then sat down in the library to work, at which point he started to feel, in his words:

a bit more uncomfortable and anxious than usual. Around this time I start to feel more scatterbrained too. I'm writing an essay

and I noticed the sentences I'm typing are muddled, like I'll forget
to write the last word or instead of writing the word I intended I'll
type a word that starts with the same letter.

ANDRÉ, JANUARY 12

The last two days were a haze. It all started yesterday. I woke up in the middle of the night, severely jet lagged. I tried to get back to sleep, but it was futile. Maybe I had moved beyond the 5:00 a.m. miracle and was now pioneering the 2:00 a.m. miracle.

There's got to be a way of being productive with jet lag, I thought, and typed "productivity + jet lag" into Google. Pages of advice appeared, but they were all about how to look fresh for a business meeting, or how to prevent jet lag in the first place. So, I had to come up with my own strategy, which was to go with the flow, and, instead of fighting it, I would surrender to the jet lag and try to use it for my own benefit.

I went up to my study and started to write, working all morning. In the afternoon, after twelve hours at my desk, I skyped Carl and explained that I was going to attempt a twenty-four-hour work marathon.

"Really? How?" he asked.

"With the help of this," I said, showing him an aluminum strip.

"Ah, Modafinil! That's the one I've been using. How did you get it?"

"From a friend," I said, and swallowed my first pill. "He used to work in this think tank and had a crazy boss who would email him at 3:00 a.m. The pills were the only way he could keep up."

I returned to work. Soon enough, I felt more clearheaded and focused. I liked it. No unpleasant side effects. Maybe I felt a bit clumsier than usual, but apart from that, nothing. I continued working all evening, listening to David Bowie, whose death had been announced earlier that day. I was in the zone. Nothing seemed to exist except work. I continued working until about 1:00 a.m. I was nearly there now.

Twenty-four hours of pretty solid work were coming to an end. I had lost track of how much I had done.

As I listened to the last song on Bowie's last album, Rita woke up. She was jet-lagged and hungry. I put aside my work and made her some scrambled eggs. When she'd finished her meal, I lay down next to her in bed. It was well after 2:00 a.m. She snuggled up against me.

I must have dozed off, because the next thing I knew, it was 4:00 a.m. But I wasn't tired. I returned to my desk, thinking I should perhaps go for a 48-hour work marathon. Night turned into morning, and I took Rita to her babysitter. I walked slowly down the street, like a ghost, drifting through space.

When I got back home I swallowed another pill and worked until lunch, at which point I started to feel distracted and restless. I went out for a walk, but that didn't help much. I tried to get back to work, but I was no longer in the zone. I didn't really know where I was, or what I was supposed to be doing. At 9:00 p.m., I gave up and threw myself into bed, falling asleep instantly. I had been working for the last 40 hours.

CARL, JANUARY 12

To kick-start my brain after lunch, I went for a walk along the water. It was minus 15 degrees. The canal was frozen, covered in a light layer of glittering ice. All I could hear was the squeaking of the snow beneath my boots. I was thinking about the drugs. They seemed to require discipline. You couldn't ignore your sleep and then rely on them. It also seemed dangerously easy to get stuck in the wrong activity. I had experienced that on a couple of occasions. If I had to check something in a book, I found myself continuing to read. If I started writing an email, I didn't seem able to stop. Which was a good thing, of course, but only as long as you could control it. I wanted to think of the pill as a subtraction instead of an addition. It didn't enhance wakefulness as much as it removed tiredness.

ANDRÉ, JANUARY 13

I slept for seven hours straight, waking up at 4:00 a.m., taking the third and final pill. I was nearing the end of the first book now.

After leaving Rita at school, I stopped at a café for breakfast. It seemed like a good idea to take a relaxing break. But I was too restless. I finished my eggs and coffee as fast as I could and rushed home to continue working.

After a few more hours, I was done. The book had been sent off to the publisher. The drug was wearing off. A few weeks of hard work was coming to an end. But then I thought about the other book on which I now had to start. There really was no end to this.

CARL, JANUARY 16

Modafinil wasn't for me. Sure, it had made me energized and focused, but it also made me anxious.

But I was not yet ready to give up. I had received another drug from a friend, called Attentin. It was described in the medical dictionary as a psychostimulating medication, designed to improve concentration and attention. It was prescribed to people with ADHD, especially children between the ages of seven and fourteen. It could be detected on drug tests. The active substance, it said, was dexamphetamine.

A bit later, my friend Jenny came over. She was a psychologist and author. Last week, we had tried Modafinil together. Like myself, she wasn't impressed. We swallowed the Attentin, sat down by our computers, and started a Pomodoro.

It didn't take long for the effect to set in. It was quite different from the Modafinil. I no longer felt anxious. I became calm. Distractions faded away. I was immersed in my own private space. I wrote effortlessly. It was not as though everything went faster, but more like time and space ceased to exist. I wondered if the text I had produced was any good. During a short break, I asked Jenny if I could read it out loud.

"It's good," she said, "you won't even have to edit that."

I asked her what she thought about the drugs. She said she hadn't worked as effectively in a very long time. But her experience was different from mine. Whereas I had become mellow—in a pleasant, solipsistic sort of way—she was more energetic and talkative. Everything worked for both of us, except for the Pomodoros, which no longer seemed useful. Each time the alarm went off, we got irritated and decided to skip the break and keep going. At 12:30 we had a quick lunch and went for our scheduled walk. It was snowing and we didn't really feel like walking, so after only five minutes, we decided to return home. We carried on working until 6, when we sat down and had a glass of wine, celebrating what might have been the most productive day of our lives.

I need to be careful with these pills, I thought to myself later that evening. The doctor I had talked to said there was nothing to worry about if I was planning on using them only for a couple of weeks. But they were worryingly good. In the late evening, I met up with the friend who had given them to me. My reaction was the typical response among those who have ADHD, he said. I was surprised. I had never thought I had a problem with concentration.

ANDRÉ, JANUARY 18

I had completed half of a different book about a year ago. After two months of intense work, a sense of lethargy set in and I stopped. It had been hanging over me ever since.

I was back to it now. By noon I had written a whole section. But then I became distracted, lurking on social media. There were no more pills, so I opted for a session of mindfulness instead. It was supposed to be good for productivity and dealing with anxiety. I found a "body scan meditation" on YouTube. The guide was Jon Kabat-Zinn, a Buddhist doctor and best-selling author.

I switched off my phone, changed into a tracksuit, and lay down on my office floor. When I hit play, Kabat-Zinn's soft voice came through my laptop speakers. I thought about my big toe—as he told me to do. Then my little toe. Then the rest of my toes, one after the other.

I could hear one of my cats walking into the study. She looked at me, making sure I was still alive, then left again. Some emails came, making a pinging sound, but none of this worried me. I was slipping into a wonderful moment of pure nothingness, as though I was immersed in a dark, limpid pool. It seemed like the opposite of being productive, but as soon I was done, I found myself back at my desk, writing another section. When it was time to collect Rita from her babysitter, I had written 3,000 words. And that was without drugs.

CARL, JANUARY 18

So far, I had stuck to my plan religiously. I had produced about 2,000 words every day—on par with Stephen King. But I was beginning to feel exhausted. I was stressed out, I had not slept enough, I wasn't doing any exercise.

Instead of going out for a short walk early in the morning, as the productivity expert had advised, I went straight from bed into the kitchen, where I swallowed a pill and made coffee. As the caffeine and drugs began to kick in, I was already immersed in work. There was something liberating about treating myself as a machine. I didn't have to ask how I was feeling or if I was in the mood for writing. I just did what I was supposed to do.

It reminded me of Andy Warhol's words: "Machines have less problems. I'd like to be a machine, wouldn't you?"

On good days, I managed five or six Pomodoros before my wife and daughter woke up. After I had dropped off Esther at school, I would return home and continue working, adding another ten Pomodoros to my schedule. I had finished three chapters now. Three more to go.

The previous evening, as I was sitting with Sally in the kitchen, I had felt a buzz on my wrist. It was my Jawbone, sending me a personal message:

You've been turning in late recently. Remember, your brain needs plenty of pillow-time to sort new information. Get in bed at 9:27 p.m. tonight.

"What does it say?" Sally asked.

"It says I need to go to bed soon."

"So you're going to do what it tells you?"

"Maybe."

"Let me get this straight. Your wristband tells you when to go to bed?"

I did go to bed early that night. The next morning, as we had breakfast, a new message from my Jawbone flashed up. It was from my "Smart coach":

Great work. You turned off the lights on time. Remember, every bit of shut-eye helps concentration. Today's going to rock.

My wife looked at me inquiringly. I showed her the next message:

Bedtime success. You're in the groove. Way to nail that 9:27 p.m. bedtime. Carry that success with you all day.

Underneath was a smiley face with both arms raised in the air. My wife shook her head and returned to reading the newspaper.

ANDRÉ, JANUARY 19

Early this morning, Carl sent me an email proposing a writing competition. The challenge was simple: Who could produce the most words in a day?

By lunchtime I had 2,000 words. After thirty minutes of mindfulness I sat down for another session at the keyboard. The words were flowing. By about four p.m. I had 3,700 words. Carl only had about 2,000. I had won. That would show him!

CARL, JANUARY 21

I was a machine, and my life was lived in numbers. I woke up this morning at 5:00 a.m., after seven hours and six minutes of sleep. Deep sleep: one hour, thirteen minutes. REM sleep: one hour, fifty-eight minutes. Light sleep: three hours, fifty-five minutes. Woke up one time, awake for forty-six minutes. In the morning, two cups of coffee, and 200mg Modafinil. Five Pomodoros before breakfast at 8:00, then more work between 9:00 and 12:00. Thirty-minute break for lunch and six more Pomodoros. At the end of the day, I had 2,000 new words.

I had also acquired the habit of electrocuting myself, every now and then, but it was having the opposite effect of what was intended. In fact, I had started to enjoy it.

ANDRÉ, JANUARY 22

The last couple of weeks had been the most productive I could ever remember. I didn't want to take a break, but Carl had booked me into a three-day self-improvement seminar. Something called the Landmark Forum. He said it would make me more productive.

I didn't know much about Landmark. Carl filled me in on the phone. "It's an offspring of est, he told me. "Another self-help program created by a salesman-turned-guru who calls himself Werner Erhard. His motto is 'What is, is. What ain't, ain't.'"

I could hear the excitement rising in his voice.

"It was hugely popular in the 1970s, when hundreds of thousands of Californians went for weekend-long training sessions. It's a bit like Scientology. You're broken down, then built up again."

After our call, I looked into it further and found that Werner Erhard had licensed his "intellectual property" from est to Landmark in 1991 after allegations of tax avoidance and incest. Since then, 2.4 million people had participated in Landmark Forum. I was curious about what would go down.

At 9:00 a.m. I walked into a low-ceilinged conference room on the fifth floor of a building in North London. Over a hundred people sat on chairs facing the stage. Most were in their early thirties: healthy, attractive, and well-dressed. A big African-American guy in a brown suit sat on the stage. He was to be our coach for the next three days.

"Some people say this is a cult," Coach Brownsuit said. "Landmark is not a cult. Cults *take* you from the family. We *send* you to your family." Then he turned to the audience. "So, why are you here?"

One of the older guys in the room leapt to his feet. "I'm a director of a successful company, but I'm dissatisfied. I want to leave and start working with horses."

Coach B. nodded empathetically. "I hear you, man."

Half a dozen others leapt up and shared intimate details about their lives, explaining why they were there. Coach B. scanned the audience. "Now turn to the person next to you and share the problem that brought you here."

I introduced myself to a young Italian guy in black sitting next to me. "My boss sent me on the course," he said stoically. "What about you?"

I wanted to say I had been sent here by Carl, as a questionable gesture of friendship. But I opted for something much simpler.

"Well, I'm unable to deal with my many commitments."

He nodded, looking at his hands.

Our attention shifted back to the stage when Coach B. hauled himself off his hemorrhoid cushion, walked to the whiteboard, and drew a circle with a black pen.

"This is you," he said. "What is it filled in with?"

He paused, examining the audience.

"Your conversations," he said.

He scribbled inside the circle until it was full. "What we're going to do is rub that out."

He was rubbing out the circle. When he got halfway, he stopped. "This is when you freak out." He rubbed out some more of the circle. "This is when you *really* freak out." He continued rubbing out the circle until it was gone. Was he going to erase our entire sense of self? I wasn't sure I wanted it rubbed out by Coach B.

After a twenty-five-minute break, Coach B. was looking as perky as ever. "By the end of this course, we should be able to complete these sentences." He pointed to the whiteboard and read:

I've been pretending that . . .
When in fact . . .
The impact of that inauthentic way of being and acting is . . .
The whole time I've been being and acting this way, what's been missing is any sense of . . .
Standing here, the possibility I am inventing for myself and my life is . . .

As I read through the statements on the board, I started to try to fill in the blanks:

I've been pretending that I want to be here at Landmark Forum.
When in fact I would be rather sitting in a coffee shop reading Joan Didion.
The impact of that inauthentic way of being and acting is that I feel disturbed and angry.
The whole time I've been being and acting this way, what's been missing is any sense of intellectual stimulation.
Standing here, the possibility I am inventing for myself and my life is to never take this nonsense seriously.

During the next break, I wrote an email to Carl asking him what he thought my blockage was. He responded with one word: *yourself.*

As I took my seat for the next session, Coach B. roamed the floor. "Your problem," he said, "is that you all spend too much time telling yourself nonsense." He then started speaking in tongues. For a moment, I thought I was in a Pentecostal revival meeting. He continued babbling for five minutes. "This is what it's like in your head," he said. "And we need to stop it. *Now!*"

A woman in her thirties, dressed in expensive clothes, raised her hand. "I recently lost my job, but I haven't told anyone."

The audience turned their attention to her.

"You need to get rid of your negative self-talk," Coach B. said. "See, that's your problem. Negative self-talk." The woman looked confused. I was confused, too. Changing her self-talk would surely do little to change her employment situation.

After two more grueling sessions, the day finally drew to an end. It was 10:30 p.m. I had been in this room for over twelve hours. I was exhausted. On my way back home, sitting on the train, I began a homework assignment Coach B. had given us: write a letter to someone we had an unresolved issue with. That someone was going to be Carl.

CARL, JANUARY 22

"Do you think André is strong enough to go through it?" my father-in-law asked, as we had lunch. "I'm serious. People are brainwashed at that place. It breaks them down."

"I don't know," I said, concentrating on my food. "I really don't know."

ANDRÉ, JANUARY 23

The next day's Landmark session began at 9 a.m. A woman in her sixties, who looked like a typical middle-class English empty-nester, leapt up.

"I think my son is gay, and he won't tell me." She was weeping.

"Okay," Coach B. said, "take out your phone."

The woman dug into her bag.

"Now get your son's number up on the screen."

She started fiddling with her phone.

"Now go outside, and call him."

I saw her walking out the door with her phone to her ear.

Next, an ex-military type in his late thirties jumped up. "I need to call my dad!" he bawled, grabbing his phone before running out.

Soon almost everyone got to their feet. "Go and call someone you have unfinished business with," Coach B. ordered. One hundred people started fumbling with their phones while heading out of the room. I just sat tight thinking about the massive and unsuspecting emotional carnage that was about to take place.

Later in the day Coach B. asked the empty nester what happened.

"Oh, my son was skiing." She looked a little relieved. I couldn't help thinking about her son, being on a ski slope, suddenly receiving a call from his mother asking if he was gay.

Next up was a woman in her fifties wearing a cream cardigan. "I find it hard to communicate with my son," she said.

"Is it just your son? What about your husband?" Coach B. asked.

"Well, my relationship with my husband is really good."

Coach B. asked a few more questions and then she suddenly broke down.

"I was abused as a child by a family member," she said, sobbing. The crowd was silent.

"The problem is that has become your story that you carry around with you."

She was crying now.

"What happened thirty-eight years ago is not happening now but you live like it is."

Coach B. turned to the audience.

"Ever heard of Humpty Dumpty?" He looked around. "It's a fairy tale! Do you get upset by fairy tales?"

Coach B. turned to the woman again: "You're trapped in a fairy tale. What happened, happened. The real damage is done by the story you tell yourself."

Her face changed, as if she had just understood something important.

"I'm not punishing my rapist," she said. "I'm punishing myself."

"You need to forgive your rapist," Coach B. said. "You did it all. You created the story and you can create forgiveness."

During the break I went to a nearby café and sent Carl a message: *why the fuck did you send me on this course?*

When I returned, I found that my badge had been put aside. It had a piece of paper attached to it. Would I like to sign up for a follow-up seminar? I had refused to sign up when we were asked earlier in the day. I was even more annoyed by the idea now.

At 10:00 p.m. I walked back to the station feeling empty. Could I really force myself to return tomorrow for the final day?

CARL, JANUARY 23

Early this morning I received an email from André. It was part of his homework. The task was to confront his inauthentic being.

Dear Carl,

I've been pretending that I am on top of everything—multiple work projects, family life, etc.—when in fact I'm not. I feel dragged along by a set of commitments which are not mine. I'm basically doing what others want of me. The impact of this inauthentic way of being is that I feel anxious—as though some impending disaster is about to occur. I also feel like I am just trying to keep others pleased. I no longer want to feel like I am a spectator or task manager in my own life.

Your friend,
André

I had never heard André talk like this before.
Around lunch, I received a new short message from him:
Fuck you Carl for making me do this!

And later in the afternoon, he sent a longer email. The one was more confused. In the last paragraph, he wrote:

Do you portray me as uncommitted just to make yourself feel better? Or do I empower you to dictate the direction of our project just so I don't have to face the anxiety of having stood for anything?

Maybe Sally's dad was right. Maybe André was about to break down.

ANDRÉ, JANUARY 24

It was 9:00 a.m. and I was walking up the familiar staircase for my final day of the Landmark Forum. Coach B. turned to look at us: "If you really want to change your life, you need to recruit."

On Tuesday we were going to have our "graduation," and we had been asked to bring along friends and family and encourage them to sign up.

"Now let's handle this marketing thing," Coach B. said. "It's just about sharing something important with the people you love. It's not sales."

"But what if they think it's a cult?" a skeptic in the audience asked.

"Well, they are the ones who need it the most," Coach B. responded.

"But what if they say no?" someone else asked.

"Tuesday's graduation is an opportunity to move forward and share your transformation. It's *not* about marketing," Coach B. said firmly.

Having dealt with the "marketing thing," Coach B. turned to the audience once again. People immediately started to volunteer their stories.

"I was a stripper and hid it from my family," a young woman yelled out.

"My parents don't know I'm gay," a middle-aged man admitted.

The tragic stories piled up. Coach B. turned to the last member of the audience who had shared their story. "You've wasted your life on meaningless kaka," he said firmly. "You go around trying to convince other people of your story just so you can feel right. And it's screwing up your life."

Was that my problem? Was it my bullshit story?

Throughout the rest of the morning Coach B. kept returning to this theme. "You are addicted to your stories," he said. "If they disappeared, you think you would die. The reality is that if your stories disappeared, you'd discover yourself."

After another hurried break, Coach B. asked when we were really able to be ourselves.

"Painting," one person yelled out.

"When I'm sewing," another person added.

"Skiing," said a third.

"How long do you spend skiing?" Coach B. snapped back.

"A week or two a year," the skier replied.

"And how much of that time is actually spent on the ski runs? A few minutes? You're living for a few minutes every year? Your life has been a complete joke." He was grinning now as he turned to the audience. "So, you're wondering what you got from this course. What you got was this: you're a joke. Your life is empty and meaningless. You're not going to get anywhere. And there's no hope."

Amazing! £480, three days, and it could all be summed up in the message that my life was a complete joke.

Coach B. started practicing jazz drumming on his chair. He turned to the audience "We're chasing *It* through the whole world. This is *It*," he said, gesturing around the room. "And *It* doesn't mean anything."

The dozen assistants who had been lurking at the back started handing out small sheets of glossy paper with quotes printed on one side, including Shakespeare and Kurt Vonnegut. Coach B. riffed on *Macbeth*: "Your life has been full of sound and fury, signifying nothing."

"I still can't believe that this is it," an audience member called out in a sad voice. "This is shit!"

"That is *It*," Coach B responded, smiling as he circled in on her.

"Baby, this is *It*," he added.

She sobbed.

"There's nothing now. Nothing to do. Nothing to say. If you can get that all right now, you're home, baby. You're whole. Complete, perfect."

Coach B. paused, rocking on his heels. Tears rolled down the woman's cheeks.

"How do you feel?" the Coach asked.

She breathed out, "Quite relaxed."

"Just be with me," Coach B. said, taking her hands. They looked into each other's eyes like two long-separated family members standing on the abyss.

He clapped her on the shoulder and looked out at the audience. "You can only create from nothing. With your words. But the most important thing is this: you make promises to yourself that you know how to keep."

When we walked out of the room, people were overawed. Many seemed euphoric, as though they had finally found meaning in their life. From what I understood the basic message was that all is nothingness and there is no meaning, so we can create anything just by saying it.

When the show finally drew to a close, the participants milled around, hugging each other. I headed for the door. As I sat on the train on the way home, I read through the quotes on the glossy white handout again. They included part of a poem by E. E. Cummings: "Everything (dreamed & hoped & prayed for months & weeks & days & years & forever) is Less Than Nothing (which would have been something) what got him was nothing."

CARL, JANUARY 24

Luckily there were no more crazy messages from André today. I was on dexamphetamine, writing feverishly, having no time or inclination to support his personal transformation.

It was the day of my graduation from Landmark, and I had brought my close friend Peter along. We walked into the packed room and found seats behind a woman and her father, who I knew had been the recipient of a few disturbing calls during the weekend.

Coach B. took the stage and welcomed everyone. "So, what were some issues you sorted out during the course?" he asked the graduates. People were calling things out:

"My relationship with my father!"

"My motivation!"

"I can now imagine a future!"

I turned to look at Peter. I was surprised to see that he was enjoying himself.

"So, what have people achieved after the forum?" Coach B. asked. The ex-soldier stood up: "I've organized a work volleyball tournament." Another woman stood up. "I'm going to create peace in the Middle East."

"I've got a video to show you," Coach B. said as the lights dimmed. Upbeat music came over the speakers and people appeared on screen with subtitles like "Scientist," "CEO," "Scholar and Teacher," "Olympian." They all described how they had benefited from the Landmark Forum in glowing terms.

When the film finished, Coach B. was center stage again. "Now, I'd like the graduates to turn to the people they brought along today. They are going to invite you to participate." I turned to Peter and read out the questions that had been given to us in advance. I tried to be sincere. Peter played along, answering sarcastically. When we left, I thanked Coach B. for his work. "Good for you," he responded.

Ten minutes later, Peter and I were sitting in a nearby pub. I'd been friends with him for nearly twenty years and this was the most open and honest conversation we had ever had.

CARL, JANUARY 28

It was dark when I parked the car outside my parents' seaside house, an hour's drive from central Stockholm. I put the food in the fridge and sat down at the kitchen table and wrote down a schedule for tomorrow:

5–8 Finish last section of Chapter 6
8–9 Breakfast. Short walk. Shower
9–12 Writing introduction and Chapter 1
12–1 Lunch and short walk
11–7 Read through the manuscript. Edit.
7–8 Dinner
8–9:30 Read manuscript. Edit.
9:30 Bed

ANDRÉ, JANUARY 29

Early this morning, Carl proposed another writing competition. I accepted his proposal and kept going all day, ignoring lunch. By about 2:30 p.m. I had 3,500 words. At 4:00 p.m. I went out to pick up Rita and came home to cook some food. After dinner, I went upstairs and kept working until midnight. Another 2,000 words. I was getting seriously tired now. Or was my tiredness just a story I was making up? Either way, 5,500 words had been added to the book, 2,000 words more than Carl. That was a fact. Not a fairy tale.

CARL, JANUARY 29

I kept to my schedule. I woke up at 5:00 a.m., swallowed a pill, and then sat down to write for three hours. Breakfast at 8:00 a.m. Then a short walk and hot shower. At 9:00 a.m. I was working again. I took a short lunch break and went for a rapid walk along the seashore. Then it was back to work. It was close to 7:00 p.m. when I closed my computer. The manuscript was almost done. I had written and edited 3,500 words today, a new record.

ANDRÉ, JANUARY 30

Mel had been reading a book about psychoanalysis. She wanted to talk about her childhood. She rarely talked about the topic. I should have listened, but I thought *this could take forever* . . . and I had a book to finish. I spoke with her for fifteen minutes then returned to my computer.

CARL, JANUARY 30

I woke up at 5:00 a.m., ingested five milligrams of dexamphetamine, and sat down to work.

Five hours later, I was beginning to feel strange. My brain was slow. I realized I had not eaten anything. I had no appetite. I continued working, but something was wrong. I was freezing. I lay down on the couch, underneath a blanket, with the laptop on my stomach. I was drifting off. When I woke up, it was dark outside. I stumbled into the kitchen, poured myself a glass of water, and then went to bed.

ANDRÉ, JANUARY 31

At about 8:00 a.m., Carl Skyped. He was lying on a couch under a blanket. He looked pitiful. I instantly started feeling better about things. This always happens. When Carl feels bad, I feel good. Buoyed by Carl's illness, I continued writing. At 4:00 a.m., I clicked save. The book was done.

CARL, JANUARY 31

The alarm went off at 5:00 a.m., as usual, but I couldn't get out of bed. It was too cold. I was too weak.

It was day now. I staggered around the house in my underwear looking for a thermometer, but all I could find was one of those cold ancient rectal instruments.

It showed 104°F (39.8°C).

Was the month going to end like this?

I had woken up at 5:00 a.m. every day of the month. I had not seen my friends and I had not gone out. I had not watched films and I had not read any novels. I had lived in my own private bubble of work, shutting everything else out.

And I was so close.

I woke up again. It was dark now. The sheets were soaked. My glass of water was empty. I checked my temperature again. It was now over 105°F (40.4°C).

I didn't know what time it was, but the month was nearly over, and I had not sent off the book to the publisher. I closed my eyes and surrendered, drifting off.

This was not how it was supposed to end.

FEBRUARY

BODY

ANDRÉ, FEBRUARY 1

I was alone at home in my armchair, mindlessly scrolling through the Internet on my phone. I opened my Fitbit app and discovered that throughout January, I had walked on average just under 1,000 steps each day, far short of my 10,000-step target. This was going to change now. The next area of optimization was the body. My challenge: to run a marathon by the end of the month.

This was not an unusual goal. 1.8 million people across the world run a marathon each year. But was it possible? I typed "one month marathon" into my phone. The first page to pop up was titled: "The 30-Day Marathon Training Schedule—or—Are You Crazy?" Running a marathon with only one month of training was dangerous, it said. I should not attempt it unless I could pass some basic tests, it warned. I ran through the questions: *How tired do you get walking up four flights of stairs?* Not very. *Have you been running regularly?* Yes, but not in the past year. *How fast can you run a mile?* I had no idea.

I opened my drawers and found some tight black leggings, a fleece top, a beanie, and a pair of socks that were once white. I put on my worn running shoes and took out an old iPod from the top of my bedroom drawers.

It was a cold, gray day. I walked up to Victoria Park, a large expanse of parkland less than a kilometer from my home. When the park first opened in the nineteenth century, an article in *Harper's Magazine* described it as a place for public preaching where you could find acolytes of "Malthusianism, atheism, agnosticism, secularism, Calvinism, socialism, anarchism, Salvationism, Darwinism, and even, in exceptional cases, Swedenborgianism and Mormonism." They were all gone now. Today, you would find a new breed of ideologues in the park: cyclists, CrossFitters, roller-bladers, tightrope jugglers, meditators, yogaistas, and, of course, runners.

I hit the timer on my iPod, and set off, keeping a fast pace. At first it felt good, but after a few hundred meters, I wanted to vomit. When I had reached a mile, I yelped, then slowed down to walking pace. Less than seven minutes. Not bad. With that pace, I had the basic fitness to train for a marathon in one month.

The serious marathon runner trained five or six days a week: four days of shorter distances between five and ten kilometers, one day of a long run, and one day of a medium distance run. On the final day, I should rest. My plan was to start off with short distances, then build up to a maximum of thirty-five kilometers, then taper my distances back down just before the big day.

CARL, FEBRUARY 1

I was still in the seaside house on the couch underneath a blanket, with my laptop on my stomach. At noon, I sent a short note to my publisher. *Here's the final manuscript.* I attached the book, and pressed send. Done!

I cleaned up and headed back into town.

ANDRÉ, FEBRUARY 3

Today, as I ran nine kilometers around the park in the half-light of winter, I tried my best to remember how I had first come to running.

Throughout my adolescence, I would forge sick notes to get out of sports at school. It was only when I was at university that I started to run to get in shape. But after a couple of months, I lost interest. Years later, when I had moved to England, I took it up again as a cure for the boredom of living in a provincial city. And then, a few more years down the line, as professional responsibilities mounted, running had become a way of dealing with anxiety.

After a particularly difficult winter, I started to run longer distances. Five or ten kilometers became an escape from the pressures of having a young child and an increasingly demanding job. That summer, I surprised myself by signing up to run a half marathon. As I ran the twenty-one kilometers through the streets of Hackney on an unseasonably hot day, a middle-aged man collapsed in front of me. I made a mental note not to do this again. But when the race finished I proudly showed off my medal to a couple of Jehovah's Witnesses who approached me on the street. Maybe it was this misplaced pride that made me sign up for a marathon in Amsterdam that autumn. The following year I ran the London marathon.

But that was the end of it. After the race, Mel said she was sick of me spending my spare time out running. So, I gave it up. This was nearly a year ago, and now I was training again. In the past, it had taken me three or four months to build up to a marathon. This time, I had only one month.

CARL, FEBRUARY 5

I was feeling better now, and it was time to pay my first visit to the gym.

I had been to a real gym only once before, at the age of fifteen, after injuring my knee while snowboarding. I remember standing by the wall bars, kicking my left leg back and forth like a figure-skater—just as the doctor had advised—when a group of bodybuilders in the free-weight section caught sight of me. They pointed at me, laughing scornfully. I never went back.

I packed a sports bag and headed out. When I walked into the gym, I saw no weight machines, no treadmills, and no mirrors. It was just a big basement room with concrete walls and black carpet. There were metal racks along one side of the room. There were barbells and kettle bells on the other side. This was how a gym should look in 2016. A real CrossFit gym. Later that day, I would learn that CrossFit had been created by two California fitness entrepreneurs in 2000, and had since spread to over 13,000 gyms across the world.

I found the two guys who would be my new personal trainers in a small kitchen talking to each over a pot of steaming coffee. One was tall and agile; the other short and beefy.

"You *have* to taste this," the agile coach said, turning to me with a cup of the fresh brew.

After a short lecture about their philosophy, they led me into the main space where I assumed various positions: on my knees, on my back, flat on my stomach, legs up in the air, on my side, upside-down. All the while they took photos, made notes, whispered to each other.

"Step up here," the beefy coach told me, pointing to a piece of equipment that looked like a sci-fi hover board.

"When were you born? Year and month?"

"October, 1980," I said. The coach typed it into his laptop.

"How tall are you?"

"195 centimeters."

"Now, pull out the handles, and hold them firmly in your hands."

He came over, made sure my body was erect and that my arms were straight, and then he went back to his computer. "77.6 kilograms," he read out. "11.3% body fat. 65.4 kilogram muscles."

I stepped off the scales and leaned over the computer.

"Seventy-seven!" I said. "I guess I need to put on some weight."

"Yes. You need to eat. I mean, *really* eat."

"How much?"

"If you want some real change: 750 grams of protein each day. Fish, chicken, meat. There's no other way."

ANDRÉ, FEBRUARY 6

They called it baby disco.

Saturday morning, underneath Waterloo railway station. We entered a small door, covered in graffiti. Only a few hours earlier, this place had been crowded by young, beautiful, happy people flirting and dancing. Now it was filled with anxious parents running after their children.

I took Rita to the dance floor. The DJ played house music, nodding along. This was probably as close to hell as I could come. But then, after about twenty minutes of compulsory dancing, I realized that this was actually the perfect workout. I was moving from side to side with a fifteen-kilogram weight (aka, my daughter) on my shoulders. You would normally have to go to the gym for this! I was jumping up and down, moving around the room. Sweat poured down my back. My daughter loved it. I loved it. My Jawbone loved it so much it gave me a buzz. 10,000 steps. Fitness goal achieved!

CARL, FEBRUARY 7

I was going back to the house at the seaside over the weekend. But I wasn't alone this time. It was me and my sister, and our kids.

When we stopped on the way to do some shopping, I explained to my sister that I would now be eating massive quantities of food.

"Why?"

"I'm building muscles," I said, and headed into the meat department.

Later in the evening, when the children had finished their dinner, my plate was still brimming with roasted potato and slow-cooked lamb stew. I continued eating, methodically, shoveling the large pieces of meat into my mouth. I was back into robot mode. Trying to forget that I was full from yesterday, full from breakfast, full from lunch, full from the two plates I had just eaten.

When I had finished my third portion, I took a photo of my empty plate. "What are you doing?" my sister asked.

"I'm logging my food. Take a look." I showed her my new app, MyFitnessPal. It seemed to be the most popular food logging app on the market with an astonishing 85 million users. It helped me keep track on what I was eating, breaking it all down into calories, carbs, protein, and fat.

"So take this dinner, for instance: 2,242 calories, 100.6 grams carbs, 117.1 grams fat, 114.7 grams protein. The day as a whole: 4,349 calories."

My sister looked at the screen, unimpressed, not saying a word.

"I've downloaded an app for my poo, too," I told her. "It's called Poo Keeper."

ANDRÉ, FEBRUARY 8

I had read about high-intensity interval training in *Runner's World*, and I had become intrigued by one particular technique called the Mona Fartlek. Following the technique, I began running slowly, then I sped up and ran as fast as I could, then I slowed down, then I sped up again. The first few bursts were easy, but then, after a couple of sixty-second bursts, I began feeling sick. A woman walking her dog looked at me with concern. I ran and yelped, jogged and panted, repeating the pattern until it was all done, and then I dropped to the ground.

CARL, FEBRUARY 8

I was making huevos rancheros for breakfast. I chopped an onion and fried it with crushed garlic. Then I added three big chorizo sausages (150 grams each), sliced into small pieces. As they browned, I added one can (400 grams) of tinned tomatoes and some chipotle paste. When the sauce was thick and nice, I cracked in three eggs, and added a full fist of grated cheese. I typed the items into my app: 1,800 calories. Pleasant meal for four people. Perfect start of the day for me.

I phoned up André on Skype. As I was force-feeding myself he explained what he was up to. He said he was focusing on running this month. I tried to conceal my disappointment. *Running?* That's what he'd been doing for as long as I'd known him. He said he might run a marathon. *Marathon?* He'd already run a bloody marathon.

I finished my heart-attack breakfast, and went back to the gym for some more tests. They wrapped a band around my chest and asked me to step up and down on a box. After ten long minutes, they took off the band and wrote down some numbers, whispering. Then the agile coach took out a twenty-kilogram barbell and asked me to move in all sorts of unfamiliar ways. For each new exercise they added more weights, writing down numbers, looking unimpressed.

When I was in the shower, still exhausted, the beefy coach appeared with a pink plastic shaker.

"Protein shake. Drink it," he said.

ANDRÉ, FEBRUARY 9

After three laps around the park, I slowed down and stretched my legs. I checked my new app, Runkeeper. I was one of 40 million people using this fitness app. *Activity completed*, a woman's voice said, telling me the precise distance and time. A prompt popped up on the screen and asked me whether I would like to take a picture. *Why not?* I thought. The app asked: *would you like to share your run with your friends?* No thanks, I replied. I was not convinced my friends wanted to be kept abreast of my fitness pursuits.

CARL, FEBRUARY 9

I was lying on the gym floor, panting, with the taste of blood in my mouth.

I had been in the gym for nearly two hours when the beefy coach suggested I round the day off with a special exercise technique called

Tabata. It was discovered in the 1990s by a Japanese scientist, Izumi Tabata, who, at the time, was working with the Japanese speed skating team. The scientist had compared two groups: one exercising at a moderate level over a longer period of time; the other exercising in intermittent high-intensity bursts. Turned out, my coach explained, that the intensive routine was far more effective.

The technique was easy: twenty seconds of intense exercise followed by ten seconds of rest—repeated eight times.

I climbed on the rowing machine and strapped my feet in.

"Row like you've never rowed before," the beefy coach shouted. I followed his orders, sliding back and forth on the machine, puffing and groaning. After twenty seconds, I let go of the handle, panting.

"Row!" he shouted again. After about five rounds I no longer knew where I was. When I had finished the eighth round, my body was dissociated from my mind. My legs and arms were shaking, sweat was pouring down my face. As the coach liberated my feet from the machine, I fell onto the floor like a pair of soaked underpants.

ANDRÉ, FEBRUARY 10

I was watching the last light drain from the winter sky when Carl called. He said I wasn't committed enough. While he was on this crazy diet and spending huge amounts of money on personal trainers, I had just done what I would normally do, going for a run around the park.

"Look, I'm just following my training plan."

"But it's boring. You've done a marathon already. Try something new."

"Like what?"

"What about a magnetic finger implant?"

"What?"

"I sent an email to a body-hacker yesterday, and he said magnetic finger implants are the new cool thing. It adds a sixth sense!"

"Why would a marathon runner need a sixth sense?" I responded.

"That's not the point," Carl replied. "The point is, you should test your limits."

I said nothing.

"An Ironman then?"

"Carl, people train for over a year to do an Ironman. I only have one month. I think running a marathon is already pushing it."

"Whatever," he said, and hung up.

CARL, FEBRUARY 10

"We have a surprise for you," the agile coach said.

"What's that?" I said, dropping the barbell to the floor.

"We've signed you up to a weight-lifting competition."

"You've done what?"

ANDRÉ, FEBRUARY 12

Outside the bagel shop, Brick Lane, 6:45 a.m. A few of us were already there, waiting, when a middle-aged guy in fluorescent running gear with flashing lights on his shoes came jogging up. "Hiya guys," he yelled, pop music flooding out of his phone. He worked his way around the small group giving everyone a hug. I saw what was coming and ducked his intimacy with a preemptive high-five.

I had joined one of the hundreds of running groups across the UK. The group was part of a new wave of collective fitness groups that mixed working out with other activities. There was GoodGym, where you ran and did social useful activities, Run Dem Crew, which was a mash-up of running and a hip-hop posse, and the Midnight Runners, which mixed partying with running. The bagel runners mixed socializing over bagels and coffee with a ten-kilometer run.

We set off at 7:00 a.m. sharp and threaded our way past commuters to the riverside. Every few hundred meters, we stopped, and the leader started taking photos. "Jump!" he said, "Throw out your arms!" Later I would find these photos on the group's Facebook page.

We looped back through the city, and after about an hour, we ended up at the bagel shop again. I was feeling tired, but satisfied. Most of the runners headed into the shop to buy a bagel. Not me. I was on a low-carb diet, and bread was off limits.

CARL, FEBRUARY 12

Nine days to the weight-lifting competition. There were two kinds of lifts I had to learn. The first was called the snatch. In one continuous movement, the bar had to come up above my head. To pass, the arms had to be perfectly straight. The second lift was called the clean-and-jerk. First the bar would land on the chest, and then, in a second movement, the bar would be lifted over the head. We were practicing with light brooms, going over the technique step-by-step. Straight back, chest up, bent knees, straight arms. Pull the barbell up over the knees and then jump. While the barbell travels upward, you have to squat underneath the bar, catching it with straight arms.

On my way back from the gym, I stopped by a retailer and bought ten t-shirts, ten pair of tube socks, and two pairs of shorts. I was showering twice a day now, changing clothes all the time. Our apartment looked like a locker room. Moist t-shirts and socks were draped over the doors, drying.

And I was sweating all the time. I wasn't only sweating when I was supposed to sweat, but also when I slept and ate and lay on the couch.

ANDRÉ, FEBRUARY 13

Morning Gloryville was a strange hybrid of a dance party and a wellness retreat.

The website advised you to "dress to sweat." I wasn't sure exactly what that meant, so I watched a few videos of past Morning Gloryville events. 1980s fitness-wear seemed popular. I settled on tracksuit pants, a muscle-tee, and a hoodie to keep me warm. I completed the look with a baseball cap I found at the bottom of my drawer.

The venue sat under an elevated freeway leading into central London. At the entrance, I was greeted by a hipster gondolier who put a bindi sticker on my forehead. Then a woman in a pink fur-suit gave me a deep and sincere hug. I handed over a twenty-pound note. Two more hugs and I was in.

I had my face painted by a woman in pink hot pants, then I rushed to the dance floor. Bright prayer flags, giant love hearts, and outsized Hindu deities were hanging from the roof. The crowd was still thin: there was a tall hippie with flowing dreadlocks, a psychedelic American Indian, a space rhino. More dancers arrived. Most looked like regular gym-goers.

As I started dancing, my Jawbone vibrated approvingly. Soon an MC appeared on stage and began peppering the music with motivational slogans: "We are a rave-olution! Sober raving! Feel amazing!"

After an hour of dancing, I headed for the "smoothie station" and ordered a green delight juice and a beetroot protein ball. A fire twirler appeared. The music went up a notch and the crowd whooped.

"This is the most perfect moment of our lives!" the MC yelled over the music. "We are sober. Our hearts are open. It's eleven o'clock on a Saturday morning!"

By about midday, I headed for the exit. As I passed the professional hugger in pink fur, she pretended to be disappointed. Two staff members stood outside smoking. I heard them swap cynical comments. I checked my Jawbone. I had more than passed my fitness goals for the day.

CARL, FEBRUARY 15

It had been one week since I first weighed myself. I was 77.6 kilograms then. Now, after a week of intense training and a 4,000 calorie diet, I was 82.9 kilograms. I had more body fat (12.8 percent), but my muscle mass had shot up, too.

All in all, I had gained 5.3 kilograms. It was a remarkable increase. If I carried on like this, adding five kilograms each week, I could probably qualify for a sumo competition by the summer.

Back home, I made my lunch of 400 grams of fried chicken served with 250 grams of steamed broccoli, and then I sat down and watched weight-lifting on YouTube while mechanically working myself through the plate.

ANDRÉ, FEBRUARY 15

It was my day of rest, and I was in a Buddhist café, relaxing after a session of dynamic yoga. According to my new bible, *Runner's World*, yoga was the ideal complement for marathon training. As I sat down to eat, Carl sent me a picture of a huge plate of chicken. I sent back a picture of my green smoothie and vegan cheesecake, hoping he might learn something.

CARL, FEBRUARY 16

After a couple of hours at the gym, I went with the beefy coach to buy a singlet. They were required in professional weight-lifting competitions. I looked at myself in the mirror. The singlet was black and stretchy with no arms and a plunging neckline. Sadly, there still wasn't much by way of muscles underneath.

We parted ways and I walked slowly through the city, feeling anxious and paranoid, imagining that there might be a drug test at the weight-lifting competition. What if they found traces from the smart drugs I used last month?

I sent a text to my friend who had given me the pills. He replied saying they should be out of my system within days, but recommended that I google for more detailed information. He was right. After about four or five days, there would be no way to trace the substances through urine or blood tests. They could, however, be found in my hair.

Later in the evening, I was sitting down at the kitchen table, still feeling anxious. All this work that I had neglected. I had stopped adding items to my to-do list. My email app informed me that I now had over 6,000 unread emails. I twisted around in my chair and looked at the big bag of protein powder which was taking up half of the sink. It was time for my third and final protein shake. But I wasn't in the mood. I decided to rebel against myself and skip the drink. It was a small but symbolic act of defiance, and I felt invigorated.

ANDRÉ, FEBRUARY 16

I eased into the hot bath and opened a book on running by the famous Japanese novelist Haruki Murakami. I had just returned from a twenty-nine-kilometer run. My longest yet. Murakami said he hated competition and craved solitude, which was why running was perfect for him. I liked that, and marked the page with a dog-ear. He then described running a one-hundred-kilometer ultramarathon. As he went past the forty-two-kilometer mark, he had to fight every part of his body, but once he had broken through the barrier of pain, he could carry on running in a state where he was "me, and at the same time not me." It was a "very still, quiet feeling," he said. Running was not just an escape from home or death, it seemed, but a retreat into an existential mode of non-being. I wondered whether I too would have that experience by the end of the month.

CARL, FEBRUARY 17

At 4:00 a.m., I woke up from a horrible nightmare. I was in a weight-lifting tournament. Three men entered the room. They were referees, wearing black-and-white striped shirts.

"Doping control," my beefy coach whispered in my ear.

The referees were heading our way. They walked in a line. They came closer. They looked at me. Then they took out scissors. They were going to cut my hair and send it to the lab. Then they'd find the drugs. I'd be disqualified, and maybe they would turn me in to the police!

ANDRÉ, FEBRUARY 17

Late afternoon. Raining. I still hadn't been out for a run. Dark thoughts spun around my head. But then I remembered the key lesson from Landmark: *narrative is your enemy*. Don't think. Just run.

I switched to autopilot: *put on your running gear, head to the park, run!*

On the way home, as I passed a group of teenage boys smoking, a thought crossed my mind: *if only they could come to their senses, stop wasting their lives, and start exercising!*

A couple weeks of training and I was already a jogging moralist.

CARL, FEBRUARY 18

Late afternoon, in the supermarket. After another long day in the gym, I was strolling up and down the aisles, stocking up on chicken and milk, when my phone vibrated. It was an email from the academic publisher.

"We have now read your manuscript," it began, "but I'm afraid that we've decided that the manuscript in its current state would not pass muster for publication." The editor explained that it was "not sound enough as a piece of scholarship," adding, in what I thought was a patronizing tone, that "we're sending you back to the drawing board."

When I came back home, I opened my laptop and wrote a short email asking the publisher to rip up the contract. This was not how I would normally react. What had prompted this violent response? I wondered this as I brushed my teeth. Maybe it was all the chicken I was eating. Or the creatine powder. Or the protein shakes. Or just the fact that I spent all my days in the gym.

ANDRÉ, FEBRUARY 19

I was working at home when a knock came at the door. A delivery man handed me a large cardboard package. I returned to my office and tore it open. Three books. The first one: *Lore of Running* (fourth edition) by Tim Noakes, MD. A medical textbook for runners. Close to thousand pages, and almost four pounds. I began leafing through the thin pages. Illustrations of bone structure. Diagrams comparing the VO_2 max values of different elite runners. Tables of training.

The second book was *Running and Being* by Dr. George Sheenan. A much thinner volume with chapters on "Understanding," "Becoming," and "Suffering." The author (a jogging doctor) described himself as a descendant of philosophers like Kierkegaard and Emerson and Bertrand Russell. It was published in 1978, at the end of the 1970s running boom, when 5 million Americans took up jogging. This was the period that Tom Wolfe dubbed the Me Decade, a time when many people became obsessed with self-improvement. I recalled a line from the 1960s yippie Jerry Rubin. In his 1976 autobiography, *Growing (Up) at Thirty-Seven*, he explained that, after years of over-indulging in hippie hedonism, he "gave himself 'permission to be healthy' and quickly lost thirty pounds." Jogging, Rubin explained, was part of his "journey into myself." A journey which people like Tom Wolfe no doubt dubbed narcissistic.

The third book, *Running: A Global History* by Thor Gotaas, mapped out a longer time scale. Here the 1970s running boom seemed insignificant. Gotaas's text was packed with fascinating tales: Japanese monks spending years running around a particular mountain searching for Zen, messengers running long distances in the ancient Inca empire, naked runners in seventeenth-century England, the creation of the first modern recreational running club in Auckland, New Zealand in 1960. The roots of running ran much deeper than I could have imagined.

CARL, FEBRUARY 19

On the scales again. I was down a little. From 82.9 to 81.7. But I had more muscles. I now had 70.5 kilograms, compared to 68.8 last time, and 65.4 kilograms before that.

"It's not all muscles," the beefy coach said.

"Water?"

"Well, it's not all water, either," he said, smiling.

ANDRÉ, FEBRUARY 21

Today was my first real test. Could I run thirty-five kilometers? Yesterday evening, before going to bed, I had mapped out my run using a website called mapmyrun.com. The website told me the precise distance, the approximate time based on my pace, and the number of calories I would burn.

I got off the train in Richmond, walked to my starting point on the riverside, and set off.

Just about three hours later, as I crossed the finishing line on the other side of London, I felt a surging sense of achievement. If I could do this, I should be able to do the marathon. I opened my running app, checked my data, took a selfie, and walked home.

CARL, FEBRUARY 21

It was early Sunday morning when we climbed over a young man sleeping outside the train station in an outer suburb of Stockholm. The streets were empty and desolate. The sky was gray. Snow lay thinly on the ground.

We found the door, a small sign outside reading Athletic Club, and we walked down a steep flight of stairs. I placed my polished Blundstones next to a mountain of sneakers and walked into a room, lined with benches and lockers. A couple of sturdy weight lifters in gray hoodies looked my way. I changed into my singlet and warmed up. My name came over the speakers. I marched through a long corridor and down a couple of stairs into the main hall. My coaches were following me.

One minute, the speaker said.

I walked down into the big gymnasium. I stopped by the bowl and covered my hands in magnesium. I stepped out onto the podium, my back against the Swedish flag. I looked out at the three referees. They were only sitting a few meters away from me, and behind them was the audience.

Beeeeee. Thirty seconds.

I gripped the barbell, back straight, chest up. I pulled the barbell vertically, and, as it reached the level of my knees, I jumped, making the weights fly up into the air. Meanwhile, I threw myself underneath the barbell with my knees bent and my arms stretched, catching the barbell above my head.

Beeeeeee.

I dropped the barbell onto the ground, looked at the judges, and then at the scoreboard. I had passed. My two personal trainers cheered from the side. I had made my first correct lift, and it felt great.

After a two-minute break, I returned to the podium, now attempting forty kilograms. Same procedure—barbell over the knees, stretched arms, jump—another correct lift.

Then forty-five kilograms. Attempting a personal best. I pulled the barbell with all my power and got it flying up into the air above my head, but as I was going to catch it with my straight arms, something went wrong. It was too heavy. My arms folded and the barbell, with all its weight, fell down, with menacing force, straight onto my head.

Bang!

Then onto the floor.

Boom!

I turned around and stumbled out, feeling dizzy. One of the functionaries ran up, asking how I was doing.

"Fine," I said, my voice breaking a little. I touched my head. No blood.

"Attempt failed. The barbell fell on his head," I heard over the speakers, as I disappeared into the corridor, back into the small gym.

I was disappointed. Humiliated. My coaches tried to cheer me up.

No time for weeping. I had to get ready for my next set of lifts. The clean-and-jerk.

My name came over the speakers. I passed forty kilograms without a problem. I asked for fifty kilograms, my personal record so far. It was easy. I felt strong. My self-confidence was returning.

"Put on sixty," I heard myself say to the functionaries. This wasn't the plan. The plan was to make forty-five kilograms in snatch (which I had just failed), and fifty-five kilograms in clean-and-jerk (hence reaching a total of one hundred kilograms).

"Take it easy now, relax," the agile coach said.

"No, Carl, don't relax. Use that adrenaline and go out and kick ass," the beefy coach intervened. "You can do this!"

I was feeling strong. My adrenaline was pumping. Yeah, let's kick ass.

I walked out, straight onto the podium, with more than a minute to go.

"C'mon Carl, you can do it," I heard people shouting from the audience, clapping their hands. I grabbed the barbell, staring straight ahead. All sounds disappeared. Nothing was there; nothing except the weights, and my body, which felt strong, stronger than ever.

I got myself into position. Chest up. Straight arms. Shoulders over the barbell. And then, with all my strength, I pulled the weights, gave it a perfect hit with my hips, and then jumped, as high as I could. The timing was good. I could feel how the barbell was flying high up into the air, landing on my chest. More shouts from the audience. Some applause. *C'mon you can do it.* I squatted and jumped, once more, as high as I could, pushing the barbell up, throwing myself underneath, with straight arms. Adrenaline was still pumping. The barbell was there, I could feel it, above my head. I could feel my face turning red. My hands were tightly wrapped around the steel.

Beeeeee.

I dropped the barbell onto the podium. I had broken my personal record with sixty kilograms. As I jogged off stage, I couldn't conceal my joy. I stretched my arms above my head.

I ran up to my coaches. They hugged me. Was this the happiest moment in my life? In the contest, I came in second to last overall. I was last in my weight group. But that didn't seem to matter. It felt like a great victory. I had done one hundred kilograms in total. Forty in snatch, and sixty in clean-and-jerk. I felt a strange impulse to write a letter to my publisher who had rejected my book and tell them I could lift one hundred kilograms in total. *Eat that, pricks!*

ANDRÉ, FEBRUARY 22

Yesterday, I managed to run thirty-five kilometers, but that didn't mean I could make the 42.195 kilometers of a marathon. A widely-shared axiom among runners was that the first thirty-five kilometers was the easy part. It's during the last seven kilometers that runners come unstuck. At that point, when the body is screaming to stop, the mind has to be strong.

When I would run my marathon next week, there would be no crowd and no other runners to carry me along. All I would have to rely on was my own willpower.

As part of my mental preparation, I had studied the psychology of marathons. Visualizing the last 25 percent of the race was crucial. At this point you had to shut your brain down. One technique was to repeat a positive mantra. Murakami's mantra, which he used during his ultra-marathon, was: *I'm not a human. I'm a piece of machinery. I don't need to feel a thing. Just forge on ahead.* It seemed a bit long and complicated so, perhaps drawing on what I learned at Landmark, I settled on: *don't think, just run.*

Another important marathon mind-hack was to break up a longer run into smaller goals. This was what Roger Bannister, the first man to run a four-minute mile, had done. Mentally, he was running four races of 400 meters in one minute each, rather than running one mile in four minutes.

That evening in bed, I set myself a psychological task: I would imagine the last 25 percent of my upcoming marathon. I pictured the landmarks. The House of Parliament, the National Theatre on Southbank, the Tower Bridge, the old riverside warehouses in Wapping. I would pass through central London as if piloting a drone, mindlessly closing in on my goal.

CARL, FEBRUARY 26

The month was coming to a close, and it was time to register my progress. My coaches gave me the same tests I had undergone at the beginning of the month.

"This is *amazing*. Look here," the agile coach said, pointing at the screen excitedly.

Bench press (10 reps): from 40 to 47.5.
Squats (10 reps): from 45 to 60.
Snatch: from 30 to 45.
Clean-and-jerk: from 40 to 60.
Training heart-rate: from 170 to 155.

"You've improved almost all indicators by 50 percent."

I blushed. Sure, the sacrifices were considerable. I had done little else than think about my body, work on my body, log my body, even dream about my body.

But it had paid off. It was all there. The figures didn't lie.

ANDRÉ, FEBRUARY 27

I had bought a new device. A running watch. It cost £159, a tiny fraction of the 9.6 billion Euros spent on running every year across

Europe. It looked like a gigantic sweatband made of rubber with a digital face on it. As I wrapped it around my wrist, Mel came into the living room.

"What the hell is that?"

"A running watch."

"What for?"

"Lots of things," I said. "It keeps track of my distance and my pace. It maps my run. It can even play music! Listen."

But Mel had already left the room.

CARL, FEBRUARY 27

I had just arrived in London, and tomorrow was André's big day. He was going to run a marathon. It was a big deal, and yet it wasn't.

I had told quite a few people that André was going to run a marathon as part of the project. They were all impressed at first. Then, when I told them that he had done it twice before, they seemed less impressed, as if this whole thing had lost its magic.

ANDRÉ, FEBRUARY 28

Today was my ultimate test. 42.195 kilometers. From Hampton Court all the way back home to Mile End.

I was facing the Thames. But it looked nothing like the ominous churning river I knew from the city. Here, the river looked like a pleasant country waterway.

Go. I pressed my watch. After about an hour, as I reached Richmond, I was really getting into the run. I rounded Kew Gardens, my watch counting down the steps. 21.1 kilometers. Half a marathon completed; another half to go.

I crossed the river to the Chelsea embankment. This was where my mental visualization began: only 25 percent to go. I passed Parliament (landmark 1), then Southbank (landmark 2), and when I reached Tower Bridge (landmark 3) I knew I was going to make it. My watch was counting down to 42.2 kilometers. I entered Wapping. I was practically there now.

Soon I reached my final destination: the Prospect of Whitby, an old pub by the river. I had done it. *I had done it!*

I took a selfie and entered the pub, ready to celebrate with a well-earned beer. Yet all I could feel was a strong sense of anti-climax.

Carl had been saying that I had not done enough this month. *Fuck it!* I thought. *I'll do fifty kilometers. A proper ultramarathon. That will show him how committed I am!*

I set out again, Bowie in my earphones, running up to Victoria Park. I felt like a machine. It was all just one step after another. I was completely empty now, drifting around the park.

After touching the gate, my finish line, I stared blankly at an ice cream truck. Fifty kilometers. Done. Now what? I took a selfie. Then another. Then another. Then I walked home like a crippled man.

CARL, FEBRUARY 28

When I got back to André's place in the evening, he opened the door in training clothes. He looked sore but happy.

"I did an ultramarathon," he said.

"Wow, an ultra—that's what?"

"Fifty kilometers!"

"Wow! Come here," I said, and gave him a hug. He knew I had been hoping for something more than a marathon, and this was, strictly speaking, something more. Though it was definitely not an Ironman.

André stretched out on the couch. His feet were damaged. They had been through a great deal.

Later in the evening at a local pub, while we were celebrating our respective achievements and feeling both triumphant and relieved,

André asked me what the most ridiculous thing I had done during the month was.

I paused, then took out my phone and showed him a picture. It was my poo. I had logged it on Poo Keeper.

MARCH

BRAIN

ANDRÉ, MARCH 1

Early morning, on my way to Heathrow airport and then Hamburg. The sun peeked through the taxi window. Spring was on its way. There was a new month ahead: this time, it would be dedicated to the brain.

Neurohacks, I typed into my phone, and a long list of articles appeared. "Caffeine, alcohol, over-the-counter medicine, and other drugs are all forms of neurohacking," I read. "Every one of these substances alters or 'tricks' the brain into desirable conditions." By the time I stepped out of the taxi at the airport terminal, I had compiled a long list of hacks promising to make me smarter. Some were simple: avoiding mental clutter, keeping news and social media to a minimum, listening to classical music. Some sounded a bit strange: speaking in the present tense, taking thirty-minute power-naps every four hours. And some sounded downright dangerous: transcranial direct current stimulation, or tCDS, which involved running an electrical current through your brain.

Once I had passed through the empty airport security, I headed directly for the bookstore. I found a shelf called "smart thinking" and picked out three books: *The Organized Mind, Mindsets,* and *Thinking, Fast and Slow.* After boarding the plane, I settled into my seat and opened *The Organized Mind.* I read about hapless people whose drawers were filled with junk, who often lost their keys, who couldn't remember their passwords, who were overwhelmed by emails, and who constantly missed appointments. It was basically about me: my sad disorganized life was laid bare.

CARL, MARCH 1

I said goodbye to André and jumped in a taxi to Heathrow on my way to New York City.

As I ate my breakfast at the airport, I downloaded brain.fm, an app that combined, they said, "music with auditory neuroscience to produce an innovative non-invasive digital therapy application for consumers." I downloaded their white paper, "Behind Brain.fm: Theory & Algorithms," and started reading: "Brain.fm music," it said, "influences cognitive states by entraining neuronal oscillations." There were pictures of brains in different colors, and there were graphs and figures on sound waves and brain waves. I didn't understand a thing, but I signed up for a one-year contract nonetheless. I opened the app. There were three modes: focus, relax, sleep.

I finished my meal and went to a book shop, all the time listening to brain.fm in "relax" mode. I picked out two titles: *Brainhack: Tips and Tricks to Unleash Your Brain's Full Potential* and *The Idiot Brain: A Neuroscientist Explains What Your Head Is Really Up To.*

Outside the gate, with an hour to kill, I put on another thirty-minute session of brain.fm. I set it to "focus" mode this time. When it was time to board, I had already flicked through more than half of the *Brainhack* book, but it was all drivel. It rehashed old clichés, such as the delusional claim that we're using only 10 percent of our mental capacities. As I was waiting in the line, André (who had just arrived at Heathrow, but in a different terminal) sent a link to a podcast. It was about the journalist Joshua Foer, who, after practicing memorization techniques for one year, signed up to the USA Memory Championship—and won. I picked up my tablet and downloaded his book, *Moonwalking with Einstein: The Art and Science of Remembering Everything.*

As we flew in over JFK, I was deeply immersed in the stories of memorization experts. They could memorize the order of a deck of cards in less than a minute, remember presidents and capitals, remember endless strings of numbers, and memorize long passages from books. Could I learn to do this, too?

ANDRÉ, MARCH 2

My challenge this month was to learn computer coding. But which language should I tackle? A week earlier, I had met with a friend in a hipster beer hall. He was a self-taught computer programmer. Pushing his beer to the side, he pulled out his silver laptop covered with anarchist stickers: "This is what you need to learn," he said. "Python. It's so easy even a kid can get it." He opened up a black screen and typed in a few lines of green text, then pressed enter. "Hello world!" flashed up. He then opened up a website, learnpython.org. "This will help you to learn. Just do all the lessons and you'll have the basics soon enough."

Python was invented in 1989 by a Dutch guy, Guido van Rossum, to cure his boredom during the Christmas holiday break. Python coders now called the Dutchman the "Eternal Benevolent Dictator."

I found an online book, *How to Think Like a Computer Programmer*, meant for high school students. It explained some elementary issues, such as the difference between formal and natural language, and the basics of syntax. Reading about programming was one thing, but I knew if I wanted to call myself a coder, I would need to start doing it.

CARL, MARCH 2

"I've been demoted to *this*!" the professor cried out, theatrically pointing his hands at the long empty bar. We had originally planned to go out for a nice dinner. But after he rejected my book, I suggested we meet briefly for a quick drink.

"I'm not sure you're meant to write books," he said.

"Why?"

"I mean, a *book*."

"What do you mean? *Book?*" I imitated his emphasis.

"For me, a *book* is an intervention among other interventions that needs to make a *lasting* mark. I'm not sure that's for you."

I said nothing.

"Maybe you should start a blog instead," he suggested.

I downed my beer and ordered another one.

"I was planning to maybe learn French this month."

"French?"

"Yes, it's part of a project I'm doing with a friend."

"Ha. French. That's *too* easy. Why not Arabic or Russian? That would be a *real* challenge."

I looked out the window onto Sixth Avenue. Fashionable women walking past. The professor continued talking, but I had stopped listening. We were alone in the spacious bistro, sitting at the bar, bottles and glasses reflecting in the mirror.

"Do you know where I can find a brain?" I finally intervened.

"A brain?"

"Yes, I would really like to see a brain. I've never seen one before."

ANDRÉ, MARCH 3

Today I started my first coding lesson. Sitting in my office at work, I logged in to learnpython.org. The first exercise was not difficult. I followed the directions and soon I saw the words "Hello world!" flashing on the screen. Then a slight alteration to the program and I had: "Fuck you Carl!" I sniggered like a schoolboy, took a screenshot, and emailed it to him.

"Excuse me," I said, "I was wondering if there is a brain here that I could see."

"Try the Hall of Human Origins," the woman said from behind the reception. I was on a brain hunt at the American Museum of Natural History adjacent to Central Park in Manhattan.

I walked past the enormous cases with wild animals, down the stairs, through an empty room with a gigantic, ancient canoe hanging from the ceiling, and into a dark room. Stuffed human ancestors stared at me. Each one was taller than the next, and they got less hairy and more upright the more recent they were.

And then, behind showcases of skulls, I finally spotted a human brain. It was lit up, in a shade of blue. When I got closer I could see it was just a piece of plastic with a lamp inside.

Disappointed, on my way back, I saw a sign. *Meet the neuroscientist.* I looked inside the harshly lit lab.

"You open?"

"Sure," a woman in white coat answered.

"I'm looking for a brain."

"Then you've come to the right place."

Next to her papers, on the desk, I could see three small showcases.

"Here," she said, and pointed at one of them. I came closer. A small sticker on the box read, *Real human brain.*

Next to it, another brain, cut in two. Small stickers of numbers pierced into each part. She gave me a laminated paper listing the names of the different brain parts.

"Touch this," the neuroscientist said, handing me a small plastic bag. It evidently had a brain inside.

"Sheep's brain?" I asked, reading from the small sticker on the bag.

"No, I don't think so. I found it here in the lab. It must be mislabeled. Too big for a sheep. Pretty sure it's a human's brain. I'm going to analyze it in a bit."

"It's so hard, like dried clay," I said, moving my fingers through the plastic. "I reckon it feels quite different when taken freshly out of the head?"

"Yeah, it'd be a lot softer then."

I started to think about Ulrike Meinhof's brain. It had been preserved in formaldehyde for a quarter of a century, then it disappeared without trace. Scientists wanted to understand how a peaceful journalist and mother had turned into a revolutionary committed to acts of violence against the state, and they believed the brain would give them the answer, the key to understanding the nature of evil.

"Look mummy, a brain!" I heard a child shouting from behind, elbowing his way to the desk. The neuroscientist lost interest in me and turned to the boy instead.

ANDRÉ, MARCH 4

I looked up from my computer screen, my eyes stinging. I had been doing the same simple exercise for two hours and had got nowhere. Coding was much harder than I expected.

CARL, MARCH 4

I had finished the book on memorization, and it was now time to practice what I had learned. My first challenge: remember all the American presidents. I had to construct a memory palace, based on a space I knew well. I chose the place where I grew up, a two-story suburban house with a garage.

I imagined walking up to the house. But the entryway was now blocked by a big *wash*ing machine. I peeked inside the small round window, *George* Costanza inside, trapped, spinning round and round. *George Washington*. I continued up the driveway, opened our mailbox, and picked out a computer. On the screen, an image of a two-headed monster: one face belonging to my friend *John*, the other to *Adam*. *John Adams* (the computer helped me remember I watched the television series John Adams on my computer). I climbed the few stairs up the porch, where, outside the entrance, our neighbor, *Thomas*, was fast asleep. *Thomas Jefferson*. I walked inside. To my left was a small cupboard. Inside was a miniature scene resembling *Madison* Square garden, and, at the center, on stage, *James* Brown singing. *James Madison*. I walked into the hallway. *James* Bond dancing the waltz with Marilyn *Monroe*. *James Monroe*.

I took a short break from the mind work and looked around the café. People were sitting in booths talking, but I had neither heard them nor seen them for the last thirty minutes.

I continued filling up my memory palace with strange scenes. In my old room, I imagined a dark nightclub and a performance by a Chinese punk imitating Frank Sinatra (called *Frank-lin*). His face covered with piercings. *Franklin Pierce*.

With only eleven more presidents to go, I was running out of space. I walked out of the house again, onto the driveway. Outside the garage lay Franklin D. Roosevelt, buried in a pile of roses. The remaining ten presidents had to be packed into the two cars parked in the garage.

ANDRÉ, MARCH 7

Late afternoon, at Piccadilly Circus, a thin guy in his twenties with a bony face walked up and introduced himself.

"Hello," he said intensely.

A few days earlier I had sent an email to a neurohacker and we had agreed to meet.

"Want to go for a beer?" I asked.

"Coffee," he snapped back.

Five minutes later we were in the Nordic Café, with two coffees and one cinnamon bun. He disappeared to the toilet. A minute later he returned.

"You know exercise is the best mindhack. I'm a climber, and I run every day. My aim is to climb the seven highest peaks in the world. Including one on Antarctica! My other goal is to give a TED talk within the year."

He was a PhD student doing research on human attention. As I ate the cinnamon bun, he retreated to the bathroom again. There would be at least three more bathroom trips before the meeting was over.

"You've heard of 23andMe," he asked.

I shook my head.

"It's a DNA test you can do through the post." He reached for his laptop, logged on to a website and showed me his genetic profile. "You should also take a blood test. They can help to optimize your bodily functions. I do one every six to eight months."

He paused for a second, thinking long and hard while looking up the ceiling. "What else could you do. Let's see. *Hmm?* Well you could try different *diets*, of course. What else? Oh yes, *posture* is important. You need to sit up straight. You know, it increases your brain waves," he straightened his back, searching for more mind-hacks. "And yes, of course, you need to eat less sugar and, by all means, avoid processed foods. What else, what *else?*" He was thinking again. I put the last piece of the cinnamon bun in my mouth, looking around the café. "Yes, that's it, you need a healthy social environment."

I was expecting advice such as running electricity through the brain. All this guy was giving me was lifestyle tips.

CARL, MARCH 10

I was back in Stockholm and had tons to read: fifty student essays and two books. But instead of confronting the task head-on, I had a different book in my hands, Tony Buzan's *The Speed Reading Book*, which promised I could read as fast as 1,000 words a minute.

Next to me sat Marcel Proust's *In Search of Lost Time*, all seven volumes. I had read through the first four volumes, and it had taken me over a year. *In Search of Lost Time* was 1,267,069 words, over 4,000 pages. If I could read 1,000 words per minute it should take me no more than twenty-one hours to get through the whole thing. The current world record holder in speed reading, Anne Jones, could read 4,700 words a minute. With that pace, she could finish Proust's suite in less than five hours.

The secret to this technique was to get the "voice" out of your head. When we first learn to read, Buzan explained, we vocalize the words. Then, as we begin to read silently, we continue to vocalize in our head. Once you get rid of this "bad habit," you can start swallowing words as a chunk, rather than one word at a time.

Eager to practice the method, I downloaded a speed reading app on my phone, Acceleread, and started the first lesson:

Focus on the center of the screen and try to read the words at once, rather than left to right.

Groups of two to three words began to flash, in the middle of the screen, against a white background. I had to digest all words at once, without moving my eyes. But watching blinking words appearing on a screen felt more like staring into a strobe than actually reading.

Next lesson:

Follow the guide as it highlights words from left to right. Try to read the entire group of highlighted words, rather than one word at a time.

The text was divided into three columns, each highlighted at a time. I had to move my eyes from the left-hand column, with one group of words, to the middle column, and then on to the right-hand column.

After a couple of practice rounds, it was time to measure my own reading speed. I skimmed through a short text about the Battle of Pea Ridge, then answered a set of questions. I read as fast as I could, jumping from one group of words to the next, not turning back, just as I had learned from Buzan.

425 wpm, comprehension 66%.

Did I understand the text I had just read? Not really, but well enough to get a 66% comprehension score, which was the same that the world record holder had achieved, although she was reading ten times my speed.

It was already late in the afternoon, and the fifty essays and the two books were still unread.

ANDRÉ, MARCH 11

Things were getting desperate. I had tried most of the lifestyle neuro-hacks I could find, and I wasn't getting any smarter. I needed an alternative.

During my meeting with the young neuro-hacker a few days ago, he had briefly mentioned tCDS. At the time, I had no idea what it meant, so when I got home I did a little research. tCDS stood for transcranial direct-current simulation. It involved placing electrodes on your scalp, then running a small steady electrical current through your brain.

In an article published in *New Scientist* a journalist described how she had used tCDS while picking off targets with an M4 assault rifle at a shooting range. Her hit rate improved dramatically when the electrical current was on. There were more articles describing how sports teams used tCDS to improve player performance, how computer gamers ran electricity through their brains to boost their kill rates, how research subjects in a lab upped their results on cognitive tasks when receiving tCDS.

Worried that this was dangerous, I dug into the medical literature. I learned tCDS did not have significant adverse effects. It did, however, have a positive impact on people with depression, alcoholism, fibromyalgia, Parkinson's, and schizophrenia. My mounting excitement was dampened when I came across a meta-analysis that concluded tCDS had little or no impact at all.

Could running a stream of electricity through my brain improve my coding? Or was it just another neuro-hoax? I felt confused.

CARL, MARCH 13

I was in the car with my mother, on our way to go skiing in the mountains. It was a three-hour drive and, to use the time effectively, I decided to memorize the sixteen digits of my bank card. When reading *Moonwalking with Einstein* I had come across a system that was used to translate numbers into symbols, which I now memorized:

0 = C or S
1 = D or T.
2 = N
3 = M
4 = R
5 = L
6 = Ch, sh
7 = G or K
8 = V or F
9 = B or P

I was going to memorize four digits at a time, placing them in a new memory palace, which, this time, was our kitchen. I used the hob and placed the first group of four digits in a nonstick frying pan, the second group in a large pasta bowl, the third group of digits in a smaller sauce pan, and, finally, the last four digits in an iron skillet.

After about half an hour of intense silence, I opened my mouth and recited the sixteen digits.

"Correct," my mother said. But she was already bored.

"Do you want to know how I memorized this?"

"Er, not really."

"Well, I first have to translate each digit into a consonant, so 0 for example is S and 5 is L and 6 is *shhh!*"

"Eh, okay."

"And then I have to place these figures somewhere, and I'm using the stove at home, and guess how I remembered the last four digits?"

"How?"

"I took your brother, dressed him in an SS uniform, and put him in an iron skillet."

"Why?"

"The last four digits are 5600, right?"

"Right."

"Your brother's name is Lars. So that's 5, L; and 6, *shhh!* And then S is 0, so to remember two zeroes I just dressed him in an SS uniform. Cool, huh?"

My mother sighed.

"Could you take out my other bank cards," I said, giving her my wallet. "I'd like to memorize them, too."

"This will undoubtedly be the most boring car journey in my entire life," she replied.

ANDRÉ, MARCH 13

Today my brain was hacked by a Russian. I had read about him in numerous articles and had seen him in videos hacking people's brains.

I arrived at the Russian's apartment late in the afternoon. He offered me some plastic flip-flops and we walked into a living room that had been converted into a lab. Technological equipment and books were scattered on desks and tables. On the wall, next to a samurai sword, hung a framed poster, mapping out the regions of the brain.

"People have been using tCDS for over a century," he explained, reaching for a small, dark wooden box with some wiring in it. "This is an electrical brain stimulator from the nineteenth century." He handed me the box. "Russian children with ADHD were given tCDS from the late 1960s onward," he added.

"I've been interested in Soviet-era neurotechnologies, such as lasers and magnetic coils," he continued, pointing to various devices around the room. One looked like a small white cone. Others were in boxes.

"Can I try these out?" I asked.

"Sure." He'd been expecting this question. "We can apply a laser to your visual cortex and add in a Kasina simulation. It's the same laser we used on depressed Ukrainian pensioners."

He laughed as he disappeared into the next room. A minute later he returned with a box. He laid out the laser, which reminded me of an oversized white plastic spoon with a cluster of large LED lights on one end. He then unfolded a sun lounger. "I use this for my guinea pigs."

I laid down in the guinea pig chair. He wrapped a band around my head. "It's a Muse scanner," he explained. He then handed me a tablet computer. A horseshoe-shaped image showed on the screen. When all the lights appeared in the horseshoe, he pressed "scan." It ran for about twenty seconds. I felt nothing. Six circles marbled with different colors showed up on the screen.

"There's lots of activity in the alpha section in the front of your left hemisphere," he said. "You probably have some anxiety."

"I don't feel anxious," I replied.

"Well, we know from Freud and Jung that feelings can be unconscious."

The Russian then put a set of goggles and a pair of earphones on me. The gentle sound of his breath reminded me of being examined by my family doctor as a child. He laid the spoon-like laser behind my head. I reclined.

I waited for what seemed like ten minutes. Then hypnotic techno sounds started to come through the earphones. The goggles lit up. First there was a yellow field with a barely discernible pattern that slowly started to move. Then the images and sounds became more intense. The colors changed, and the simulation became all-enveloping. I could see the blood capillaries at the back of my eyes. It was like an LSD trip. At some point, it occurred to me that I was sitting in a Russian man's house who I had only just met, and I had no idea what he was up to.

After what seemed like an hour, the simulation slowed down. A neutral sound and soft colors returned. I started to wiggle my fingers and toes.

"So, what are you thinking and feeling?" he asked, as he removed the goggles and headset.

"That was very intense," I replied.

"Hmm," he said, as he took another measure of my brain using the Muse. My brain activity was now much more balanced across each hemisphere. The anxiety was gone. More activity in my visual cortex at the back of my head.

"What's that?" I said, pointing at a helmet with wires sticking out of it.

"A God Helmet. It stimulates all regions of your brain at once to give you a religious experience." He went on to tell me about a breakthrough experience he had a few years ago when he applied sixteen magnetic coils to his head for about twenty minutes.

"Afterward I had an intense individuation experience," he explained. "I felt like Superman. I read 600 pages of very difficult technical manuals in one night. I didn't sleep. This continued for a week. During that time, I developed the core hypotheses that I'm still working on. At the end of the week, I tried sixty-four coils."

"Wow," I said.

"Yeah, but the result wasn't good. I became depressed for a month. I learned that simply adding more coils does not necessarily improve the results."

A few hours later, as I walked through the night back to the tube station, my vision seemed to be clear and intense. Once home, I started some housework, washed the dishes, made dinner, and cleaned up, all with great efficiency. I had an unusual amount of energy and focus, similar to my experiences taking Modafinil.

CARL, MARCH 15

Today I read one book and fifty student essays, using the speed-reading method I had just acquired. So, I should probably rephrase that: today I skimmed one book and fifty student essays.

ANDRÉ, MARCH 15

I ran up to my study, like a teenager with a new porn magazine, and ripped open the package I had just received in the mail. Inside was a white box with clear casing containing my very own Muse.

I downloaded some apps, entered my personal information, and put on the Muse. It looked like a plastic hairband, like something that a younger David Beckham would have used to keep his hair in place.

On my iPad, an image of a Hawaiian beach appeared. Soft waves were rolling in.

Settle in. Take a few moments to relax by becoming aware of your breathing, a woman with a California accent said. *No need to change your breathing, your body knows how to breathe.*

The gently lapping waves became stormy, a sign that my mind was overactive. *To focus on your breathing, count each out-breath up to ten.* I tried to focus by counting my breaths. The wind quieted down for a moment. Then the storm returned.

When the winds get stronger, your mind is overactive. Don't worry, just start the count back at one without judging how you're feeling. I was breathing deeply, trying to calm the waves.

All done. Tap the screen to see your data, the calm voice said. A graph showed my brain activity over the five minutes that I had been meditating. There were a few moments when it dipped into the relaxation zone, but mostly it was up there in the overactive range.

I opened another app called Opti Brain, and the same horseshoe-shaped graph that I had seen at the Russian's place appeared. I pressed scan and six brain images popped up, filled in with different colors. I had no idea what this meant, but I was delighted I could now scan my brain.

CARL, MARCH 15

At home, I was testing my IQ online using the Mensa Sample test. After answering twenty-four questions in ten minutes, this message flashed on the screen:

Your IQ is estimated to 116.
This corresponds to the 85th percentile, i.e. 85% of the population has an IQ less than 116.
To become a member of Mensa an IQ of 131 or more is required, which is achieved by 2% of the population, i.e. the 98th percentile.
The probability that you will qualify for membership of Mensa is small.

ANDRÉ, MARCH 16

The Russian brain-hacker asked me to meet him at a place called Hackspace. Before going, I checked the website, which described it as a "community run workshop where people come to share tools and knowledge." I matched the address with a graffiti-covered door facing out onto a busy road. I was led in by a young guy who looked like an American professor: navy blazer, chinos, chambray shirt, a white t-shirt underneath.

About twenty geeks were sitting in an open-plan space talking intensely. I saw the Russian. He was sitting at a table with a friend in typical Goth attire: black hair, makeup, black clothes, and one of those plug-like earrings. The Russian led me into a separate room and began unpacking his bag. Out came wires, cables, a Muse, a laptop, goggles, and many other unidentifiable objects.

"What would you like to do today?" he asked.

I threw the question back at him, asking what he might recommend.

"A Kasina simulation with tCDS."

"Okay," I replied.

"Basically, I'll run a low-level electrical current through your brain."

"Okay," I said pulling up an office chair and sitting back. The Russian did a few scans of my brain using his Muse. My brain waves looked more balanced today, he said, gluing two sticky pads to my forehead and wrapping gauze around my head. *I must look like a psychiatric patient from the 1950s*, I thought as I leaned back in the chair. The Russian helped me put on the goggles and headphones. I surrendered to the technology as it started working on my brain. I could feel a light pulsing on my temples before pink and blue patterns appeared in front of my eyes.

After what seemed like hours I started wondering whether the Russian had gone outside for a cigarette and forgotten about me.

The noise died away and I heard two people in the corner of the room talking about real estate prices. Soon the Russian was there, next to me, helping me take off the goggles.

"What did you think?" he asked.

"Well, it was longer and a bit more boring than last time. And there was pink and blue instead of yellow."

"Strange," he said. "It was exactly the same simulation we did with you previously."

I was surprised. He did some more scans using the Muse and started to explain what they meant. He pointed to a part of the chart and said: "Could be signs of depression."

The Russian turned his attention to the Goth now. He doused a couple of wool pads with a liquid drug called Piracetam and pushed them up the Goth's nostrils. Hanging from the wool were two wires connected to a machine. He then attached a small computer chip to the Goth's forehead and another wire to the back of his neck. Once all the equipment was in place, he set the electrical current going.

It was getting late and it was time for me to head home. As I left, the Goth was still sitting calmly in his chair with the electrified cotton wool up his nose. The Russian studied the data on his computer that was being transmitted from the chip on the Goth's forehead.

CARL, MARCH 16

In my office, I prepared myself for the upcoming IQ test, now only a day away.

Your IQ is estimated to 119.
90% of the population has an IQ less than 119.

This was the second time I had done the same test, which, technically speaking, was not fair practice, because I was answering the very same questions as once before. Despite cheating, I had only managed to improve by three points, and I was nowhere near Mensa's entry barrier of 131.

In a desperate attempt to improve my IQ, I had bought *The Ultimate IQ Test Book: 1000 Practice Test Questions to Boost your Brain Power*, which claimed that, even though it was generally accepted that our IQ is constant from the age of eighteen and onward, it was indeed possible to train our minds and boost our brain power by practicing.

I spent the next five hours working through long and tedious tests. At the end of the day, when I felt properly prepared, I returned to the online Mensa test one last time.

Your IQ is estimated to 126 or above.

This was the best score you could achieve, and I was told I had a good chance of qualifying for Mensa. The arrow on the bell curve suggested I was there, on the very far right corner, in the company of Einstein, Sherlock Holmes, and E.T. I took a screenshot and sent it to André.

ANDRÉ, MARCH 17

In the evening, I met up with a friend, who talked about recent problems in his life. He clearly needed distraction from his woes, so I offered to scan his brain. He agreed. I took out the Muse from my leather satchel and put it over his head. After five minutes of struggling with it, I managed to get a signal. Then I ran the scan and showed it to him.

"What does it mean?" he asked.

"I have no idea," I replied.

CARL, MARCH 17

I was in the foyer of a new university campus, two hours' drive from Stockholm. A group of young men stared into their mobile phones, pretending to be busy.

"Here for the Mensa test?" I asked a young guy in his early twenties.

"Yes, er, that's right." He looked nervous, then continued. "It was my friend. I mean, my friend did it first, a few months ago, and then I thought I should do it, too. You know, it's good if you apply for jobs. It looks good on your resume."

An older man came down the stairs, wearing Birkenstock sandals and white socks. "Are you waiting for me?" He tucked in his checked shirt, sharpened his belt, and tugged up his jeans.

We followed him up the stairs, then down a linoleum-tiled corridor. No one said a word. Our eyes remained glued to the floor.

The test room was a physics lab, cluttered with machines. The leader sat down at a table, facing us. He smiled, correcting his glasses. "You've done the sample test on our website?"

We nodded.

"And you had a good result?"

Everyone nodded again.

"There's no point in taking the same test more than once. Some people do it three or four times."

Everyone laughed. Me too, although more nervously than the others.

"Given your test scores on our website," the test leader continued, "you are all extraordinarily gifted."

He gave us an emotional speech about the difficulties that came with having a high IQ: "You have probably found it difficult in school, right? No stimulation? You were probably done with your math exercises before all the others?" He paused, letting us nod in agreement. "Yep. That was the case for me, too."

He read three mock questions, and then the test started. We had twenty minutes.

I went through the first questions with ease but as it became more difficult I was beginning to feel strangely nervous. With more than fifteen questions to answer, I noticed I was running out of time. *Fuck!* I went back to the unanswered questions and filled something in, then answered the last few questions at random.

Time was up and I had screwed up. Whatever naive fantasies I may have had of passing the test, they were now dead.

As the others left the room, I lingered in the back.

"Do you have a minute?" I asked the test leader once we were alone.

"Sure."

I told him about our project and that I was interested in attending some of Mensa's social events.

"Well, join me now. I'm going to the pub to meet other members."

It was a short walk to the pub. It was dark but not cold. Spring was in the air.

They were already waiting for us, a man and a woman, at the back of the pub, drinking beer.

"What made you want to join Mensa?" I asked.

They all seemed to have similar stories: they'd had a difficult time in school, they'd not been able to fit in, and the school jocks had given them a hard time. After graduating from school, they had still struggled socially. When they had first heard of Mensa, they thought that maybe this was a place for them. And they had been right. The man described his first social meeting at Mensa. He had met with another member, and they were meant to go out and have dinner with the rest of the group. Several hours later, they realized they had missed the dinner. And when he later met other members, he had similar experiences. It was as if he was set free for the first time.

"Are you ever ridiculed for being members?"

"All the time," they said in chorus. The woman explained that, at work, if she would do something wrong, her colleagues would never fail to make fun of her, saying: *Oh, but I thought you were so intelligent.* I asked what they made of accusations that Mensa was an elitist club. They said it couldn't be further from the truth. The man said that, among themselves, they often referred to Mensa as a club for the socially impaired.

I asked if they spent much time with mind puzzles and other IQ-boosting activities. Only one of them did, the test leader. The other two didn't seem interested in any way whatsoever.

"So what do you do," I asked?

"We hang out. It is just a social thing," the man said.

"And it's a great opportunity to date," the woman said, laughing, alluding to the numerical imbalance between men and women.

I spent a couple of enjoyable hours chatting with the three Mensa members. Just as I was about to leave, the man said that once I received my letter of acceptance, he would love to chat with me at the pub again.

"Sure," I said, knowing this would never happen. I liked that they thought of me as an equal, but the hard truth was that my IQ was only about average.

ANDRÉ, MARCH 18

A few days earlier I had noticed Bulletproof Coffee on the menu of a café in central London and wondered what on earth it could be. I learned that its creator, Dave Asprey, promised that the beverage could boost your IQ by twenty points. He stumbled onto the idea while trekking in Nepal.

He had drunk some of the local yak butter tea and found himself feeling unusually enlightened. After returning to the US, this cloud-computing entrepreneur had come up with a recipe of coffee, butter, and coconut oil. Each hit was over 400 calories. But despite the high-fat content, Asprey claimed that the beverage would make you thinner as well as smarter.

So, I gathered the necessary ingredients, brewed the coffee, spooned out the butter, and then chiseled some coconut oil from a jar. I then blended it all together with a newly acquired hand mixer. When it was done, it looked approximately like something you might order at Starbucks. The first sip was more pleasant than I had expected. It tasted slightly tropical and very rich. Ten minutes after consuming the drink I noticed a definite improvement in my hitherto sluggish mood. Was I becoming bulletproof?

Later that day, I began reading Asprey's new book, *Head Strong: The Bullet Proof Plan to Activate Untapped Brain Energy to Work Smarter and Faster—In Just Two Weeks.* The coffee, it turned out, was just part of a much larger system. If I really wanted to boost my brain power, I had to follow a strict ritual. Each morning I should begin by exposing my bare skin to sunlight for ten to twenty minutes, followed by twenty-five squats, and five rounds of deep breaths. I needed to upgrade my diet: avoid sugar, eating lots of brightly colored food, and drink Bulletproof Coffee. To become completely bulletproof, I should exercise each day, meditate, and reduce all digital distractions. It was vital that I maximize my sleep by avoiding screens before retreating into a completely blacked out, temperature-controlled room for a full eight hours of sleep.

CARL, MARCH 18

I had just learned to solve the Rubik's Cube when I had to run off to a café for a meeting with Mattias Ribbing, the three-time Swedish memorization champion.

I told him about my memorization practice. He said I had to be more effective in my use of symbols. The stories were too long. I should also find ways of integrating these techniques into my life, so I could start remembering everything, at all times.

I asked him about remembering the order of a shuffled card deck. His personal record was just over one minute.

"I no longer find these things important."

"No?"

"They're just party tricks."

I didn't care whether they were party tricks.

"I want to learn to memorize the first five hundred digits of pi," I said.

"That's going to be really difficult. You will need an entire system of symbols, from 1 to 100. It will take time to construct one," he replied.

He explained how, years ago, preparing for the Swedish championships, he had designed his own system, from 1 to 1,000.

ANDRÉ, MARCH 20

I hated programming! No amount of bulletproof living could change that.

CARL, MARCH 21

So, if I wanted to memorize pi, I first had to construct a system of symbols, from 1 to 100, and the symbols should be personal, to make them easier to remember.

I already knew how to translate figures into characters: 0 = S, 2 = N, 3 = M, and so on. But that was the easy part.

What I had to do now was to take two consonants, and join them with vowels, making them into a memorable noun. It would become my own idiosyncratic symbol.

I started with 11, 12, 13, 14, 15, 16. Eleven became tits. (11 = tt.) I just had to squeeze a *i* in between the two *t*s and add an *s* at the end. A tit should be memorable enough, and it could be made larger and smaller. Besides, I had learned from *Moonwalking with Einstein* that, the more bizarre and obscene a symbol, the easier it would be to recall. Sexually charged symbols were especially strong. I then constructed a series of nouns in Swedish. 12 = barrel (tunna), 13 = thumb (tumme), 14 = panties (trosa), 15 = turd (tolle), and 16 = Tarzan.

After about six hours of intense work, I had constructed individual symbols for all the numbers, from 1 to 99. It was now time to start memorizing pi. I picked our own apartment as a memory palace and began outside our front door, memorizing the first six digits (3.141592). On the door handle I hung a pair of knickers (trosa = 14), and inside the knickers I placed a turd (tolle = 15) and a banana (banan = 92). I could see it in my mind's eye and, yes, this was going to stick in my memory. I opened the door and carried on in this fashion, filling up the wardrobes in our hallway.

As I went to bed, just before midnight, I had memorized 204 decimals.

ANDRÉ, MARCH 22

Today I did some online IQ tests. The first was easy. I received a score of 100%, which I immediately sent to Carl. Then I tried a longer test on iq-test. dk. Thirty-nine questions to answer in forty minutes. The first part was simple, but after about twenty minutes I was struggling. I tried to use meditation techniques to refocus my mind, but all I wanted to do was escape.

When I was finished, I received my result. 106. Which was just above average, and quite far off a genius score. I sent it to Carl. I was sure this would make him pleased.

CARL, MARCH 22

I had memorized the first 300 digits now.

Angela Merkel (10) was in our bath, nuns (22) balancing on the showerhead, sliding down a long leather belt (64), into the sink. George W. Bush (96) was sitting on the toilet, eating an umbilical cord (28). Our apartment had been turned into a mental asylum, filled with crazy animals and celebrities engaging in the most unspeakably disturbing activities. Was I designing my own haunted place, like the hotel in *The Shining*—a place to go mad in?

ANDRÉ, MARCH 22

I had to cancel the Mensa test. Mel was ill and I had to take care of her. I was feeling increasingly torn between Carl's demands and Mel's. Whatever I did, I seemed to disappoint.

CARL, MARCH 23

Immediately after waking up, at about six, I went to the kitchen and sat down to continue my memorization. I wrote everything down: the numbers, the symbols, and how they were connected. It was like a story-board for a film. At this point, there were too many numbers and stories and symbols to keep exclusively in my head. After lunch I had passed 500 digits. I sent André an email telling him I was now going for 1,000.

As I was sitting in our kitchen, late at night, staring into the wall, memorizing more numbers, it dawned on me: André would never do what I was doing. He'd never put the same amount of time into this project. He would probably see it as a waste. I had wasted hundreds of hours in the gym last month (running up a tab of close to $2,000). And this month, I had spent an endless number of hours on memorization. Learning the Rubik's Cube had taken me at least twenty hours, probably more.

I couldn't help feeling let down. He was working on other projects, with other people, whereas this was now my sole occupation.

ANDRÉ, MARCH 24

Today I got a long message from Carl. He wanted me to quit all other projects I was involved with and focus only on our project. He used the word "monogamy." That seemed like a strange choice of word to me. But I couldn't think about our relationship now. I only had a few days left to learn Python. We could deal with this next month.

CARL, MARCH 25

Hi André,

    Done! I've now memorized 1,000 decimals of pi.
    Best
    Carl
    P.S. What have you achieved this month?

ANDRÉ, MARCH 25

This was the worst day of the year so far. I was woken at about six a.m. by my screaming daughter. I gave her some food and an iPad and sat down with my coding. I was running through a fairly simple exercise. At the start of the month, I had seemingly mastered it. But now it made no sense. My mind felt like a stagnant pond in a garbage dump. The whole month had been a failure.

Later in the afternoon I realized that Rita had not been outside the entire day, so I took her to the playground. She was playing in the sand, while I sat staring into the distance, thinking about my failures. I was on the verge of crying.

CARL, MARCH 26

I had memorized the capitals of the world, the American presidents, the Swedish prime ministers, and the first 1,000 digits of pi. I could now solve the Rubik's Cube, and I had completed (and most certainly failed) the Mensa test.

But I had not learned French yet. Was it too late to do something about it? The academic I met in NYC had said it was easy.

ANDRÉ, MARCH 29

Today I accepted the fact that I had failed. That meant I needed to take my punishment. During the day, I emailed Carl suggesting I could do one of those Maoist self-critique sessions where you admit to your faults in front of a crowd of people. Carl responded enthusiastically, saying it was a great idea. I asked him what the title might be. "Why I'm an Asshole," he suggested. I said I could do it at Speakers' Corner.

"Great," Carl said, followed by the nail in my coffin: "When?"

How had this joke become a plan with a prospective deadline?

CARL, MARCH 30

André had failed to learn programming and was now going to punish himself at Speaker's Corner. My goal for the month had been to learn French, which I had not done, so I suggested my punishment should be to learn French in April. To make sure I didn't escape, I had to accept an invitation to appear on French radio by the end of April, giving an interview in French.

ANDRÉ, MARCH 31

Carl called me up and I watched him recite 1,000 digits of pi, blind-folded, which took him close to an hour. He then recited all the American presidents while solving the Rubik's Cube.

What did I have to show for myself?

I had spent over a hundred hours trying to learn coding. I had read a bunch of self-help books about mind improvement. I had tried Bulletproof Coffee. I had tried a regular exercise regime. I had tried to get a decent amount of sleep. I had tried neurofeedback. I had tried meditation. I had tried tCDS. I had tried applying a laser to the back of my head. I had tried brain food. I had tried mindfulness. And the only result of all these smart interventions was that I felt more stupid than I had before.

APRIL

RELATIONSHIPS

ANDRÉ, APRIL 1

March was over, and I could now forget about coding. But there was one thing I couldn't get away from—my faltering relationship with Carl. We'd had our conflicts in the past. But now, only three months into this project, things between us were at an all-time low.

We had to deal with our relationship, and that probably meant therapy. I knew we both secretly loathed the idea, but we needed to do something if we wanted to get through this year.

CARL, APRIL 1

"I'd prefer a woman," I said to André as we browsed through the long list of therapists on skypetherapies.co.uk.

"Why?"

"I'm sick and tired of men. This whole project has been about men."

"Fair enough."

"And I want a therapist who specializes in Cognitive Behavioral Therapy."

"CBT?" André said, sounding genuinely surprised.

"Yeah, why?"

"It's just that . . . " he paused. "Well, it's a bit weird that *you* of all people would suggest CBT."

He was right. I had written my doctoral thesis on the French psychoanalyst Jacques Lacan, who, more than anyone else, despised the kind of therapists who were committed to improving human beings. Human engineers, he derisively called them. Lacan and CBT were about as compatible as oysters and chewing gum. I was, in theory, on Lacan's side. But now, as we had to fix our relationship fast, CBT seemed like the right route to go down. Critics like Oliver James had called it a quick-fix fantasy with no lasting effect. But the market spoke a different language. It had been the most popular method of therapy for years, with an annual revenue of US$8 billion, and all reports seemed to suggest that, as depression and fatigue from work grew, the method would continue to grow in popularity, too. What people looked for now, in an era obsessed with work and productivity, was not philosophical musings on the unfathomable depths of human nature. Instead, they wanted no-nonsense strategies for making them better, more efficient, and more functional.

"This is the one," I said.

"Are you sure?"

"Yes, listen to this. *Experienced Cognitive Behavioral Therapist. Accredited.* And here: *I provide individual programs for clients enabling them to resolve their difficulties and move on with their lives.* Well, wouldn't you say that's exactly what we need?"

"Okay," André said, and we hung up.

I sent an email to the Skype therapist, describing our situation. An hour later, she got back to us and we scheduled our first meeting for Monday next week. André and I would talk to her individually first.

ANDRÉ, APRIL 2

I had failed to learn coding and following the contract I had drawn up with Carl at the start of the year, failure meant punishment. During the last days of March I had joked about giving a public speech on the topic of "Why I Am an Asshole." Carl took me seriously.

When I arrived at Speakers' Corner, I found a couple of hundred people milling around in the beautiful spring weather. Most of them were crowded around a Muslim preacher. There were smaller clusters listening to a suited Christian, a bearded Libertarian, and a fat guy talking about British Politics.

My rising anxiety was tempered when my friend Simon showed up. "Everyone has something to stand on," he pointed out. "Do you?"

"Ah, no," I replied.

"Don't worry, I'll sort it out," he said as he disappeared. A few minutes later he returned with a small kitchen stepladder.

"That guy over there lent it to me," he said, pointing to an elderly Muslim gentleman. "I told him you wouldn't say anything bad about Islam."

No problems there. I would only be speaking badly about myself.

I picked a spot between the Islamic preacher and the libertarian. I stepped up on the ladder and began. "I'm going to talk about a topic you have never heard here. Why I am an asshole." Within a minute, I had a crowd of about fifty people. They laughed as I started describing my failures. "I take advantage of others," I explained. "I do this systematically and I have an entrenched sense of personal entitlement." My script was lifted from Aaron James's book *Assholes: A Theory*. The crowd in front of me quickly lost interest as I started laying out the evidence. One by one they drifted off to listen to an Islamic preacher who had just started his peroration. One man continued listening to me as he swigged from a can of Jack Daniel's and Coke and pointed a video camera in my direction. When I finished, I was rewarded with polite applause from the ten people who remained. I descended from the stepladder, feeling a curious mixture of exhilaration and shame.

CARL, APRIL 2

I was in the seaside house again. It was raw, cloudy, and wet. Sally and Esther were in the garden, raking leaves. I was inside, on the couch, under a blanket, watching a video clip on my phone. The clip was of André explaining to a crowd of people why he was an asshole. It was a rather wonderful scene, not because he embarrassed himself, but because it showed his commitment to the project.

My punishment was different, but no less humiliating. Our previous book had just been translated into French and we had been invited to go to Paris for the launch. When speaking to the press officer this morning, she had asked if I'd be willing to give interviews in French. I said yes.

This was absurd. I had studied French for two years, at the age of fourteen and fifteen, but that was once or twice a week, halfheartedly, and, to be frank, I couldn't remember much of it. I'd say my French was as good as my German or Italian or Spanish, which is to say that it was a tiny bit better than my Russian or Arabic or Esperanto.

I had to learn fast and so the best place to start, I reckoned, was Tim Ferriss. I found a post on his website. *12 Rules for Learning Foreign Languages in Record Time—The Only Post You'll Ever Need.* It was a guest post, written by a guy called Benny Lewis, who did not begin learning languages until he was an adult, but now, just a few years later, had mastered eleven languages.

First, I had to learn lots of words. He recommended a flashcard app, Anki, and I downloaded the 5,000 most common words in French and started to practice. Theoretically, this should take me a long way, because, in English, only 300 words made up 65 percent of all written material.

The other trick was to immerse yourself in the language, Benny said. If you want to learn French, listen to French radio, watch French television, read French news, talk to French people online. In short, create your own private France.

Benny then recommended a language-learning app, Duolingo, which he described as "wonderful and completely free." I downloaded it and set five lessons as my daily goal. This was the most ambitious goal available, called "insane."

Many hours later, when Sally and Esther came in from the cold, I realized I had not moved an inch the whole day. I had not done five lessons, but fifty lessons, and I had gained five hundred points.

Before going to bed, I wrote down a set of rules for the month:

Only listen to French radio (France Culture)
Only read French newspapers (Le Monde)
Only watch French television and French movies (France 24)
Only listen to French music
Only read books in French
Eat lunch with a French person twice a week
Speak on the phone with a French person three times a week
Do fifty lessons of Duolingo every day

ANDRÉ, APRIL 4

Today I had my first session with the therapist. I had only visited a therapist once, years ago, so I was nervous about what was ahead. Before the session, I filled in the A4 form that the therapist had sent us. *Think of a key event you found hard*, it asked. "Facing Carl when I had not lived up to his expectations," I wrote down. Next question: *What emotions did that spark in me?* "Anxiety." I moved on to the next question: *What behaviors did that lead to?* "Avoidance," I wrote. The final question: *What were your physical responses*? I thought hard, then began writing: "Feeling jittery, restlessness, washing dishes."

I went up to my bedroom, pulled up a stool, and faced the window. The therapist skyped me. On the other end of the line was a soft-spoken middle-aged woman, sitting on a couch in her house. She introduced herself and asked why I was doing therapy.

"Well, I'm working on a year-long project with Carl. We're having a lot of conflict at the moment," I explained.

"How long have you known him?" she asked.

"About ten years."

"So, how have things been in the past?"

"When we worked on our first book, there had been a few clashes. But when we began this project it was different. Carl assumed I wasn't going to do enough from very beginning, from the first day. I don't feel like any of my efforts have really been valued by Carl."

"What's been happening recently?"

"Last month Carl accused me of not being committed enough."

"So, what did you think about that?"

"It was unfair," I said. "I felt like I had achieved some things this year—I've written a book, I've run an ultramarathon, I tried to learn coding. But Carl doesn't register any of that. He seems to think I have been doing everything but working on this project."

"Mmm," she said.

"I've also been worried whether I am really good enough to carry this project off. I've been working hard during the last month, but I've been getting nowhere."

"So, what does this mean for the therapy we will do together?" she asked.

I thought for a second: "I guess the real question is whether I should continue, and if so, how."

CARL, APRIL 4

I had my first session with the therapist today. I told her my side of the story. Which was really rather simple. I had spent at least four times as much time on this project as André. I had pushed everything else aside. He hadn't. I told the therapist that, when writing our previous book, the same thing had happened. We scheduled meetings on Skype that he missed. Then he promised to send chapters, which he didn't. And when he finally did, they were often in terrible shape. When I pointed these things out, he would become defensive and evasive, blaming me for making him feel bad.

"Did you take the lead when writing your previous book?" she asked.

"Er, take the lead? Well, yeah, I suppose I did."

"And you're taking the lead now, with this project?"

"Er, yes, probably."

"How would you feel about reversing roles, so André takes the lead?"

"I'd love it!"

"And how would you feel about continuing to be the leader of the project?"

"Well, that'd be fine too. But not if he's unwilling to work hard, and not if he's going to blame me for making him feel bad."

"I see, you think it's unfair."

"Yeah, I'm sacrificing a lot for this project."

"And you feel André is not invested in the project in the same way?"

"Exactly. Take today for example. I was asked to write an article for a newspaper, which I really wanted to do, but I said no because it would interfere with our project. There's no way André would have done the same thing."

She said nothing.

"You see, for me, this project is very special. I just hoped that he'd feel the same way."

ANDRÉ, APRIL 5

As I sat in front of a screen in a gigantic IKEA showroom picking out kitchen units, I started thinking about a scene in *Fight Club*. Edward Norton was ordering furniture from an IKEA catalogue and he realized how pathetic his life was.

I felt a sense of rising anxiety. I whipped out my phone and sent a message to Carl asking whether there was a Swedish word for IKEA anxiety. He replied: "No, but there was a guy who stabbed two people in an IKEA store last summer." At this point I was so agitated that I started randomly grabbing things to buy: two umbrellas, four light bulbs, three plastic bags, a folding stool.

When we got home, I headed upstairs and started searching for information about self-help for confused and anxious modern men like myself. One website caught my interest. It was for a man camp that promised to transform someone like myself into a "new warrior."

It sounded perfect! I sent off an email. A guy called Brett responded quickly, saying there was a place on their camp in a few weeks, and I could join. For some reason, I felt joining a male warrior cult would be the best way of dealing with Carl's crazy demands as well as my IKEA anxiety. After all, that was effectively what Edward Norton did in *Fight Club*. Then another thought occurred to me: does that make Carl the psychotic Tyler Durden—my double?

CARL, APRIL 5

I was at home, flicking through Baudelaire's *Fleurs du Mal*, not understanding a word, when Sam, our French publicist, phoned.

"Listen, I'm in a hurry. I just wanted to let you know that I've arranged a radio interview."

"In French?"

"Yes, of course. It's okay, right?"

"Er, yes."

"And you will present your book in a lovely bookshop."

After we hung up I went out to the kitchen and heated a French microwave dish, Confit de lamb, and poured myself a glass of French white wine to calm my nerves. Serge Gainsbourg flowed from the speakers. On the table, next to my plate, was a pile of books I had just bought. Balzac's *Le Père Goriot*, Françoise Sagan's *Bonjour Tristesse*, Albert Camus's *L'Étranger*, and David Bisson's *L'enfant Derrière La Porte*, which, despite being labeled an easy read, was far too complicated for me.

I rather enjoyed living in this Frenchified bubble. What I didn't enjoy was the thought of having to break out of it and expose myself to real French life.

ANDRÉ, APRIL 7

At about four in the afternoon, the therapist rang on Skype.

"How have you been since our last conversation?" she asked.

"Okay," I said. "But I feel like I have been losing my direction."

"How so?" she replied.

I described how each month seemed to have a familiar cycle. We started out on a new topic with enthusiasm. Carl threw himself into it, but my own efforts were halfhearted. Carl got angry. I got anxious. Only then did I start to really try.

"So where does the conflict happen in this process?" she asked.

"In the middle, I guess."

"Couldn't you address it earlier on?"

"I guess, but how would we do that?"

She went on to explain how we might be able to restructure our interactions.

When the call was finished, I went back downstairs feeling lighter. Mel looked at me with a mixture of amusement and disdain.

"What have you been doing?" she asked.

"Having a session with my therapist," I replied.

"What about?"

"How I can improve my relationship with Carl."

"That's depressing," she said, and turned on the TV.

CARL, APRIL 7

Our Skype therapist was on her couch. She wanted to talk about ideas.

"Generally speaking. . . ." She paused. "Who comes up with the ideas?"

I was thinking back on the project, and how it all started, a few years ago, in an airport taxi, me talking and André taking notes. And with the previous book—was that all my idea, too? Where was André?

"I guess most of the ideas have been mine," I said.

"Mm-hmm. Okay," she said softly. "Has that been the case all of the time?"

"Not all of the time, no, but most of the time."

"Mm-hmm. Right. And why do you think that's been the case?"

"Okay so here's one theory." It felt strange to talk about André in this way to a total stranger but I was paying money for this, sixty pounds an hour, so I felt inclined to speak without censoring myself. "He sees pretty much everything in his life as things that he needs to do. Things that other people have told him to do. So, for instance, the other day he sent me a text from IKEA. He was there with Mel, his partner, looking at a new kitchen. He complained about being there. Saying she had forced him to go."

"So, he doesn't like to take the initiative."

"Well, it's more complicated, I think. This is how he has structured his whole life. He turns everything into obligations. So all he does is *attend to* things. He uses that word a lot. *Attend to*."

"So now he has to attend to you?"

"Yes, and that's pretty depressing, to be honest."

ANDRÉ, APRIL 8

Carl had challenged me to a boxing match at the end of the month in Paris. It was a horrible idea. He was nearly a foot taller than me and had a much longer reach. But if the fight was actually going to happen, I wanted to be prepared, so today I took my first kick-boxing lesson, then signed up for ten more.

CARL, APRIL 8

Today was my first real test. Lunch with a French person, a guy who was working in the French department at the university.

I had practiced my French for a week now, day in day out, and I had kept to the rules: I was listening to no other radio channel than France Culture, reading no other newspaper than *Le Monde*, and cooking no other food than French.

After about fifteen minutes I was exhausted, and we switched to Swedish.

Later that afternoon, on the subway, making my way to my first boxing practice, André called. He sounded low. He said he had no direction.

"But I thought you would do something on parenting."

"Yes, but I've looked through all this stuff and I don't seem to go anywhere."

"But there's tons of stuff you could do."

"Like what?"

"You could do the tiger-mom thing and try and teach your daughter computer programming?"

"She's three years old, Carl."

"That's not the point. The point is that you need to try."

André was sounding more and more depressed the longer we talked. I was standing outside the boxing club now, feeling increasingly frustrated.

"But there's only two weeks left."

"There's more than two weeks. Three weeks. The month has just begun. Look, I'm learning fucking French this month."

André was silent. I was silent.

"My boxing lesson starts in two minutes," I said, and hung up.

ANDRÉ, APRIL 9

I was completely sick of being immersed in this project day and night. Thinking about it, feeling it, doing it all the time. As these thoughts swirled around me, I remembered some of the therapist's advice: "Try to take a realistic perspective." I asked myself *what is planned this month, and what actually needs to be done.* I wrote out a list: *Speakers' Corner, therapy, kick boxing, man camp, Paris.* That seemed like a lot already. But still I couldn't help feeling like I wasn't doing enough. Why was this? I couldn't blame Carl for everything. I had to think about my own motivations. That was the only way to fix things.

CARL, APRIL 10

I opened the envelope with the Mensa logo stamped on the upper right corner. It read:

Test result: 35/45
Your result is higher than 82% of the population.
This corresponds to an IQ of 114

I had failed. I was almost twenty points short of the entry requirement of 131. But I didn't care. All I could think about was the night that I did the test. Sally had been working. I had to find someone to look after our daughter, while I had to drive four hours there and back to take the test. André had also been going to take the test. But he canceled at the last minute. Something had come up, another obligation, another thing he needed to *attend* to.

ANDRÉ, APRIL 11

"So, how have things between you and Carl been?" the therapist asked. "Have you two been talking recently?"

"Yeah, we spoke on Friday. It started out positively, but then we fell into old patterns."

"How are you feeling now?"

"Pretty overwhelmed. The project's become my entire life. I wish I could just step back sometimes."

"What's this project about, for you?"

I didn't know what to say. I started giving a vague, abstract description. Words were coming out of my mouth, but I had no idea what they meant. Did I have any idea what I was spending this year doing, and why?

"What is your role in this?" she asked.

Again, I had no idea. Was I Edward Norton's character in *Fight Club*, having my life taken over by my own Swedish version of Tyler Durden?

CARL, APRIL 11

"So how have you been?" the therapist asked.

"Not good."

"No, why?"

I explained the situation. André was accusing me of all sorts of things. He said I had forced him to give a talk at Speakers' Corner, which was not true, and that I had enjoyed seeing him humiliated, which was not true, and that I was now training at a boxing club so I could beat him up when we would meet in Paris. Another lie.

"You know what, I've had enough of this. I'm going to pull the plug now. Quit the project."

"Are you sure?"

"I don't know. All I know is that things can't go on like this. Also, it's come to my attention that he's been speaking about me to a mutual friend, explaining how I'm bossing him around and doing everything I can to make him feel bad."

"How does that make you feel?" she asked.

"Awful."

"Maybe you need a pause. Maybe you should stop talking to André for a week or so."

ANDRÉ, APRIL 18

When the therapist called, she began by asking how my week had been.

"Things have improved," I said. I didn't want to mention the fact that Carl had not been talking to me for most of the week. "I've been trying to focus on my behavioral patterns, especially my avoidance."

"Why avoidance?"

"Well, I think I often avoid things that are hard. Even small things. I often put them off until it is just about too late."

"Why is that, you think?"

"I commit to things, and then I pull back. I guess I end up asking myself whether something can happen without me. If it could, I pull out."

"Is that possibly just a way of trying to make yourself feel needed?"

I paused to think. It was only ten minutes into our session and already I wanted it to be over.

The moment we hung up, I rushed off to the gym and worked on my punches and roundhouse kicks. Which was a hell of a lot more satisfying than working on my relationship with Carl.

CARL, APRIL 18

"So how has your week been?" The therapist was on her couch again.

"Better," I said. "Your idea of not talking to André really helped. I had to distance myself."

"Good."

It was strange. I felt that the therapist was on my side. I felt as though she was also frustrated with André. Maybe it was just a projection. Maybe it was a therapist's trick. Either way, it made me like her all the more.

What the therapy had helped me understand was that there was nothing I could do about the situation. André would not change. I had to accept that he was going to work on other stuff at the same time. I had to accept that I would be pushing the project forward. And I also had to accept that he would blame me for it. I would have loved to do things differently, but whenever we had tried, it had failed.

"I think you are now ready to talk to André again," she said as our session was coming to a close.

Was this the point of CBT? To make you accept the situation as it was?

ANDRÉ, APRIL 21

As part of the preparation for the man camp, I had to cook a meal for three men. Something "healthful," it said. I settled on risotto. Not a particularly manly meal, but it would have to do. As I packed my bag, I remembered how much I hated camping.

CARL, APRIL 22

In the absence of emails from André, I was enjoying the encouraging messages I kept receiving from Duolingo. Today it congratulated me on my twenty-two-day streak, saying I was "on fire." It then challenged me to spend another day on the app, aiming to reach level fourteen, a challenge I immediately accepted.

ANDRÉ, APRIL 22

The door opened, and I was led into a darkened room. More than a dozen men were standing around, wearing black clothes with black paint smeared on their faces. Black fabric covered the walls.

"You're number 21," a shadowy man said as he bustled me to a desk where I had to hand over my personal items. As they were thrown into a black plastic bin, I wondered what the hell I had signed up for.

A craggy-faced man in a kilt led me up a flight of stairs and into a pitch-black room. "Sit down," he said. Just before the light disappeared, I realized there were about thirty other men sitting on the floor with me. I couldn't help feeling we were about to be executed.

After half an hour, we were led out of the darkness. "Line up!" one of the black figures yelled. "Put these around your eyes!" Bandanas were forced into our hands. Were we about to be sacrificed to some ancient He-God?

Blindfolded, we marched along. The sound of drums got louder as we picked up the pace.

"Remove your blindfolds," someone yelled. I found myself on the floor of a large room, surrounded by about fifty men. All of them were dressed in black with blackened faces.

"Who didn't bring food?" a dark figure on stage yelled.

A small guy in the back slowly raised his hand.

"I had soup . . . but they confiscated it at airport security."

"Why did you prioritize yourself over others?" the dark figure on stage shouted back.

The soupless man tried to defend himself. But after a barrage of abuse, he broke: "Sorry. I should have thought of the other men."

Then another dark figure ran through a ceremonial speech. "Men have been performing initiation rituals for thousands of years. But today masculinity is broken. It is caged. We need to change that by becoming men who have a mission."

The last thing I wanted to become was a man with a mission. But after all the ordeals I had been through in the last few months, I was convinced that if I was going to make it through this year, I needed to do something drastic. Maybe this crash-course in manliness was exactly that.

A German with shoulder-length hair took to the stage. "Close your eyes," he said. "Imagine you are an adventurer. Get into his posture."

I stretched my arms out and stood like Leonardo DiCaprio on the bow of the *Titanic*.

"Now, imagine you are a wild man! Find your inner wild man! Stand like your wild man!"

I spread my legs and thrust out my crotch.

"Yell like your inner wild man!"

Arrrrrrrrrrrrgghhhhhh. I tried to go deeper. *Arrgggghhhhh! Oh yeah! Aaaarrrrrrrrrgggggggggghhhhhhhhh!*

"Be a little boy," he said next. "Throw your ball in the air!"

I threw an imaginary ball in the air.

"Make the sound of a boy!"

Weeeee, ahhhhhhh, yaahhhhh. I was feeling great.

During a short break, I sipped an herbal tea and tried talking with a bald middle-aged man. His only response to my questions about why he was here was: "Iron John." At the time I had no idea what he meant. The story of Iron John, I later learned, came from a classic book about masculinity by the American poet, Robert Bly. It spent sixty-three weeks on the best-seller lists and was a major inspiration for the Men's Movement. This movement emerged in the 1980s in response to the rise of feminism. Men, it was claimed, had lost connection to what it meant to be a man. To reclaim their manhood, they had to be initiated into a community of other men, and get in contact with what Bly called "Zeus Energy." I was now participating in one of these initiations.

We were called back. One of the men in black instructed us to imagine our inner animal. A monkey came to mind.

"Describe the qualities of that animal," he instructed. *Thoughtful?* Yeah, thoughtful would do. "Thoughtful Monkey" would be my name.

One by one we jumped into the middle of a large circle and called out our new animal name and acted it out. There were wolves, hawks, eagles, tigers, lions, and foxes. One guy became "Intuitive Alien." Another was "Unfuckwithable Rhino." I jumped in the middle and shouted, "Thoughtful Monkey." As I was monkeying about the center of the circle, the men around me roared in unison: "You are Thoughtful Monkey. Aho!"

That evening when I lay on my stretcher in the large open barn, I wanted to cry like my inner little boy. Was this a sign I was finally getting in touch with my Zeus Energy?

CARL, APRIL 22

I was in the house by the seaside again, on the couch, reading *Le Monde diplomatique*, when Sam, our French publicist, called.

"Carl, ça va,"

"Ça va bien, et toi?"

Sam was speaking to me in French. Fast. Words were flooding from the phone.

"Sam, sorry, could you say that in English instead? I'm still struggling to understand."

"Yeah, sorry, I was just saying I have now booked you into three radio interviews. The first one will be on the same day as you arrive."

After we hung up, my heart was pounding and my hands shaking. What the hell was I getting myself into?

ANDRÉ, APRIL 23

Bang Bang Bang. Drums beating.

"Get up!" two men yelled. "Shower time."

We walked out into the freezing morning light.

"Take your clothes off!"

In front of us were three shower nozzles attached to a sinister-looking concrete wall.

"Line up!"

We were all naked and shivering. The first group of three men stood under the shower screaming, while the rest of us counted out loud to sixty. Soon it was my turn. The cold water took my breath away. Once it was over, as we huddled together to keep warm, I felt a strong sense of brotherhood. I wondered whether this was Anthony Robbins's inspiration for his cold morning showers.

We returned inside. The German was back on stage. "Lie back and imagine you are floating up into the air, then flying fast through the sky," he said. Disney music played over the sound system. "You come to a forest. There's a cave. You enter the cave. You keep going down. Then you are stuck!" The Disney music climaxed. "Start digging," the German yelled. "Dig for your life."

I dug like I was doing circuit training with a sadistic coach.

"Head toward the light! There he is. He is you . . . as a little boy."

I tried to imagine myself as a boy of about eight.

"Now imagine what that little boy wanted, deep down."

I thought of a few words: courage, play, creation.

"They will become your mission," he said.

As I repeated these words to myself, they sounded like a lame corporate values statement.

"Imagine a picture projected up into the sky. It is your little boy's perfect world. What would it look like?"

The first thing that came to mind was my adolescent obsession with designing huge buildings. I remembered how, as an eight-year-old, I had planned to develop a shopping mall on a vacant piece of land near my boyhood home. Then it struck me: I had been a little Howard Roark, the self-assured architect at the center of Ayn Rand's libertarian classic, *The Fountainhead.*

Later in the afternoon, as we walked silently across a recently ploughed field, I contemplated the little Howard Roark inside me. *What had happened to that little property developer? Why I had neglected him for so many years?* Then I snapped out of it. *What the hell was happening?* I came here to discover my Zeus Energy, not my inner libertarian!

When we arrived back inside, we were given some drums. Soon we had a rhythm going. The dozens of men who had already been initiated walked into the room and circled around us chanting "guts, guts, guts, guts." The chorus faded and a man yelled, "Bring out the rugs!" Three large circular rugs were carried in and we split into groups. One new initiate stepped forward.

"What's your mission?" our group leader asked in a thick Cockney accent.

"Creating a loving world," a brooding initiate answered.

"Who was the first person who made you feel this wasn't possible?"

"My mother."

"He is going to be your mother," the Cockney said as he pointed at another man. "Tell her how you feel."

The brooder started yelling at his stand-in mother. Soon he was sobbing uncontrollably.

"Do you want to get rid of this now?" the Cockney asked.

"Yes," the brooder responded.

The more experienced men gathered together, whispered, and started to pull items out of a large wooden box. Sports pads, a hockey stick, large blankets. They gave a hockey stick to the brooder. He took it and attacked his pad-wearing mother.

I was getting worried now. I didn't want to attack my mother with a hockey stick. Nor my father. Not even Carl deserved the hockey stick treatment.

A similar routine was repeated for each new initiate. One was reborn through a birth tunnel made out of a rolled-up rug. Another was held in our arms as we sung "Amazing Grace." There were moments I felt like I was in a Caravaggio painting—men yelling and screaming for their lives.

It was my turn, but I couldn't think of anything to say, like an actor without lines.

"Get out of your head," the Cockney yelled.

I was thinking hard.

"I need courage," I said.

"I know what we'll do," the Cockney replied. I was blindfolded and led up to the top of a tall stack of boxes. I stepped off a ledge, fell backward and was caught by ten other men below. I couldn't help feeling disappointed. Wasn't this a cheesy team-building standard?

But just as the sense of guilt for my ungratefulness began to bite, my brothers lifted me up above their heads. I started bellowing like a tenor in full flight. I'm not sure I had any great breakthrough, but I certainly felt some of that Zeus Energy pulsing through me.

As the dusk fell over the Scottish mountains, it was time for the initiation ceremony.

"What was your name?" an old man with a white beard asked.

"Lone Wolf," an initiate responded.

"What name are you now?"

"Loving Wolf."

The whole group chanted "Loving Wolf, Loving Wolf, Loving Wolf, Aho!" I took to the stage and heard the old man saying "You were Thoughtful Monkey. Now you are Courageous Monkey." The other men shouted "Courageous Monkey!"

After receiving our new names we were handed a pen and paper to write letters to ourselves, which were going to be sent to us in 6 months' time. I wrote the letter and finished it with a line from the poet Rilke. *You must change your life.*

It was dark as we were led outside, naked and blindfolded. The cold hit me. We walked slowly for about ten minutes. Then I heard the beat of drums and the crackling of a fire.

Take off your blindfolds, a man shouted.

I saw a huge fire surrounded by fifty men. All naked, all wearing the same necklace. We joined them and started running around the fire, faster and faster. After about fifteen minutes, we stopped and stood shoulder to shoulder. We were a tribe of nude men in a circle facing each other.

"Men have been doing this for thousands of years," an old white-bearded man said. Then each new recruit was given a necklace. It was our sacred talisman, we were told. Our face was marked with ash, and our new names were called out. When my time came, I received my talisman and I heard my brothers calling: "Courageous Monkey, you are Warrior!"

CARL, APRIL 23

Today I completed the final lesson on Duolingo. I had used the app every day of the month, from morning to evening, and now, with only a few more days to go, I had come to the end of the tree, and reached 51 percent fluency.

I was curious to assess my performance. I logged into the social community where Duolingo buffs boasted about their feats. I found users who had finished the whole tree in two or three months. Then I came across one user who was doing nineteen languages at the same time, including Norwegian and Welsh. "My first tree took three months to finish," the digital polyglot said, "Then I finished others in one to two months."

I wanted to brag about my achievement. But to whom? I couldn't tell my wife and child, who, at this point, were sick and tired of me spending all my days staring into my phone or computer. And I couldn't brag to

André. He was at some man camp. I was considering adding a post on the Duolingo community site but it seemed pointless.

ANDRÉ, APRIL 24

It was early in the morning and we were dancing around a large room to "Mr. Brightside" by the Killers. Naked. After letting our inner wild men loose, we formed two circles and sat down, still naked. A middle-aged man who looked suspiciously like Jeremy Clarkson was sitting at the head of the circle holding two large wooden phalluses. Each man in the circle took turns holding a phallus and talking about their sexuality. Little slices of individual sexual histories were revealed one by one. When it was my turn I said that, despite having been raised in a liberal household that was open about sex, I didn't like to talk about it. "Amen," Clarkson said.

Still naked, but now with our shoes on, we walked through the freezing fields until we reached a small clearing with a large fire in the middle. As we circled around the fire, the goose bumps on our skin disappeared. Pieces of papers were thrown into the fire. They were the questionnaires we had filled out at the beginning of the weekend. Was that my old self going up in flames?

A few hours later, I sat in a taxi on the way to the airport, holding my talisman. I still wasn't sure what to make of my experiences over the last two days, or what it might mean for my relationship with Carl. But for the first time in years, I was feeling a little more in touch with masculinity, whatever that was.

CARL, APRIL 27

On the train from Paris-Charles-de-Gaulle into the city, I tried to speak to Sam in French. But I was too slow and too bad. She switched to English.

"Change of plans, the interview you were supposed to give today has been canceled," Sam said.

"Thank god," I said.

"Tomorrow you will present your book in a bookstore. And then, on Friday, you will do a longer radio interview."

Phew. That meant I still had some time to practice.

ANDRÉ, APRIL 28

I had come to Paris to spend a few days with Carl in the hope of putting our relationship issues to rest.

Late in the evening, we had our book launch at a small bookstore tucked down a little side street. About forty chairs were packed into the small space. They were all taken and there were people standing at the back.

Carl was reading his entire speech in French. He answered a few questions in French, then switched to English. It was hard to believe that Carl had only started seriously learning French less than a month ago. I was proud to be working with him. But secretly I felt a little ashamed. Carl had learned French in one month. What had I done? Danced around a campfire naked with fifty other men?

CARL, APRIL 28

"Je suis très heureux d'être ici," I began. We were sitting in easy chairs, me and André, facing the audience. The small bookshop was packed. My heart was pounding.

"J'ai une confession que je veux fair." Yes, I had a confession to make. About my French. My poor broken French. A month ago, it was even worse, I explained. It was nonexistent. "Je n'ai pas parlé un mot de Français il y a un mois." But I had been working hard to improve it, I assured the audience. Still, I'd understand if they'd find my way of speaking annoying. It felt like a necessary precaution.

I was terrified. The whole day had been an ordeal. I had been preparing the speech, sitting in a bistro, trying to calm my nerves with small quantities of red wine.

"D'apres l'application de Duolingo je parle 51 percent Francaise."

They were laughing now, even giving me a small encouraging round of applause. I told them about André's ultramarathon and my own adventures in the world of weight lifting, then went on to explain the main argument of our previous book.

I was relieved it was over. But it wasn't over. Tomorrow was going to be worse.

ANDRÉ, APRIL 29

For the entire month, we had been trying to work on our relationship while we were in two different countries. But today we were together, and we had arranged an appointment with our therapist.

We sat next to each other, on a couch, speaking to our therapist on the screen. "I can only sustain this for a year," Carl said. "And besides, André has a second child on the way." I was taken aback. I had told Carl this news in confidence. Now there were five people who knew about our unborn child: Mel, me, the doctor, Carl, and our therapist. If everything went well, the child would arrive just before Christmas.

Later that day, we walked into a building that smelled of pot. It was home to a small alternative radio station. We were greeted by two older women. They were going to interview Carl in French. I was amazed that he had agreed to do this. We sat in the studio as Carl answered questions. When the music break came, I congratulated Carl.

Later that night we stopped by a nightclub on our way home from a long, expensive dinner. As we danced, my Zeus Energy rose up. I started grunting like a wild man—*huh uhhh huh, AHHHHHH! Uhh, huh, huh, AHHHHH!* A group of guys gathered around me. One joined my howling.

After a while I took him aside. I stared into his eyes and told him he was a man. This news seemed to please him. Feeling a sense of manly connection, I gave him my talisman, then left.

CARL, APRIL 29

"So what should we talk about with the therapist?" I asked André as we were having breakfast in a classically Parisian bistro.

"Hmm. She seems really keen to talk about behavioral patterns, so I guess we could talk about that."

I laughed.

"What?" André said, looking confused.

"This is sooo you!"

"*What?*"

"We're paying for therapy. It's supposed to be for *us*. And all you can think about is what *she* wants to get out of it."

An hour later, back in the flat, we started our session:

"So how do you feel now? Have things changed?" the therapist asked.

"I'd say nothing has changed. And everything's changed," I said.

"How so?"

"I feel like I'm one of those unhappy but resigned wives who accept that their husband is cheating on them, because they know deep inside that at the end of the day, they'll come back anyway." Both André and the therapist looked disturbed. But it felt good saying it out loud.

"And André, how are *you* feeling about this?"

"Um, I don't know," he said.

After we finished, I had to prepare myself for the radio interview.

A couple of hours later we walked into the studio. I met with the two radio presenters in a small room. They were cheerful and started casually talking to me, assuming I could actually speak French. When they understood that this wasn't really the case, they began to worry. Sam intervened, explaining that she could help.

We were in the studio now. Sam was gone. They asked me a question. I didn't quite understand, but I made a guess and started answering the question as well as I could, looking down at my notes, hesitating, reading a sentence out loud, repeating myself, stumbling on the words, pausing, flicking through my notes again. I was trapped in here. There was no escape.

Sam came into the studio. She was carrying a bag of beers. She gave me one. Soon I had found a new tone. More theatrical. I imagined myself as a drunk Serge Gainsbourg. That should do the trick, I thought, but the presenters looked confused. Then I insisted on reading a long passage.

After an hour, it was done. I wanted to throw up. My head was spinning. André rushed forward and gave me a hug. I wanted to cry.

MAY

SPIRITUALITY

ANDRÉ, MAY 1

As I stepped across the threshold of the nineteenth-century church, I was handed the standard issue Church of England hymnbook. Thirty people sat quietly in pews. I found an inconspicuous spot and sat down.

Attending church on a Sunday morning is the most normal thing in the world for many people. Every Sunday, 760,000 people in Britain attend a service in the Church of England. But it was a big deal for me. I was raised an atheist and could not remember setting foot in a church until I was about twenty.

The vicar climbed the pulpit and the parishioners began singing. I hummed along as I desperately searched the hymnbook for the right song. An elder man stood up and began reading, name-dropping characters I didn't know. After the sermon ended, some elderly folk came up to me to shake my hand. I grinned and shook their hands.

As I stepped out of the church into the brilliant morning light, I felt lighter. My mind was clearer but I did not have the kind of transcendental experience I had hoped for. Walking across the park, I wondered whether it was possible for me to have a real spiritual experience by the end of the month.

CARL, MAY 1

I was in bed, phone in hand, searching for spiritual activities. Sunlight was angling in from the window, warming my legs. It was spring now.

An hour later, I had booked a three-day new-age retreat. This month was going to be difficult. I was about as spiritual as a toaster. I had no religious beliefs. I regarded new-age theories of energy and chakra as delusional. And I hated the smell of incense. Sure, there were some spiritual things that I liked. The films of Andrei Tarkovsky, Alexander Sokurov, and Terrence Malick. I recalled enjoying Herman Hesse's novels when I was in my early twenties. I also read the Upanishads and Bhagavad Gita at around that same time. But dancing barefoot in a forest, hugging strangers? That was not for me. Not yet, anyway.

Later in the afternoon, I was having a late lunch with a friend at a vegetarian restaurant overlooking the harbor.

"I'll probably become a vegetarian this month," I said as we sat down.

"Yeah, why?"

"As part of my spiritual journey. Then maybe I'll become a vegan."

"Okay?"

"And I should probably try raw food, too."

My friend said nothing.

"And maybe finish off the month by not eating at all."

"So this would make you more spiritual?"

I was looking at a wooden sign on the wall, which read: *Live, Laugh, Love, the most important things in life are not things.*

"I think so, yes," I said.

ANDRÉ, MAY 2

"Check this out," Carl said over Skype and sent me a link to a new-age retreat he was going to attend. Cross-legged hippies were on the floor, facing a leader. "My plan is to spend the month diving straight into new-age spirituality."

"But you hate new-age stuff, don't you?" I said.

"Well, I've never given it a serious try." He paused. "So, what's your plan?"

"I'll try out the established religions."

"Eh, okay," Carl said. I could tell he was skeptical.

"I thought I could try one new religion each week for four weeks."

He was silent.

"I'd focus on the most popular religions in the world. Christianity, Islam, Buddhism, and Hinduism."

"Okay?"

"And by the end of the month I'll gather all my spiritual insights together and climb to the top of the highest mountain in Britain, where I hope to have a spiritual experience. I've never had one of those before."

"I'm sorry, but I don't get it. What does this have to do with self-improvement?"

"Come on Carl, religion is the oldest form of self-improvement there is. All that self-help stuff is just a thinly disguised rip-off of things that religions recommended centuries ago."

My voice grew louder.

"What are the hot things in self-help now? Mindfulness, right? That's just rebranded meditation—something Buddhists have done for thousands of years. Waking up at five a.m.? Millions of Muslims do that every day. Chanting aphorisms to yourself? Hindus have done that for millennia. Taking long contemplative walks? Christian pilgrims have been doing that for centuries, too."

Carl was silent.

"And the message is basically the same. Take the classic self-help books. Norman Vincent Peale's *The Power of Positive Thinking*. It's all about God. And *The Alchemist* by Paulo Coelho. It's all about a boy going on a personal pilgrimage through North Africa. God is mentioned on every second page."

I could hear that Carl was still there, so I kept going:

"Religions have also incorporated all the techniques from the self-improvement industry. I just read an article in the *Financial Times* that said churches in central London take inspiration from TED talks to make their services more engaging."

"Fine," he said, then hung up.

CARL, MAY 2

I was sitting on the couch next to my daughter, browsing through Tim Ferriss's blog on my phone. "Never been able to meditate?" he asked. "These guided meditation apps make all the difference." He recommended Calm and Headspace. I downloaded both, then signed up for a ten-day program on Calm.

Now I was on the carpet, my legs crossed, headphones in my ears.

"What are you doing?" Esther asked.

"I'm meditating."

"Why?"

"To become calm. To find inner peace. It'll only take ten minutes."

I closed my eyes and surrendered to the soft voice in my ears. She spoke about work and mounting pressures. The demand to always be switched-on, running from one thing to the next. She spoke about the need to relax, to calm down, to meditate. I was surprised by these remarks. Was she a social critic? It seemed odd that an app should save me from the perils of capitalism.

The guided meditation started and I followed her instructions: breathing in through my nose and out of my mouth, scanning my body, noticing sensations, counting my breaths. After ten minutes, she asked me to open my eyes again. I felt remarkably calm. Esther was still on the couch, watching a film, looking my way, smiling, asking if I was calm now.

"Yes, I think so."

Later in the evening, I listened to a podcast called *The Seven Chakras*, which told the story of an ordinary American who, thanks to mindfulness, had left his old life of poverty and depression behind and entered a new era of success and personal fulfillment.

I continued my research. Mindfulness would not only help me focus better, I read in a *Forbes* article, it could also combat anxiety, depression, body shame, racism, and ageism. Practicing mindfulness would make me a more present father, a more focused employee, a forgiving friend, and a compassionate lover. It would also help me experience "mind-blowing sex," I learned from *Huffington Post*.

If all this was true, it was no wonder meditation had become big business. In 2015, the market for meditation and mindfulness was worth almost one billion dollars. Headspace, which was the most popular app on the market, had been downloaded six million times.

ANDRÉ, MAY 5

After walking through a small village full of quaint little tea shops, I came to the Pilgrims' Way, a Neolithic walkway that runs for nearly 200 kilometers between Winchester and Canterbury cathedrals. Parts of Chaucer's *Canterbury Tales* were set on this trail.

As the week had worn on, I was struggling to find a way to connect with Jesus Christ. I had been reading the bible and visiting churches to prey. But that wasn't enough. WikiHow suggested I should spend quality time with him by attending church, receiving the sacraments, reading the Bible, and talking to him directly through prayer. I could also fast, be frugal, give alms, chant, use beads or . . . whip myself. Then I found what seemed to be a perfect option: a pilgrimage. It promised the ideal mash-up of spirituality and workout. There was even a study by neuroscientists at Stanford who had found that walking in nature significantly reduced people's levels of negative ruminations.

As I began my thirty-kilometer mini-pilgrimage toward Canterbury, I tried to keep my mind blank, focusing on my steps, my breath, the wind, and the dappled light. As I emerged into an open field, I took a selfie and sent it to Carl. After a few more kilometers, I came to a sign that told me I was on a path of European significance that went all the way to Rome.

I passed a farm shop, strawberry fields, a dead baby rabbit, a hiker struggling with an ordnance survey map, and an older couple swearing at their dog.

Then another sign: from here, you can see the Canterbury cathedral. I could pick it out in the distance, but it was still ten kilometers away. I knew I would struggle to get there for the evening service if I continued walking, so I started running.

The path turned into a wider road leading up to a pretty village. The church bell tolled three. I passed through hop fields and a forlorn caravan park used by migrant workers and crossed a motorway. My energy was beginning to wane. I tried to find my inner wild man, and I yelled as I ran up a steep hill.

When I entered the cathedral, the service had already started and I was drenched in sweat. A woman in a black cloak showed me to a seat in the back, far from the other people attending the service. I was in shorts and t-shirt, panting loudly. At the front was a full choir. Around the altar sat ten priests in their finest gowns. It was an important saint's day.

On the way home, I sat on a train drinking a can of beer. It felt like I was returning from a hard day of work. But what was my work? Tending to my soul? Had my long walk today helped to make my soul flourish? Had it brought me close to a spiritual experience? I wasn't sure about these things. But I was sure that I felt glad to spend a glorious spring day walking in the English countryside.

CARL, MAY 7

I was at the seaside, behind the house, alone, eyes closed, listening to the virtual mindfulness woman gently speaking to me. I was there, in the moment, immersed, feeling my body, counting my breaths. Then, suddenly, someone rushed up from behind, shaking my shoulders and screaming "Boo!" right into my ears. It was Esther. She had found me.

"Very funny," I said, irritated.

Later in the afternoon, having finished the first fifty pages of Paulo Coelho's *The Alchemist*, I climbed the roof and sat down on the ridge, shirtless, ready to finally do my meditation. Ten minutes later, calm and refreshed, my phone buzzed. It was a notification from Facebook, saying I had been tagged in a post. I opened it. A picture of me half-naked on the roof, taken just a few minutes ago from the terrace. This time it wasn't Esther making fun of me. It was my sister.

The following day at lunchtime, I cycled to a spirituality center, located on an empty side street in central Stockholm. I walked up a few flights of stairs along a wall of framed posters, neatly arranged, with prints of Buddha, flowers, and words of wisdom. I took off my shoes and moved into the main lounge with its blue-painted floor. On a long couch lined with cushions, a young man sat meditating. He was in his underwear. His legs were crossed, his eyes were closed, and his hands rested on his knees. His index fingers and thumbs were pressed together, forming small circles. The rest of his fingers were straight, stretched out into the air, into the universe, into the cosmos. He was slim, agile, and good-looking. His brown curly hair fell down on his shoulders.

I walked up to the small reception area, my back turned to the young man as he continued meditating.

"I'd like to become a member."

"Yes, of course," the young blond woman said. "You can try all of our courses for one month for only one hundred dollars."

"Good. Thanks. You have something starting soon?"

"Mindfulness. It starts in twenty-five minutes. You can help yourself to some tea while you're waiting." I walked into the lounge, poured myself some ginger tea, sat down by a large dining table, and flicked through a book about chakras.

Twenty-five minutes later, I entered a small, white-walled room and sat down on a meditation chair, my legs crossed, facing the instructor.

She was an older woman with white hair and white clothes. She spoke in the same generically calm, soothing voice as the woman speaking on the Calm app and the man on Headspace. We sat there for thirty minutes, scanning our bodies, paying attention to our breath, letting our minds go. It was just me and three other middle-aged professionals who all seemed to be there on their lunch breaks.

In the locker room, changing my clothes, a German banker asked why I was there.

"I was curious to try something new," I said.

"You don't end up here by accident," he said. I felt as though he was testing me.

"No?"

"No, this is a very special place. A *very* special place."

He looked straight into my eyes, making me feel like a traitor, a spy, a mole, like I was just about to be found out.

ANDRÉ, MAY 8

When the house was quiet, I retreated upstairs and opened my Bible. Over the past week, I'd experienced moments of profound calm while praying in different churches. I had felt a deep sense of purpose when walking through the countryside toward Canterbury Cathedral. But I had yet to have the transcendental spiritual experience I hoped for.

Before my week as a Christian ended, I wanted to finish reading the New Testament. I had completed the Gospels, Acts, and the Epistles. The messages seemed so familiar, woven as they are into the very fabric of our culture. The struggle with death, the joy of being part of a community of believers, the promise of hope beyond suffering. Each of these messages surfaced not just in Christian religious art, but in many of the self-improvement books that both Carl and I had read this year. The only difference seemed to be that while the Bible asked you to have your faith in God, most self-help books asked you to have faith in yourself.

Before ending my week as a Christian, I read the last section of the New Testament, the Book of Revelations. It freaked me out. The scenes were horrifying, as if invented by a Dungeons & Dragons master on acid. After reading the last words, I closed my small green Bible.

How could these bizarre visions of destruction be squared with the gentle calm of the Sunday services I had attended at the start of the week? I much preferred the gentle Christianity to this apocalyptic horror show.

CARL, MAY 9

It was late afternoon when I entered the spirituality center for a session of chakra meditation dance. From a site called chakradance.com, I had learned that it used "spontaneous dance, to specific chakra-resonant music" in order to re-tune my whole energy system and put me in touch with the sacred within myself. I wasn't sure what that meant, but thought it'd be worth a try.

I changed into running tights and a t-shirt and walked into a large white room with inspirational words painted on the walls and ceiling:

CONNECT, RADICAL, ENGAGE

We were facing the instructor, standing barefoot, in front of a Ganesh statue. He was tall and slim, in baggy sweatpants and a yellow t-shirt with STAY TRUE written over his chest. He had long gray hair, worn in a ponytail.

"We need to be in touch with our anger," he explained. "Society has banned anger. But anger is important. It is life. It is energy."

He explained that, here, in this room, we were free. We were all individuals. We could do what we wanted. We could scream or shout or cry. We could be ourselves, be true, be real.

"It's all about mom and dad," he said. "You have to free yourself from them." I was confused. I had just spent an enjoyable weekend with my parents at the seaside, relaxing and eating good food.

Indian music was blaring from the speakers. He was dancing now. I watched his movements, arms in the air, waving, letting loose, expressing himself, then stimulating his third chakra, the area around the stomach.

We were dancing too, all of us, but in different ways, staying true to ourselves and not copying each other. He turned up the volume. A young woman in jean shorts and a top was running around the room in circles, rotating her arms like a windmill. I was next to an older woman, pale and feeble, who was drowning in her kaftan. She was standing on the spot, in her own universe, dancing with herself with her eyes closed.

Then Jon Bon Jovi came over the speakers.

IT'S MY LIFE

A bearded man in his mid-forties with shoulder-length hair was marching around like a soldier, shouting and screaming along to the music:

IT'S NOW OR NEVER

Sweat was pouring down his face. His mouth twisted, and he kicked his legs high. Jon Bon Jovi was going straight to his heart. He was pointing his finger at himself, touching his chest, screaming:

I AIN'T GONNA LIVE FOREVER

I was dancing on my own, under the window, sweating, feeling frightened.

They were playing Queen now, and the room was boiling. They were all screaming, punching and kicking in the air. The instructor was running around in circles, touching us, then he stopped in front of the Ganesh statue and started pushing his hips back and forth, fast and forceful, as though he was humping the air, fucking space, screwing emptiness.

Then we were on the floor, under heavy blankets, panting. Meditative music played quietly from the speakers. I was staring up toward the ceiling, through the window, into the blue sky, thinking about this project, trying to understand why I was here, subjecting myself to this madness.

ANDRÉ, MAY 9

As a new week began, I was leaving Christianity behind, ready to explore Islam.

According to productivemuslim.com, a website run by a guy who lived in Dallas and went by the name Abu Productive, the Koran was the ultimate self-help book. I browsed through the site and found "the Ultimate Productive Muslim Goal Planner," a guide that helped me outline my goals in different categories: Islam, personal, family, work, community, ummah (community of Muslims). At the top were intervals of time: six months, twelve months up to twenty years and then Akhira (the afterlife).

At this stage, planning goals for my afterlife seemed a little ambitious, so I decided to stick to a slightly shorter time horizon: one week.

There were five obligations of a good Muslim: Shahada (the declaration of faith in the prophet Mohammed), Salat (praying five times a day), Zakat (charity), Sawm (fasting during the month of Ramadan), and Hajj (the pilgrimage to Mecca).

Some of these obligations were impossible for me at this stage. I could not declare faith to a religion I knew little about. It was not Ramadan so fasting was out. And as a non-Muslim, I couldn't take part in the Hajj.

That left me with prayer and charity. On top of that, I would try to find out more about the faith through reading.

So, to get started, I picked up a slender Penguin volume of the Koran. It was divided into 114 Suras. The longest, the Cow, came first. The shortest, the People, came last.

CARL, MAY 10

I went into the kitchen and poured a cup of coffee without milk. I was a vegan now. Then I phoned André.

"I found something on Tim Ferriss's website that might interest you," I said.

"What's that?" André seemed only moderately enthusiastic. Maybe he was still skeptical about Tim.

"The 30-Day Challenge, it's called. No booze, no masturbation for one month. They call it NOBNOM."

"Okay."

"You're becoming a Muslim now, right?"

"Yes, that's the plan."

"So you're in? You'll take the challenge with me?"

"Okay, whatever."

ANDRÉ, MAY 11

At four thirty a.m. I walked into the bathroom, feeling the cool tiles beneath my feet, and began to clean myself before prayers. I washed my arms and hands three times, then my face. I cleaned out my mouth with water three times and sniffed water up my nose. I poured water on my head and on my legs and feet. Again, three times. At this point, I was feeling fresh and awake. Once again, the image of Anthony Robbins taking his freezing morning showers came to mind.

I got dressed, went downstairs, and laid out a small Turkish carpet, making sure I was facing Mecca.

The previous evening, I had found an Islamic prayer guide on YouTube produced by a group of Australians. I pressed start and followed the instructions for the first prayer of the day, called Fajr.

I raised my hands, then bowed and moved back up with one hand on my heart. Then back into a bow and onto my knees. All the while, the Australian guided me. I went through the final move, acknowledging the angel on my left, then the one on my right.

It was not yet five in the morning, and I was at my desk working, feeling focused and enlivened. Maybe this was the Islamic version of the "5:00 a.m. miracle."

75 percent of all Americans prayed at least once a week. Even 17 percent of agnostics and atheists said they prayed regularly. According to

a research paper I found, praying increased one's self-control, reduced anger levels, and made one better at coping with stressful situations.

Just after 1:00 p.m., I rolled out my mat again for Zuhr, the midday prayer. After 6:00 p.m. I did the Asr, and as dusk set, it was time for Magrhib. After completing the Isha'a at 10:00 p.m., my legs were aching from all the prostration. But I was feeling calm and tired, and I was struck by the way these prayers changed my sense of duration, and I rather liked to be reminded of my spiritual essence throughout the day.

CARL, MAY 12

After the 6:00 a.m. CrossFit class and a session of mindfulness, I returned to the spiritual center to try yoga for the first time in my life.

From its ancient Indian roots, yoga had turned into a massive $27 billion industry. Over 20 million Americans were practicing it in 2012, a 29 percent increase from 2008. In the same period, spending on yoga products had increased by 87 percent. The typical yogaista was a woman (83 percent) from a middle-class background (over 30 percent of *Yoga Journal*'s readerships had an income in excess of $100,000).

I rolled out my yoga mat and sat down, facing the leader, a good-looking guy in his mid-forties who had just returned from a long, inspiring trip in California.

The instructor pointed to the ceiling above his head, where the words *LET GO* were printed. To reach this state of letting-go, he explained, we had to go through three steps: the first was to be "in the body," the second was "to be real," and the third was "to be together."

"What got you here, ain't gonna get you there," he said. Pausing. Then again: "What got you *here*," his finger was pointing downward, "ain't gonna get you *there*!" He now pointed his finger upward and grinned.

"If you do what you've always done," another pause, "You'll get what you've always got."

We nodded, gratefully.

"I want to drag out what is already inside of you."

The yoga routine started, and I peeked nervously at the others, mimicking their postures. I had just gotten myself into a new position, stretching out my legs, when the instructor spoke up again.

"Now think for a moment. Did you do that because I told you to do so, or because you really wanted to?"

I was thinking about this question as I continued to follow his instructions for the next hour and a half, at which point he said *namaste* and told us we could roll up our mats and go home.

Later in the evening, I returned to the spirituality center for a session of Kundalini meditation. The lounge was crowded, and some of the people from the Chakra Dance were sitting on the couch drinking ginger tea. I did not feel like hanging out. Instead I changed clothes and headed straight into the studio.

We were standing in a circle, barefoot. It was me, five women, and an older man who frightened me. He was grinning and staring at all of us. Then he rushed up to a woman, hugged her, and wouldn't let go. The scene disturbed me. He looked genuinely horny.

Kundalini referred to a kind of primal libidinal force. It was a Sanskrit word, meaning "coiled snake." I had spoken to a close friend earlier in the day, and she had asked me to be careful. She said a friend of hers had become possessed by the Kundalini spirit and gone mad.

The music was riveting, loud, and repetitive; it reminded me of Steve Reich's work. I mimicked the movements of the instructor, a pale older woman dressed in white. She jumped up and down on her soles while the rest of her body was relaxed. By stamping our feet on the floor, we supposedly whipped up a special energy which was meant to be traveling through our bodies, like a coiled snake, all the way up to our heads. This would awaken the Kundalini spirit, making this sexual primal force come to life. I later read on kundaliniguide.com that awakening this spirit "can be startling and chaotic, frightening or blissful, and it usually triggers months and years of new sensations and changes in the person who awakens it."

The music became faster. We were dancing around the room in circles. I was getting exhausted as it had been a long day. The music stopped and we sat down. We were instructed to remain still and not to move for fifteen minutes. This proved hard because my body was aching from the CrossFit session twelve hours ago and the yoga six hours ago. We were allowed to lie down now, flat on the floor, moving a little if we wanted to. As I lay there, underneath the heavy blanket, the words from the yoga instructor came to mind:

Did you do that because you really wanted to?

ANDRÉ, MAY 13

When I got on the train at Canary Wharf, I noticed two elderly Bangladeshi men standing among the bankers. I could tell from their clothes that they had the same plan as me and hundreds of thousands of the other 3 million Muslims in the UK: attend Friday prayers at the mosque.

So far, I had been exploring Islam alone, my only guide being the Koran and the Australian imam whose videos I had watched on YouTube. Today was the first time I would join other Muslims in prayer. In fact, it would be one of the very few times I had visited a mosque in my life.

When I arrived at the East London Mosque, I took off my shoes and put them in a vast shoe rack. This was one of the largest mosques in the country, with a capacity of 5,000 people. I was feeling nervous and clueless, which must have been visible, because a man came up to me and led me into the main prayer hall holding my hand. Hundreds of men were on their knees waiting for the prayers to begin. Then, my escort tapped me on the back, led me out of the hall up a narrow flight of stairs and into a long, low-ceilinged room. Through the large windows, I could look down onto the main prayer hall as it filled up. They could see I was out of my depth. From here, I could cause no harm.

"Would you like some coffee or tea?" the polite young man asked.

"No thanks," I replied.

"What brought you here?"

"Well, I live in the area, and I've always wanted to know more about Islam."

Staff filed into the room and a hush spread through the crowd below.

There must have been at least a few thousand men in the vast hall as the prayer began. I should have prayed with them, but I did not feel competent enough, so I stood at the side, feeling awkward.

When the service was over, the only white staff member led me out of the mosque, through a crowd of hundreds of men handing out pamphlets and selling perfumes. Despite the bustle, I had a deep sense of peace and goodwill. Despite my own ignorance, I felt very welcome.

CARL, MAY 14

Everything was going from bad to worse, strange to mad, a descent from purgatory into hell.

It was seven a.m. on Saturday morning and I had signed up for Dynamic Osho Meditation. "This meditation," I had read on osho.com, "is a fast, intense, and thorough way to break old, ingrained patterns in the bodymind that keep one imprisoned in the past, and to experience the freedom and peace that are behind these prison walls." It was invented by Chandra Mohan Jain, also known as Osho, who came to fame in the 1960s as he traveled across India, preaching a sexually open attitude. He became known as the "sex guru."

On my way into the meditation room, I picked up a pillow and a sleep mask and found a spot in the corner. When I looked around the room, I noticed that everyone was blowing their noses, which was strange because it was May now, not January or February when people usually caught colds.

The nose-blowing, it turned out, was necessary preparation for the meditation because—as the instructor explained—during the first fifteen minutes, we were going to breathe hard and strong through our noses, squeezing the air out of our bodies as though we were accordions. I was blindfolded and stooped forward, pushing my elbows up and down, breathing slow and long and fast and short, trying to avoid getting stuck in a pattern. Snot was flooding out from my nostrils and my head was spinning.

Was I doing this because I was told to, or because I wanted to? The words from the yoga session were ringing in my head again.

Bong!!!

The gong was ringing and it was time for the next phase: catharsis. Now everyone started screaming and jumping and shouting and beating their pillows.

"I hate you, you mothafucka," the woman next to me cried.

I was screaming, too. What else could I do? I was screaming, without knowing why, and I wasn't sure what kind of screaming I was doing, but it was loud and broken.

Bong!!!

We were jumping up and down now, on the spot, my palms beside my ears, like a goalkeeper facing a penalty. Each time we landed on our feet, we were groaning.

Uuh! Uuh! Uuh!

Together we sounded like an Amazonian tribe, preparing to fight, stamping the ground, intimidating our enemy.

Bong!!!

The music stopped and the room fell silent. We were ordered to stand still and not to move an inch. Sweat was streaming down my forehead, tickling my nose, dripping down onto the floor. Our hands still in the air, we looked like mannequins of goalkeepers. We were panting, and my arms were slowly falling down. I was getting weaker and weaker, at the point of breaking down.

Bong!!!

Music was playing from the speakers again, sitars this time. We were instructed to dance and celebrate. I peeked under my blindfold. The woman next to me was massaging her breasts, moving like a snake, making herself aroused. Now she was rubbing herself against her arm. I withdrew into the darkness behind my mask again, hoping to disappear.

I wasn't feeling aroused and I wasn't feeling calm and I wasn't feeling free or enlightened. I felt empty and frightened.

Was I doing this because I was told to, or because I wanted to?

ANDRÉ, MAY 14

A young Bangladeshi guy called out to me. "Hey mate!" He was probably fifteen. "Can you buy me some cigarettes?" he said as he thrust a crumpled five-pound note in my direction.

I went into the store and brought him the cigarettes. When I handed them over, I also gave his five-quid note back. He looked surprised.

As I walked the short distance home, I was feeling proud of having helped a Muslim in need. I had done my zakat, or gift, for the week. I'd also fulfilled one of the five pillars of Islam, which was charity.

When I came inside the door I told Mel about my little gift.

"Why did you do that?" she asked. "Imagine if people bought things for Rita that we did not want her to have."

"Why are you yelling at daddy?" Rita asked from the living room.

"Daddy has been naughty," Mel replied.

CARL, MAY 15

This was painful. Reading Paulo Coelho had been painful. *The Alchemist* was the most annoying book I had read in my life. Dancing around in a room with middle-aged people screaming and shouting had been painful. Listening to gurus speaking about "mom and dad," "letting go," and "being real" was painful.

I sat down and wrote a message to André, telling him how much I was hating this month.

André sent back a link. I opened it. Another Tim Ferriss challenge. "Real Mind Control: The 21-Day No-Complaint Experiment."

Fine, I'll stop complaining then.

ANDRÉ, MAY 15

It was just past midnight when I read the last sura of the Koran. It was only a few lines long, but I felt like I had climbed a mountain.

The message of the Koran seemed pretty straightforward: recognize Allah and accept his message as passed on to Mohammed and recorded in the Koran. If you did so, you could happily recline in a shady garden and enjoy a lifetime supply of cool water with a slice of ginger in it. The alternative: you would burn in the most horrible way possible.

Putting the Koran aside, I reflected back on the past week. Praying five times a day had seemed strangely familiar, like a mixture of intensive yoga, mindfulness, and religion.

Reading the Koran was a much stranger experience than reading the Bible. It was like a message from another world that I could not quite comprehend. From the part that I did understand, it was pretty clear that if I really wanted to be saved, I had to make a big leap of faith. And that was something I didn't feel prepared to do just yet.

CARL, MAY 16

I had gone from vegetarian to vegan, and now, as a new week began, I was going to adopt a new diet: raw veganism.

The first thing I saw as I walked through the doors to my local raw food restaurant, located only a few blocks from my home, was a pile of leaflets from the new-age retreat I was going to attend at the end of the week.

I ordered a beetroot burger and a no-nut wrap and sat down on a white bench, flicking through a book about raw food. It described raw food as the diet we were originally designed for.

"We are the only creatures on this planet eating cooked food," it said. "And we are most likely the most ill."

As I read through the text, I was wondering what the life expectancy might have been "back then," when everything was natural and we had no ovens, no stoves, ripped plants from the ground, and ate with our bare hands.

The recipes were long and complicated, requiring massive quantities of expensive herbs and nuts. To retain the nutrients, nothing should be heated over 49 degrees. Making crisp bread took about two days. Raw eggplants sliced into slim strings was called "spaghetti," and raw parsnips run through a food processor was called "rice." This reminded me of the bags of crisps you could find in the UK, where some marketing genius was able to make fried potatoes sound like a three-course Christmas lunch.

After about an hour of chewing, I headed a few blocks down to a bookstore and bought a raw food cookbook. Then I went back to my local supermarket, where I bought five bags of nuts, a basket full of vegetables, and a small forest of herbs.

I spent the next four hours cooking, making a "spaghetti" (thinly sliced zucchini) tossed in pesto (without parmigiano), a strawberry walnut salad with red onion, a Romesco sauce of tomatoes, peppers, garlic, and coriander, and a large salad.

It tasted good. But when we left the table a few hours later, we were still feeling hungry.

ANDRÉ, MAY 16

It was a new week, so time for a new religion.

I was at the Buddhist Center facing an Indian guy with a white sash around his neck. People shuffled around, building little towers of cushions to sit on.

Although there were only about 150,000 Buddhists in the UK, this was a belief system with which I felt more familiar. A friend had given me *The Teachings of Buddha* when I was a teenager, and it was the first religious book I owned. During my twenties, some of my friends began exploring Buddhism more seriously. One had even gone on to become a Buddhist nun. Buddhism seemed like the only religion that a member of the postmodern cognitariat could proudly talk about. Tim Ferriss discussed some of the lessons from Buddhism in his interviews with the well-known neuroscientist, Sam Harris. It seemed to be the perfect religion for an essentially irreligious soul like me.

The chanting started: "Focus on your breathing," the Indian man said in a soft gentle voice. I counted my breath. *In . . . out. In . . . out. In . . . out.*

I sat cross-legged, feeling calm and relaxed until I realized I could no longer feel one of my legs. It had gone numb. I tried to poke it awake, but it was to no avail. The Indian man read a poem by Rumi:

I am a fish. You are the moon.
You cannot touch me, but your light fills the ocean where I live.

I fidgeted like a fish, trying to bring my leg back to life. A gong cut through the silence. It was over. People around me sprang up, but not me. I still couldn't move. I just sat there and massaged my leg back to life.

CARL, MAY 21

I had been here for a day now. I was in the forest, a three-and-a-half-hour drive from home, staying in an old train station. I was on the top floor in a small room that had two bunk beds on each side. The window looked out over the rail tracks, the fields, and the forest.

I was in my bed, reading Eckhart Tolle's *The Power of Now*: "Unease, anxiety, tension, stress, worry—all forms of fear—are caused by too much future, and not enough presence."

Below me was an older, big-bellied man. He was fast asleep, breathing heavily. He was ill, and probably dying. He had told me about it yesterday, during the assembly, shortly after we had arrived. We had been in a separate house sitting in a large circle, facing the guru, a soft-speaking Englishman. He was preaching the wisdom of Eckhart Tolle and Master Mooji, another spiritual teacher originally from Jamaica. The big-bellied man said he was scared. He said he didn't have the courage to face up to what was happening and that he couldn't reconcile himself with the brutal facts of his situation. I felt a lot of sympathy for him. I wanted to give him a hug. When it was my turn, I simply said I was there to learn to let go and to live in the present.

I had turned off my phone when I arrived. Maybe that was why I had slept so well. The window was open, and the birds were singing. It was still early, and the sky was white. I stayed in bed for another hour. I finished the book and went down to breakfast.

An hour later, we were back in the meditation house, sitting on the floor and listening to music. When it stopped, the guru opened his eyes.

"Welcome," he said, smiling. He was in the front of the room, sitting in a chair. He recited a passage from Mooji: "When you can write your autobiography on the back of a stamp and still have room to spare, I wish to meet you."

Next to our teacher was an empty chair. We were welcome to go up, take a seat, and tell him about our problems.

A woman in her early thirties went up and sat on the chair. She was crying as she explained how she scared people away. All the men she met left her, she said, and now her friends had distanced themselves from her too.

Next up was an older woman. She said she had left her husband, and since she had been here the last time, she had begun to live her own life authentically. She had stopped thinking about what other people said about her. Next, a young man in his thirties spoke. He was crying. He said everything was bullshit, and that he couldn't go on like this for much longer.

After lunch, we went for a walk through the forest. I was feeling calm and peaceful now. We sat down in a glade, meditating, trying to ignore the mosquitoes buzzing around us.

I spent the afternoon in bed, reading *White Fire: Spiritual Insights and Teachings of Advaita Zen Master Mooji*. His message was similar to Tolle's, but more refined. "Who gave us this crazy idea that we should know how to live?" Mooji asked. It sounded like a harsh critique of the notion of self-improvement. Which was rather ironic since I was here to improve my spiritual powers, right? A few pages later: "Best is just be nothing."

Later in the evening, we were back in the meditation room. A woman in her fifties was now sitting in the chair.

"I am afraid to be alone," she said.

"Could you describe the feeling?" the guru said.

"I am afraid. I feel . . . I feel like I'm going to break down." Her voice was trembling.

"Could you try and stay in that feeling?"

She closed her eyes. Her arms leaning on her knees.

"How does it feel?"

She was crying now, tears flooding down her cheeks.

"That's okay," the guru said. "We're here with you."

We were on the floor, watching her, or "watching over her," as the guru put it.

She was trembling, shaking, and crying. She couldn't speak. She threw her head back and forth as she sobbed. It looked as if she was going to throw up. She appeared to be having a full-blown panic attack.

"That's alright. Just stay in the feeling. We're here with you."

On my return, at the entrance to the house, one of the men came up to me. He was a big man, probably an old weightlifter. He had a kind face, and the eyes of a puppy. He reminded me of Meat Loaf in *Fight Club*. The big man came up to me and hugged me. He squeezed hard and long, and I squeezed back, hard and long. Another line from Mooji came to mind: "Whatever comes, do not push away."

ANDRÉ, MAY 21

The Dharmapada had been sitting on my desk for a few days. This morning, I started leafing through it. When I was about halfway through, my attention was caught by the ping of an email. It was from a company called 23andme, and the subject line said, "Your reports are ready."

It was only a few months ago when the young neurohacker suggested that I should have my DNA analyzed. The next day, I had logged on to the company's website and paid just over £100. A few weeks later, I received a small plastic vial that I filled up with my own spit and sent off to a lab in the Netherlands for analysis.

I opened the report and clicked on "ancestry." A multi-colored wheel appeared, illustrating my DNA. 99.9 percent European and 0.1 percent Middle Eastern and North African. 41.6 percent British and Irish, 19.9 percent French and German, 5.6 percent Scandinavian, and 2.9 percent Neanderthal. I clicked on health conditions, and a long list of horrible diseases popped up: breast and ovarian cancer, Alzheimer's, Parkinson's, heart disease. There were stars next to each of them. My heart sunk. Oh God! I had a genetic predisposition to Alzheimer's? Heart disease? Parkinson's?

I felt as though I had just read my death warrant. I was seized by images of a sudden heart attack, or an older me shaking in a chair or wandering lost around a neighborhood.

I had spent the morning reading the Dharmapada, learning that life was an impermanent flux and that death was part of the process of life. Yes, everything was impermanent, but I was terrified.

CARL, MAY 22

I was in the car. The station house was slowly disappearing in my rearview window. I passed one of my roommates on the road, walking toward the bus stop. I would probably never see him again.

I was on the highway now. Driving slowly. No radio, no music. Just silence. "To listen to the silence, wherever you are, is an easy and direct way of becoming present," Tolle wrote.

The weekend had left me emotionally overwhelmed. There had been so much pain. I never went up to sit in that chair. I felt like I had nothing to say. Whatever my problems were, they were nothing compared to the problems of the people I had been with during the last couple of days.

Before going to the retreat, I had thought of spiritual training as a middle-class indulgence. But now, after I saw the pain that these people were suffering and how desperate they were to get better, I could no longer stand on the side and laugh.

I was ashamed. After going there and intruding on all their pain, I felt cynical and exploitative.

ANDRÉ, MAY 22

I was sitting in the main prayer room at the Buddhist center, looking up at a giant golden Buddha. He was well-toned, like he'd been seriously working out. The group leader began to read from a large book in front of him, and after each paragraph, we repeated his words. One by one, we approached the altar and bowed before the buff Buddha. Then we lit an incense stick, twirled it around our heads, and bowed once more.

Before leaving, I picked up a book—the Diamond Sutra—which had been mentioned during the lectures a few times. On the way home, I drifted into a secluded park and sat down under a tree and started to read. Small insects landed on the page. I was careful not to crush them. When I reached the final verse, I lingered on it as the sky turned black with rain clouds:

> *Thus shall ye think of all this fleeting world*
> *A star at dawn, a bubble in a stream;*
> *A flash of lightning in a summer cloud,*
> *A flickering lamp, a phantom, and a dream*

Walking home, I was repeating this verse to myself. Then I saw two boys crossing the park dressed in matching gray tracksuits. *This was the only time this will ever happen*, I thought. *Those two boys will never again stand there talking in the same way as they did then.* It was utterly unique, utterly impermanent.

Perhaps I had finally had a spiritual experience, watching two teenage boys in tracksuits, contemplating the utter singularity of this moment, all the while being aware of the death sentence inscribed in the results of my DNA test.

CARL, MAY 23

I had stopped eating altogether now. I was drinking only water, and I was trying to overcome my hunger by reading Mahatma Gandhi's autobiography. Fasting, he wrote, was a means of self-restraint that helped curb animal passion. He celebrated all forms of collective self-denial. Which reminded me of the challenges that André and I had signed up for: not drinking, not masturbating, and not complaining.

ANDRÉ, MAY 23

I had enjoyed my week as a Buddhist, but as a new week arrived, it was time to move on to Hinduism, a religion I knew almost nothing about.

I was in an Indian vegetarian restaurant in Soho, flicking through the Bhagavad Gita when an overweight Indian guy in a suit asked if I had been upstairs.

"No," I said. "Why?"

"There's a temple," he explained. "It's very clean."

Leaving my large plate behind, I followed him out the door, into another entrance and up some steep narrow stairs. My new friend took off his shoes and led me into the temple, which was about the size of an office boardroom. On the walls were Indian pastoral scenes painted into porticos. At one end was a huge statue of who I would later learn was A. C. Bhaktivedanta Swami Prabhupada, the founder of the International Society for Krishna Consciousness; or, as I knew them, the Hare Krishnas. At the other end of the room, lush curtains were draped.

My chubby friend asked me to sit down on a cushion as the room filled up.

A bell rang, and the curtains opened. Between two life-sized porcelain figures, on a bed of flowers, a shrine was revealed. Everyone stood up and started dancing.

Hare Krishna, Krishna Krishna, Hare Hare. Hare Rama, Rama Rama.

I joined in, and we danced from side to side.

CARL, MAY 24

I was in a basement an hour's drive north of Stockholm, lying on a yoga mat underneath a blanket. I was there together with seven women. We were grouped around a shaman, who was playing the drums.

I had read about shamanic journeying, or soul flight, on shamanicdrumming.com. The idea was that, beyond our ordinary everyday awareness, there was also a "second non-ordinary awareness" that could be "accessed through altered states, or ecstatic trance, induced by shamanistic practices such as repetitive drumming."

We were traveling to the underworld to meet our power animal. First there was a rattling sound, then came the sound of the drum. I closed my eyes and dived into a muddy hole, head-first, crawling down through the roots, digging myself deeper into the ground until I came out into a large black space. Blue smoke was coming from behind. I could see myself from above, small and lonely. I zoomed in again, changing perspective, as in a video game, returning to my own point of view.

Drums were banging in the background, and I imagined myself riding a motorcycle through the dark, farther down into the underworld. As I drove up a hill, the scenery became lighter, pastel-colored. I stopped to pick up a broken chair when I heard some noise from the bushes behind me. I twisted around and found my power animal, a tiger. A tiger? I was disappointed. It was so predictable. But I did not dare resist my vision. I had to embrace the tiger.

I was riding the tiger now, holding on to his mane, and I asked if it hurt, but the tiger explained that he could not feel pain. He took me through a secret portal into a futuristic complex with pillars and platforms, looking like something my daughter could have built in Minecraft.

We climbed into a hot bath, and his friends joined us: an alligator and a polar bear.

Seven loud beats sounded and then the drum stopped. It was time to return. I flew over the hill, into the dark space, up through the roots, squeezed myself through the mud, and resurfacing, I was back in the room.

"Tell us about your travel, Carl," the shaman said.

I spoke enthusiastically about the tiger and the polar bear and the alligator.

"And how was *your* travel?" The shaman turned to one of the women.

"I couldn't get into the underworld today," one woman said. "Impossible."

"Same for me," another woman complained. "The energy . . . It's so . . . There's something wrong. It's coming from here." She pointed in my direction.

"Maybe it's Carl . . ." a third woman suggested.

They all looked at me accusingly. I said nothing.

"No, it's not Carl," the shaman eventually said, coming to my rescue. "The energy was here before he arrived. I felt it, too."

ANDRÉ, MAY 24

I had been trying not to think about my DNA test, but today I logged onto 23andme for a closer look and realized I had been wrong. I had misinterpreted my results and did not have a predisposition to a smorgasbord of horrible diseases. It seems I'd invented a false death sentence for myself. Was this the result of all my Buddhist contemplation on the impermanence of life?

It was the fifth and final day of my fast, and I was lying in a large dark pod floating in salty water, trying to drift into a deep meditative mood.

The flotation tank was invented in the 1950s by John C. Lilly, a neuropsychiatrist who sought to simulate an experience of nonbeing modeled on the precise moment prior to being born. The best result, he explained, was achieved experiencing the flotation tank whilst on LSD.

Maybe it was the lack of LSD, but I experienced no such feeling. I simply felt restless and hungry, as I bounced back and forth between the walls of the pod, unable to remain still.

When the music finally came on about an hour and a half later, I opened the lid, showered off the salty water, got dressed, paid $80, and traveled to another part of the city, where I had scheduled a meeting with a psychic.

She had a kind face, and she wore a long, colorful tunic. She led me down into a small basement room with pink walls and offered me a seat by a small table, next to a bed covered in gold velvet.

"You are tense," she said, as she studied my aura and energy. "There's a lot going on up there," she said, as she pointed at my head, "and you are good at solving problems." She was silent for a moment. "Sometimes you get irritated with people who you feel are standing in your way," she said.

She drew a breath of air and then said, "You have great creative powers. But you feel as if you don't get the chance to fully realize your potential." She then fell quiet again.

She was placing tarot cards on the table. In the middle was a dark and intimidating card with a skull and a black raven. I asked if this was a bad omen.

"No," she said. She went through the rest of the cards, explaining I was a loyal and loving dog. She said that I gave a lot of love. She explained that there were givers and takers and that I was a giver. Then she got more serious again, explaining that we are like cars.

"Cars need fuel. And we need fuel, too." She listed the names of various petrol stations, saying that these were the place where cars went to get more fuel. But people also needed to go places to get energy. She said I had to be better at receiving love. I couldn't go on just giving.

More cards. A picture of a woman appeared.

"You're going to meet love. You're going to meet a woman. Someone from work."

I nodded, as though she was onto something. I didn't want to hurt her, but she was wrong. I was happily married.

Before going home to eat, I made a stop at the gym. It was nice to see my personal trainers again. I had not been there for the last week. I was too weak for CrossFit. They took out the scale and I stepped up. I had lost more than six kilograms in two weeks.

ANDRÉ, MAY 28

I walked up the narrow stairs and into the temple. When I was here earlier in the week, it was nearly empty. Today it was full.

I'd always been aware that the Hare Krishna existed. They seemed to appear with their yellow robes and strange haircuts in the center of nearly any city. It was not until now that I had actually looked into their central beliefs. They were contained in a book entitled *The Science of Self-Realization*. By adopting a Krishna consciousness, I learned, it was possible to save myself from spiritual death. This meant reconnecting with what they called the "supreme godhead." There were many ways to serve the godhead. One was studying the Bhagavad Gita, which I had done during the past week. Another was ritually chanting the Maha Mantra. "If one chants this mantra," I read, "he will never get tired. The more one chants, the more his heart will be cleansed of material dirt and the more the problems of his life within this material world will be solved." I was going to test this claim today.

The chanting was led by a blond woman in a sari who had an ecstatic look on her face. Beside her sat a young man playing a drum. He waved his head from side to side, engrossed in the rhythm. On her other side was another young man playing a harmonium. He too seemed to have disappeared into the music. The woman chanted the same words over and over.

Hare Krishna, Krishna Krishna, Hare Hare. Hare Rama, Rama Rama, Hare Hare.

The chanting moved with the music. Sometimes fast, sometimes slow.

I looked around the room and found an empty spot on the floor. I slowly began to move my lips, mouthing the words *Hare Krishna, Hare Rama*. It felt a bit forced to begin with. But gradually, with each cycle, my chant grew louder, more forceful. The pace rose and fell. After about an hour I was chanting as intensely as the woman. My eyes were closed so I didn't notice that the curtains of the shrine had opened and the audience had turned away from the musicians and were directing their chants to the icons. It didn't matter, because at this point, I had lost my sense of self, being completely immersed in the chant.

After hours of chanting, I left. On the way home, I wondered why chanting the same few words had such a strange effect on me. I found the answer in a recent study published in *Brain and Behavior*. The researchers found that when subjects were asked to chant a mantra, they experienced a significant reduction in mind-wandering. Instead of ruminating on the past or the future, people were able to focus their mental activity on the present, which had a calming effect on them.

When I walked in the door, I showed Mel my new outfit and the prayer beads I had purchased from the temple shop. She groaned.

"You look like a geography teacher," she said.

That was fine with me.

I retreated upstairs, put a Ravi Shankar album on, sat down, and chanted 108 Mara Mantras.

CARL, MAY 30

After breaking my fast, I was gradually coming back to my senses. This month had been tough. I had hated most of it. The only thing that I liked was mindfulness. It had proved rather effective. Ironically, I found myself using the technique to get through all the other madness. When gurus explained their ludicrous theories about chakra and life energy, I brought my attention to my own breathing. When surrounded by people beating up pillows and screaming, I repeated the philosophy of mindfulness: don't be judgmental.

Despite this, I was less cynical now than before. Going to the new-age retreat had exposed me to the suffering and pain of these people. They felt lonely and sad. Some were dying. There was nothing ridiculous about them. All they wanted was for their lives to be a little bit better, a little less painful.

ANDRÉ, MAY 31

It was 3:45 a.m. on my thirty-ninth birthday when I began to climb Ben Nevis, the highest mountain in the UK.

It was just light enough to see the pathway. The easy gradient quickly gave way to a steep, uneven climb. After an hour or so, I found myself on a plateau near a small lake. The sun was slowly coming up. It was a truly beautiful scene. I continued upward. The path smoothed out as I passed small waterfalls cascading down the mountainside.

When I arrived at the top, I discovered a wide, flat expanse. On one side of me were clouds. On the other side were mountains picked out by the sun. I was at the highest point for hundreds of miles in all directions.

I took off my backpack, instinctively closed my eyes, and assumed a meditation posture. As I scanned my forehead, I felt some tension, which I tried to soften. I scanned my shoulders and counted my breaths. I felt the warmth of the sun on my face. Time stopped meaning much. A sense of pleasure started to gently spread over me. The pure silence was only accentuated by the occasional chirp of a small bird.

I kept my eyes closed and floated in this I-less state for a long time, and when I opened my eyes again, I took out my prayer beads and started chanting.

OM OM OM OM OM OM OM.

I followed a lonely cloud as it passed across the sky. Everything seemed to be moving slowly and imperceptibly. I wanted to hold on to this moment for the rest of my life: the warm sun on my face, the stillness, the silence, the chirping bird, the single cloud.

The month was coming to an end, and as I was looking at the mountains in the distance, I thought that maybe this was the spiritual experience I had strived to achieve.

JUNE

SEX

CARL, JUNE 1

During our ten years of friendship, André and I had not once talked about sex. So it was no surprise that we had wanted to skip this month. But there was no way around it.

I was happy with my sex life. I just wasn't interested in examining and discussing it.

A few months back, when I first told Sally I was going to optimize sex, she said "have fun, but I'm out." For a monogamous person like myself, there was only really one option left: masturbation. I decided to spend the whole month improving my own private, autoerotic sex life. Become, as it were, a professional wanker.

On the subway, traveling to my weekly tennis lesson, I found a popular podcast called "Sex with Emily."

"Happy masturbation month," Emily screamed in a high-pitched voice.

Masturbation month?

I checked the Internet and found out that it was last month. But who cared? June was going to be *my* masturbation month.

I listened to the first few episodes, and before long, a new world started to emerge. Masturbation was more than just "release," Emily explained. It was about health and wellness. When masturbating, you should spend at least twenty minutes with yourself. Massage your sexual zones using lubricants. Get to know your arousal cycles. Emily also recommended some sex toys, especially the Fleshlight, an artificial vagina made of silicon and packed inside a flashlight-looking tube. I had heard people talking about the Fleshlight, but only mockingly, as the ultimate symbol of manly decay. The thought of using one had never crossed my mind.

Later that afternoon, on my way back from the office, I cycled into town to visit some sex shops. I'd never been to one before, but I found out that there were three in the city center, located close to one another.

I locked my bike outside on the street and entered the first store. It was like walking into a Las Vegas hotel lobby. There was red velvet carpet on the floor. Pink lampshades hung down from the ceiling. The velvet carpet continued downstairs to a basement strip show. It was early afternoon, and the show wouldn't start until midnight.

I was the only customer. The woman behind the counter stared into a large computer. I cleared my throat and told her about my project, explaining that I was going to spend a whole month trying to optimize sex.

She looked at me with an air of indifference. I listed the things I had done so far this year: weight lifting, French, memorization techniques, mindfulness. Then I explained that I wished to do something similar this month.

"I was thinking that, maybe, if possible, I could learn how to get an orgasm without . . . you know . . . touching myself?" I said.

Finally, she reacted. She left the counter and walked across the carpet. I followed her.

"Then you'll need one of those," she said and pointed to a small box.

"What is it?" I asked. It looked like a gearshift from a sports car.

"It's a prostate vibrator."

I went silent.

"A prostate vibrator?" I was feeling nervous.

"Yes."

"So, you, eh, just plug it in?" I asked.

"Yes, that's the idea."

"And wait?"

"Yes."

"And then I'll . . . er . . . come?"

"Yes."

"While watching porn?"

"Yep, that's a good idea."

Plugging a black rubber handle into my butt and passively waiting for something to happen didn't seem like an impressive feat of self-improvement to me.

"Is there anything else you'd recommend?" I asked.

She took me to the other side of the store, to a large shelf lined with hundreds of boxes. Half-nude porn stars adorned the covers. I read the caption on one box: Fleshlight.

"This is the classic version," she said, and took one out. "It's the world's most purchased toy for men." It looked like a Barbie-doll box. Only there wasn't a plastic doll inside.

"Then you have these." She moved over to the left and took down a few more boxes. "They're molded after famous porn stars," she said as she handed the boxes to me.

I told her I would probably come back in a day or two. I walked out to the street and headed up a narrow slope.

My friend was already there, waiting outside the next sex shop. I had called him earlier in the day, asking if he'd be willing to join me for moral support. We walked down the steep stairs into the basement, then through a narrow corridor lined with masturbation booths. This place was a lot rougher, catering to those interested in more extreme sex. It was just as I'd imagined a sex shop would look, with a red-painted concrete floor and an air of decadence. We studied the large display cases filled with chains, leather masks, and butt plugs the size of American footballs. There was a door at one end of the room with a red blinking sign: GAY CINEMA. CRUISING.

Twenty minutes later, we climbed the stairs and stepped out to the street again. We walked down a few blocks and entered the third and final sex shop on my list. This one was very different. It was fitted out with wooden floors, Persian rugs, cut-glass chandeliers, antique drawers, and white stucco walls.

The target group for this shop was women. They were selling sexy underwear, lingerie, dildos, erotic books, and massage oils. There was only one shelf for men. The selection was familiar—Fleshlights and prostate vibrators. We were looking around the shop when a woman came up to us and asked if we needed help. I told her about the project, and she was instantly interested. She explained to us how the prostate vibrator worked, and I asked her some more questions about masturbation tools and techniques.

Before I left, she showed me a couple of books on masturbation. One was about Taoism and sex, and the other was about achieving multiple orgasms. I bought both of them, feeling hopeful again. I now seemed to have a concrete goal: to learn how to have multiple orgasms.

ANDRÉ, JUNE 2

Sex. It was all around me, but I had learned to ignore it. I wasn't exactly Victorian about sex; I was Wittgensteinian: *of that which we cannot speak, we must remain silent.*

I had always been mystified by people who treated sex as some kind of hobby, like gardening, Italian cookery, or tennis.

So yes, I had some reservations about spending an entire month trying to optimize my sex life.

I was thinking back to our therapist and her suggestions that I should take a realistic stance. As a first step, I should learn to read and talk about sex. I had taken a small step while I was on the Man Camp, sitting naked in a circle of other men, holding a phallus and telling the other men what sex meant to me. But that was a one-off. I needed to go further. Much further.

I headed for the nearest bookshop, where I found a copy of the Kama Sutra. This was probably the most mainstream sex item you could buy, and yet I felt embarrassed paying for it. Later that night I reluctantly showed Mel my new book.

"Why have you got that? It's your stupid project, isn't it?" She looked unimpressed. "So, what are you going to do this month?"

"Sex," I said quietly.

"Sex?"

"Yes. I thought I should learn to talk about it."

"Well, I guess that might be easier for you than actually doing it," she said.

I was silent, feeling awkward.

"We only have sex about once a month," she said, "and that is when I force you."

I said nothing.

"Take the last three times we've had sex. Twice we were trying to conceive, and the other time I had initiated it," she said.

Silence. I knew I had to say something. After all, I had brought up the discussion.

"What do you think about that?" I asked.

"Well, I don't think you're that interested in having sex."

"You're probably right," I replied.

"Yes, well, you don't seem very interested in having sex with *me*. Only with yourself."

She was right again.

"Why is that?" she asked.

The question was left hanging.

After a moment of awkward silence, I tried to explain that masturbation was a boring chore—like cleaning your teeth or taking a shower. Taking care of natural needs.

"You know, as part of my spiritual development, I have not masturbated for almost a month now," I told her.

"Eh, okay."

"So how do you feel about all this?" I asked.

"Frustrated," she said.

I was feeling embarrassed by this whole conversation, so I retreated upstairs to read the Kama Sutra. As I discovered the many different ways you could use your nails during sex, it occurred to me that I was much more comfortable reading about sex than talking about it, let alone doing it.

CARL, JUNE 2

"Why can't straight men talk about sex?" a column in *Vogue* asked. When women talked about sex it was seen as "transgressive," the columnist explained, because it challenged social mores. When men talked about sex it was seen as reactionary, as though they either wanted to preserve the status quo, or just brag. If a straight man positioned himself as a sexpert, she continued, "he's generally perceived as a creep who's trying to manipulate women into having sex with him."

She had a point. I always felt like a creep when talking about sex. Which was why I normally avoided the subject. I tried to explain this attitude to my friend Jenny, who wrote regular columns for newspapers about sex. Unlike me, she had an impressive ability to talk about the subject with both insight and wit.

"Look, I can talk about sex if I have to," I said as we ate lunch in a cheap Indian restaurant around the corner from my house. "It's just that, you know, I'm not so extraordinarily interested in it."

The more we got into the subject, the more obvious it became that I had never seriously talked about sex with any of my friends. The boys who talked about sex when I grew up were usually assholes, boasting about their conquests. I had always been repulsed by that. But now, after two decades of silence, I was thinking there had to be a way of talking about sex that didn't make me into an asshole.

Later that evening, on my way to meet some colleagues for a drink, I stopped by the more elegant sex shop, with the wooden floors and the knowledgeable woman. I had made up my mind to buy the prostate vibrator and the Fleshlight. How hard could it be? I was cool and relaxed about sex, right?

When I walked in, I found another woman staffing the shop. She told me that my friend had left for the day. I passed the counter, went down the few flights of stairs, and walked up to the section with the Fleshlights and prostate vibrators. I stretched out my arms, just about to take down the products from the shelf, when I suddenly froze. I heard giggling coming from behind me. When I slowly turned around, I saw a group of three teenage boys looking at oversized dildos. Then they looked at me, laughing scornfully.

My heart started to race. I sank through the floor. Beads of sweat dropped from my brow.

The few seconds I stood there stretched into infinity. I had to get out. I threw my empty rucksack on my back and rushed up the stairs, past the shop assistant, and out onto the street. I walked for a few blocks, then sat down at a pub and ordered a beer. I called André and told him this wasn't working. I felt like a creep.

ANDRÉ, JUNE 4

I was starting to realize that I had been thinking about sex all wrong. It wasn't just a natural urge to be dealt with every now and then. Rather, it was a performance that required discipline and careful training. With this in mind, I was searching for ways to up my sex game. Soon I discovered sexercise, a technique that promised better sexual performance, increased fitness levels, and improved spiritual health. Turned out it was the favored workout of Kim Kardashian.

On YouTube, I found a video of a sexercise instructor called Ash. A huge tattoo crept down one arm. His nipples were pierced. He was very buff. Half his apartment was taken up with fitness equipment.

When Ash was coming to an end of his sexercise routine, he placed his hands together in a prayer pose and said "blessings." I closed the computer, put on my gym clothes, and headed to my local park. Where would Ash go for his sexercise, I wondered? The fake Chinese temple in the middle of a fake lake, of course.

I found a spot on the grass near the temple, then ran through the sexercise routine, alternating between humping the air and tensing up my PC muscle.

As I came to the end, I automatically went into a meditation posture, breathed slowly, and thought about the connections between spirituality, sex, and fitness. Then, all of a sudden: "Boo!"

A godless little child had come up behind me trying to scare the shit out of me. But I was relaxed and calm like Ash and not easily scared. Instead I returned to my state of sexual nirvana, breathing deeply, first through the mouth, then through the nose, which was when I started to smell something. I sniffed harder. It smelled like . . . what was it? I looked around. Shit! My sexercise spot, I now realized, also served as the toilet for a flock of geese.

CARL, JUNE 8

Sexual kung fu was developed as a branch of Chinese medicine, I read in *The Multi-Orgasmic Man*, a best-selling book described by *GQ* as a "straightforward how-to for modern men."

"To learn to become multi-orgasmic, you will need to become increasingly aware of the speed at which you get aroused," I learned. "Often men go from erection to ejaculation like race cars."

I had spent a week masturbating, trying to improve my technique. I was learning to get in touch with my arousal cycles and how to distinguish orgasm from ejaculation. I had always thought of them as one and the same thing. Not so. An orgasm was good; ejaculation bad. An orgasm was about life; ejaculation about death. As they put it, I had to avoid falling "over the edge and down into the ravine of postejaculatory stupor."

I was excited to read about sexual kung fu masters, as they referred to themselves. They boasted about having orgasms, over and over again, until their entire bodies became orgasmic. Even your brain could have an orgasm. The trick was to blow the sexual energy into my body, and let it circulate throughout my entire orgasm. I doubt, however, that I looked very spiritual when I was lying there practicing these techniques.

I followed a five-step exercise. First, I lubricated my penis ("oil is generally better than lotion"). Second, I pleasured myself ("remembering to massage and stimulate your entire penis, your scrotum, and your perineum"). Third, I paid close attention to my levels of arousal ("notice the tingling at the root of your penis, notice the stages of erection, notice your heartbeat rise"). Fourth, as I neared ejaculation, I stopped ("notice the contraction of your PC muscle and anus that occurs at contractile-phase orgasm" and "try to squeeze your PC muscle around your prostate"). Fifth, regain control and start again ("as many times as you like").

I had the multi-orgasmic book open next to me, so I could see the drawings of an erect penis, with a hand illustrating various squeezing methods such as the "scrotal tug." I set a timer to twenty minutes and put on some porn of the heterosexual vanilla variety. Porn was an excellent way of getting started, the book explained. But as soon as I was aroused, I had to switch it off. Porn was a distraction from myself, they said. "In this practice, you need to go inward and experience your own pleasure, not someone else's idea of pleasure."

I closed my computer and started concentrating on myself. I tried to treat myself as though I was my own lover, as the book had instructed, but the moment I put away my computer, I became self-aware and mildly repulsed. I put the video back on again. I couldn't help feeling uncomfortable lying in the bed, covered in lubricant, trying to pleasure myself. I could think of many people I wouldn't like to have sex with, and I was one of them.

ANDRÉ, JUNE 10

The first porn film I saw was at a neighbor's house when I was twelve. It was on a VHS cassette, and it belonged to my neighbor's father. Through the rest of my teenage years, all I remembered about encountering porn was occasionally flicking through magazines. By my twenties, I saw porn as cultural garbage involving the exploitation of women. I had only watched a handful of porn films in my life. When people talked about porn, I tried to act cool and change the topic as soon as I could.

I knew my aversion to porn put me out of step with much of society. Forty million Americans regularly visited porn websites. 35 percent of all web content was pornographic, and 25 percent of search engine inquiries were related to porn. It was a huge industry, with over $3,000 spent every second on pornography in the US. I thought pornography was just a male thing, but apparently one third of porn viewers were women. Given its vast popularity, I wondered whether taking up porn watching could help me on my quest to confront the issue of sex.

To find out, I logged on to Pornhub, one of the largest pornographic websites in the world. Each year, users watched 92 billion videos for 4.5 billion hours on this site. The first thing I saw were the eighty-five categories of porn. This was what Emily Witt, in her book *Future Sex*, described as "the most comprehensive visual repository of sexual fantasy in human history." Faced with so many types of titillation, I felt overwhelmed by choice. There were unlimited options, but I didn't understand the language. It seemed that I was lacking the precise words to connect my own tastes with the seemingly infinite range of fantasies available.

I did a quick calculation. If I spent one Pomodoro of twenty-five minutes on each category, that would amount to roughly thirty-seven hours. An entire working week of watching. Some people might have relished that. Not me. It sounded depressing, like watching daytime television for two days straight. And besides, spending twenty-five minutes on each category was more than double the nine minutes and forty seconds the average British user spent on the site during each visit.

The first category I clicked on was "British." The main characters were taxi drivers, police officers, secretaries, and grannies. I randomly picked a film. A female taxi driver picks up a male passenger. They talk about the weather. What could be more British? After some more small talk about his "policeman's truncheon," the film cuts to a parking lot.

Inside the car, she strokes his penis, then sucks it, then they have sex in various positions. The whole thing climaxes as he masturbates and she holds open her mouth, as if she's about to swallow a dose of disgusting medicine. The film finished with the woman gargling his semen like mouthwash. I had only been watching for half an hour, but I was already bored. With a sense of stoic duty, I moved on to the next category.

In the week that followed, I watched types of porn that I had no idea existed: mature, MILF, "for women," grannies, cartoons, 60FPS, Asian, Amateur, Arab—to name just a few. Later I discovered that the most popular categories on Pornhub in the UK were lesbian, teen, and MILF. Across the world, the most common search terms for men were MILF, stepmom, and stepsister. In contrast, women's top three search terms were lesbian, lesbian scissoring, and threesome.

The more I watched, the less interested I became. My Internet browser suddenly seemed to be full of adverts for "hot grannies" who lived close by and were "gagging to fuck." I waited for some kind of arousal, but it didn't arrive. It seemed I faced the exact opposite problem of the 200,000 people in the US who were classified as porn addicts. My challenge was not to *stop* watching. My challenge was to force myself to *continue* watching. I hoped my strict Pomodoro schedule would help.

There were a few genres I found more palatable. Hentai, Japanese cartoon porn, had a strange aesthetic appeal. Some genres were mildly funny. A character called the "MILF Hunter" stood out. He was a pornographic version of the Crocodile Hunter, spending his days cruising around Florida looking for "hot moms" to "party with."

There were other genres that were less appealing, like a film starring a seventy-year-old German woman. Her main role was to stand naked in the middle of a paddling pool, inside a cinder-block garage. Around her, ten men of various ages, all wearing black ski masks, were sluggishly stroking their cocks waiting for their turn.

After hours of watching these films, they all seemed to blur into one another. I was finding it hard to keep track, so I called up Carl to discuss my problem.

"You have to be more scientific about this," he suggested.

"What do you mean?"

"Keep a record of all the films you watch," he suggested. "Maybe you could use your brain scanner."

I followed his advice and created an Excel spreadsheet. I made columns for genre, aesthetics, ethical issues, number of hard-ons I had, and general sexual arousal attained. I then put on my Muse EEG headset and kept tracking my brain activity as I watched.

When I came to the end of my viewing marathon later that week, I reviewed my spreadsheet, carefully recorded my notes, and looked at my EEG images. I tried to draw some conclusions. What did I actually like? It was a lot easier to say what I didn't like. As I added up the numbers, I found that porn for women came out at the top of my list. Why? Maybe because since these films were allegedly for women, they gave me some license to watch.

CARL, JUNE 15

Half the month had passed when I met a friend for lunch. She was the only multi-orgasmic person I knew. I had told her how my initial optimism about becoming a master in the art of autoerotic lovemaking had waned. I had been a committed student. I had followed the instructions and practiced breathing and contraction exercises, and I had set aside the mandatory twenty minutes each day for masturbation. Despite my best efforts, I was stuck. Becoming multi-orgasmic had proven daunting. It required more than sheer discipline and hard work. It seemed to presuppose some kind of existential shift.

During lunch, she explained how she'd learned to become multi-orgasmic.

"It's like meditation. When you've learned it, it's really easy," she explained.

"So you can pretty much come whenever you like?"

"Yes, I could come right here and now."

"What? How?"

"I have a particular mental image of me and my boyfriend." After describing the image in some detail, she added: "I imagine that I'm looking at that image, masturbating. I concentrate my mind on myself getting aroused by the image. That's all I need."

"What, so the trick is to observe myself when fictively masturbating to an image of myself having sex." How could I learn to do this, I asked?

"You need a better understanding of how you gain pleasure. Could you film yourself while having sex with Sally? That would help."

"I could ask. But it'd be a hard sell."

"You could also do it while masturbating. Either you film yourself or you use a mirror. The point is that you need to understand yourself and how you look when you're in that mood of ecstasy."

It was then I started to understand the nature of my obstacle. For me, sex was about escape. When I had sex with my wife, I preferred to think about her rather than myself. Whenever I masturbated, I was thinking about something else. Not myself. I had located the problem: it was myself, and the fact that I wanted to erase myself from the equation of sex, whether it involved other people or just myself.

When I got home, I asked my wife if we could film ourselves in action.

"No fucking way," she said.

I had to find another strategy.

ANDRÉ, JUNE 16

Early in the month, I had been at a friend's house. As our children played together, he asked me which projects I was working on. I told him that I was trying to optimize sex. He was one of the few who didn't immediately change the topic.

"Have you looked into pick-up artistry?" he asked.

"What's that?"

"Basically, it's guys using special techniques to seduce women that they don't know."

I was skeptical at first. I had a partner and a young child and wasn't interested in picking up strangers. But all the same, I couldn't deny being intrigued.

I had always been hesitant about approaching women, and the idea of turning pick-up into an art seemed utterly foreign to me. But I wanted to find out more, so I began with Neil Strauss's classic *The Game: Penetrating the Secret Society of Pick-Up Artists*. It told the story of how Strauss became part of a small scene of LA pick-up artists and then participated in making pick-up into a global industry. Strauss described himself as a "transformational journalist" and had written about everything from being on the road with Mötley Crüe to how to make love like a porn star. I discovered that Strauss was a friend of Carl's guru, Tim Ferriss. This was my man.

As I read about the many techniques, I realized that pick-up artists drew on many of the self-improvement tools we had experimented with over this year. A serious PUA (Pick-Up Artist) should go to the gym, be authentic, chant positive aphorisms, work on their "inner game," use Neuro-Linguistic Programming to master the power of suggestion, and practice hypnosis. Really committed pick-up artists mastered tantra, zen, and mindfulness.

I also learned about "chick crack" (any kind of psychological test), "soul gazing" (looking into someone's eyes for an extended period of time), visualization techniques (imagine yourself in places where you feel really good), and the importance of improving your posture (a course in the Alexander Technique was recommended).

Even though these guys were creepy, I couldn't help being amazed by how committed they were to self-improvement. It was a very odd kind of self-help, because they weren't really interested in their *own* selves, other than as a means to pick up women.

CARL, JUNE 17

In the US alone, the sex toy industry makes over $15 billion a year. Vibrators are the most popular products, making up 20 percent of total sales. 44 percent of American women have used them, and 20 percent of men.

My own experience was nonexistent. I had never held a vibrator in my hand.

It was early afternoon when I walked into the upmarket sex shop for the third time. The shop owner was there alone, folding some underwear.

"So, I've made up my mind and would like to buy a prostate vibrator."

"Oh, okay, let me help you," she said, and took out a box. "This is the standard model." It was black and curved and intimidating.

"It's a bit big, no?" I asked.

"The size doesn't make much of a difference, once it's inside."

"No?" My voice was breaking.

"And then you have this model." She took out a blue vibrator. It was Japanese and looked more like an advanced kitchen gadget than spare parts for a car.

"Hold on," she said. "I think I have something even better." She dug through a basket full of products on sale, and returned with a large luxurious box.

"Yes, I knew it was here," she said. "I've had this for a year now, but no one has bought it. It's the Rolls-Royce of prostate vibrators."

"Rolls-Royce," I repeated while studying the box, which reminded me of expensive Belgian chocolates.

"It's half-price now. It's supposed to be superb."

Later in the evening, I was in bed, alone with my Rolls-Royce vibrator. I took it out of the box and plugged it in to charge while reading the user manual.

Nexus Revo Stealth remote-controlled prostate massager is the next step in male pleasure technology. Utilising innovative mechanics, the rechargeable Revo Stealth features unparalleled functionality, created to enable the user to reach new heights of orgasmic bliss.

This was exactly what I had been looking for. *Orgasmic bliss. Next step in male pleasure technology.* I continued reading:

It combines a 2-speed rotating shaft which gives a deep, thorough massage with a vibrating perineum massager with a choice of 6 stimulation functions. Nexus Revo Stealth also comes with a super sleek remote control enabling greater freedom for you to use alone or with a partner. The Revo Stealth will deliver discreet, targeted stimulation where you want it most.

When I had read through the user manual in detail, my Rolls-Royce device was fully charged. I felt a twinge of anxiety. I sat there for a while, studying the black rubber head as it was moving around in circles, like a dancing worm.

I took my clothes off, opened my laptop, put on a random porn clip, set a timer for twenty minutes, applied a generous amount of lubricant, and started touching myself. I tried to be as sensual and self-loving as I could. After a minute or two, as I was getting excited, I took the Rolls-Royce and moved it to the designated place.

It was an unexplored area of my body. Slowly and gently I pushed the Rolls inside. The feeling was unreal. As soon as it was in place, I reached for the remote control and pressed one of the buttons. The shaft started moving in circles. My stomach felt as though I was undergoing an internal medical examination. I pressed the other button. A low vibration started. I pressed the button again, hoping it would slow down. It went faster. I tried to focus on the film, forgetting about my own sensations, but the buzzing in my behind was overwhelming. I pressed the remote again. The vibration turned into pulse mode. I pressed once more, resulting in harder and stronger pulses. I pressed again, and now the pulses were escalating. I pressed the other button, and the shaft started to move faster. I pressed both buttons at the same time, hoping it would stop. But it didn't. I was losing control. I wanted to scream.

Just as I was about to free myself from the rectal terror, the machine came to a stop. I was relieved. I could breathe again.

I had to get back into the right mood. I concentrated on the film and caressed myself gently and slowly, as if I was trying to apologize to my body for the inappropriate things I was doing to it.

The Rolls was still in place, still and silent, waiting for my next instructions. I pressed both buttons one time each. Low vibration, like a mild breeze. The shaft moved slowly, like a gentle massage. This was much better. Just as I was getting into it, something really strange happened. I watched the man and the woman on the screen. They were still at the stage of foreplay. She let one of her fingers slide inside herself. I watched it disappear, then looked at her face as she was closing her eyes, and I couldn't help feeling strangely close to her, as though she was me or I was her.

I carried on for another fifteen minutes: slow shaft rotation and slow vibration. I added more lubricants, stroking myself gently. I prevented myself from reaching the point of no return. Two weeks of practice had paid off. I had become familiar with my arousal cycles, and I knew when to slow down, how to use my fingers, and where to push. I wouldn't go as far as to say I was now a sexual kung fu master, but I certainly did something I had never done before. I was having sex with myself. It was intense, passionate even.

And then, after twenty long minutes, the timer beeped. It was time to let go. I pushed myself off the metaphorical cliff and gave a long sigh of relief. I was mentally and physically exhausted. All I wanted now was to roll over and fall asleep. But I couldn't. Because the machine inside me was still moving and vibrating, and I couldn't get it out. I tried to calm down, but I was stiff and stressed, and started to think about all the stories I had heard about patients coming into the Accident & Emergency with foreign objects trapped in their buttholes. I took another deep breath, relaxed my muscles, and pulled as hard as I could. It popped out, like a wine cork. I was free again. Repulsed and proud in equal measures, I ran into the bathroom and washed myself.

ANDRÉ, JUNE 17

It was time to practice the art of pick-up myself. Before entering the field, I had to be prepared. First step was "peacocking." The best pick-up artists looked more like street performers than men on the prowl. I was new to this, so I just went with a long dangling scarf, a low-cut t-shirt, and prayer beads. I had prepared a cheat sheet that included a range of standard openers: "Hey, just wanted to ask you a question—my friend is still friends with his ex-girlfriend and his current girlfriend is not very pleased—what should he do?" There were also some side notes about body language ("lean back, chest out, take control") and voice ("low, slow, and loud").

I was ready.

I'd done some research and found a perfect place for trying out my pick-up skills: a large courtyard in the City of London encircled by dozens of bars. At this time of the year, many of the drinkers were interns at nearby banks and law firms, who had recently come to London and were keen to meet new people.

But the moment I arrived at the courtyard, my confidence evaporated. The thought of actually walking up to a group of women and using an opener made me feel queasy. I retreated into a bar and drank a glass of overpriced wine while waiting for my friend who was going to be my wingman. Apparently one important source of inspiration for the pick-up community (alongside hypnosis and Neuro-Linguistic Programming) was the film *Top Gun*, which was where phrases like "wingman" and "target" were picked up from.

When my wingman finally showed up, we went outside and I gave him a crash course in PUA. I pulled out my cheat sheet and began reading through the sequence of the ideal pick-up:

1. *Smile and own the space. Whenever you enter a room you need to look positive.*
2. *Three second rule. When you see a woman who interests you, approach them within three seconds.*
3. *Use a memorized opener. Ideally with open-ended questions.*
4. *Focus on the group, particularly on the alpha males. Ignore the woman you are "targeting."*
5. *"Neg" the target. Use a positive comment with a negative follow-up. For instance, "those are nice nails, are they real?"*

6. *Convey personality to the group. You can use a pre-practiced routine like showing photos of various times in your life.*
7. *Give another "Neg" to the target.*
8. *Isolate the target. Take them to a quiet place, and looking for IOIs (indicators of interest). These include the target asking you any personal details like your name, your job, or where you live.*
9. *Demonstrate value by doing something unusual. You could perform a magic trick, run a psychological test, or even pretend you have ESP.*
10. *Focus on the target's internal qualities. People's favorite topic of conversation is themselves.*
11. *Stop talking. Does the target re-initiate the conversation? If so, you are in a good place.*
12. *Close. Either with a kiss or say you need to go and get their number.*

When I got to the end of the list, my wingman leaned over to my side of the table.

"See that woman sitting at the opposite table?"

"Yes, why?"

"She's been listening to you."

"Really?"

"She looks horrified," he said, laughing.

"Oh, shit!" I felt ashamed and changed topic.

Soon after, it started raining heavily, and everyone disappeared. I convinced my wingman we should go somewhere else.

"Sure. I know the perfect place," he said.

About half an hour later, he led me into a neighborhood pub in North London. It was quite a contrast to our previous hunting ground. It was the kind of place that appealed to old men who wanted to drink alone and young people who wanted to hide. But my initial disappointment lifted when I noticed that there were a few groups of women scattered around the pub.

We sat at the bar, ordered a beer, and talked for a while. A couple of pints later, I had amassed enough courage to make my first attempt at approaching the targets: a group of women in their thirties and forties.

I opened with a question I had prepared earlier: "I'm doing some research on tattoos—do any of you have one?" There was no alpha male to focus on, so I turned my attention to the alpha female. The question seemed to spark some interest. Some of them had tattoos; some of them didn't. Having opened the group, it was time to establish rapport. They were friendly but made it clear that they weren't that interested, so I ejected and returned to the bar. My wingman laughed at me. I told him that as my wingman, he was supposed to be supportive, not mock me.

I drew up the courage to approach the next group of women. This time, they were much more attractive and much younger. None of them were interested in my tattoo question. I walked away after about three minutes of monosyllabic answers. I looked into my beer, defeated. My wingman cruelly laughed at me again.

But then a woman from the first group came over to us. She was by far the most attractive. She seemed genuinely interested and stayed talking with us for about twenty minutes. Perhaps ignoring her had worked.

After she left, I looked at the guy behind the counter. He was wearing the kind of cut-off jean shorts that were popular with German hikers. He was pumping his body up and down to the music, like a ten-year-old girl with a new pole-dancing kit. I looked around at the other men in the bar. Most of them were probably gay. I looked back at the two groups of women I had talked with. The alpha female rested her hand possessively on one of the beta-female's legs. "Is this a gay bar?" I asked. My wingman laughed at me again.

Soon it was approaching closing time. All was not lost, however, because there was a night club around the corner. I looked at my cheat sheet again: "Own the space," it said. So, when I walked into the club, I tried to project a positive attitude by giving a broad smile. I also wanted to show I was in charge, so I went right up to a guy I had never met and asked him to buy me a beer. I laughed when he asked why. I moved on to the next group. Then the next.

Soon, I noticed a very attractive woman. I walked directly up to her and used a "direct" opener: "You look interesting." She seemed to be very open, but after two minutes she told me she had a boyfriend. While studying the Venusian arts, I had learned that any persistent pick-up artist sees long term relationships (or LTRs in PUA speak) as a temporary hurdle. The music was loud, and she slipped away. Now I could see why many PUAs preferred the "day game."

I danced around with abandon and was approached by a few women and even more men. But once again, I spotted my attractive target and approached her. This time, she was with her boyfriend. "Focus on him," I thought. He said he was an Israeli soldier. Not someone you really wanted to tangle with. But I tried to think positively, as PUA experts advised: *I'm not hitting on this guy's girlfriend, I'm doing him a favor by making her feel desired.*

About this time, I realized my wingman was trying to escape from the club. I grabbed him and dragged him back down the stairs. "I need my wingman!" I cried. He returned, reluctantly. But as soon as my back was turned again, he disappeared. I guess he had had enough of watching me make a fool out of myself. Mercifully, the music stopped after about an hour. I ran out immediately, feeling relieved, and got a cab home.

CARL, JUNE 22

After an unsuccessful second attempt to use the prostate vibrator, an experience that felt more like self-rape than self-love, I returned to the upmarket sex shop. I was happy to find my friend there. I started telling her about my reluctance to use the vibrator. She said it usually took some time to get used to. I told her I was planning to try something else, maybe a Fleshlight.

Since it was invented in 1998, more than four million Fleshlights have been sold, and 45 percent of purchasers were repeat buyers. On the official website, the Fleshlight was described as the "#1 male sex toy" providing "the most realistic intercourse simulation known to man."

"You should try one of these," she said, and took out a transparent version. "It's really cool, because you can see yourself when you're inside it."

I didn't like the sound of that. What could be more repulsive than watching myself sliding in and out of a transparent plastic tube? But I followed her advice and bought the device. I cycled back home, and went straight into the bathroom. It was a big slimy thing, placed inside a cylinder-shaped cage. I took out the slimy part, and weighed it in my hand. It was moist and sticky, like a jellyfish.

I read through the instructions carefully and filled it up with hot water, which was supposed to give it a more natural feel. Then I went into the bedroom and got myself into the right mood, added lubricant, first on me and then on my new device, before connecting myself with the slime. I was on my back with a big plastic tube on my penis sticking straight up into the air. I could only imagine how ridiculous I looked.

I followed the sex shop woman's advice and glanced down at myself. But all I could see through the thick plastic was some blurred flesh. It didn't help me understand my pleasure. I looked up again and stared into the computer screen, pretending I didn't exist. It was beginning to feel nice and warm, and I could see why it had become a hit.

And then, when it was all over, the shame arrived with remarkable force. As I walked into the bathroom again, my heart sank. I felt disgusting. I took out the slimy jellyfish from the container and opened the artificial labia with my fingers, placed it under the tap, and flushed hot water through the pipe. I drowned it in cleaning alcohol, flushed some more, then left it on the washbasin to dry. An hour later I came back, patted powder on the opening, put it back in the plastic cage and the box, and finally put it into a bag, which I hid in the wardrobe.

ANDRÉ, JUNE 22

According to some regulars on the Venusian Arts, a web forum frequented by pick-up artists, tantra was great for mastering your "inner game." Neil Strauss described tantra as a spiritual experience that enabled "a release from ego, a merging with the other, a discorporation into the atoms vibrating around us, a connection to the universal energy that moves through all things." After my religious experiences in May, I was keen to find out more.

One book which was popular among pick-up artists was *The Way of the Superior Man* by David Deida, a neurophysiologist turned spiritual and sexual teacher. I had always assumed that tantra was about delaying and intensifying orgasms. But what I discovered from Deida was something quite different. By fully embracing my male inner essence, I could move beyond being either a hyper masculine King Kong or a new age wimp. His words reminded me of the man camp. "The search for freedom," he said, was the "inner sexual core of men." Reading the first chapter, I learned that I had not yet liberated my essential inner gift. I had to stop holding back, stretch out my arms and open myself up to the world. I needed to discover my inner edge and reach beyond it. If I followed his instructions I could learn how to "fuck to smithereens."

This was something I had to try out. A quick web search led me to a tantra workshop which would be held in a few days. I immediately signed up.

CARL, JUNE 25

I reached into the back of the wardrobe and took out the two big boxes. One contained the prostate vibrator. The other, my Fleshlight. I also grabbed the lubricants and my computer and flopped down on our bed.

After about five minutes, the vibrator found its place, and I started to zap around with the remote control. I then reached for my Fleshlight, added lubricant, and pushed it all the way down. I could see my penis through the transparent plastic.

I was just lying there, waiting for something to happen. I thought back to the woman in the sex shop I had met on the first day of the month, who said it was enough to just plug the vibrator in, and then an orgasm would come flying. How wrong she was!

After about ten minutes, I gave up. I grabbed the tube with both my hands and moved it up and down. Just as I was reaching climax,

I stopped. For some reason, I wanted to film myself and show André. Maybe I wanted him to see the humiliation I was going through. I hit record on my computer, staring into the built-in camera, while slowly bringing myself over the cliff. I could only imagine how ridiculous I looked, lying there, in my vain attempt to optimize masturbation.

ANDRÉ, JUNE 26

It was early Sunday morning, and I was on my way to a tantra workshop, leaving Mel and Rita at home.

A woman in her forties opened the door, and I followed her into a large community hall packed with odd furniture. In the middle of the room, forty people sat in a circle on the floor.

"Please come and join us," the leader said.

Her name was Samantha Sunsister. Next to her was a guy dressed entirely in white who had a talisman from the man-camp around his neck. In the middle of the circle sat a small brass Hindu figure nested in tie-dyed fabric.

"Now, let's start by dancing."

The sound of a didgeridoo played over the sound system.

"Get in contact with your hips."

We started moving.

"Let your hips lead you."

A woman next to me was yawning. When the music came to a stop, the yawner was right in front of me.

"Okay, you are going to work with the person in front of you. We're going to do an exercise on boundaries," Samantha said.

All the women went to one side of the room, and the men went to the other. The didgeridoo was replaced with the sound of dripping water. I was instructed to walk slowly toward my partner. I focused on the yawner and started my journey. But then she held up her hand, so I stopped. After what seemed like minutes, she lowered her hand, and I continued my slow approach. A few more steps, and her hand came up. She buzzed with defensiveness. After she lowered her hand, I set out again. It seemed to take half an hour to cover ten meters. She stopped me when I was a meter away. *What the hell was going through this woman's head?*

During the tea break, the yawning woman asked me why I was there.

"Well, I'm sort of disconnected from my sexuality," I said. "I want to explore it again."

"Mmm. So are you in a long-term relationship," she asked.

"Yes."

"So, where is your partner?"

"Oh, at home . . . logistics, you know."

Silence.

"So, you will bring back what you learn today to the relationship," she said.

"Well, ah, I guess so."

After sharing our reflections, the didgeridoo music returned and we began to dance again. This time I found myself with an attractive and athletic woman in her forties. In this exercise, we were supposed to explore our feelings about taking the lead. She was first up. She growled at me, like a panther, and I could see the sexual energy flashing in her eyes. I acted like her prey. She rose above me, ready to attack. I submitted. We were locked in a dance of death.

When the didgeridoo faded, we were both exhausted and elated. I was surprised by the sudden burst of intense energy and intimacy that I had just shared with a stranger. As we caught our breath, she told me she had been to many tantra workshops in the past, both with her clothes on and without. I guess this meant that, as you progressed, you got more naked.

In the afternoon, the men formed a small circle, while the women stood on the outside. I found myself face-to-face with a casually dressed young woman. Over the sound system Samantha gave us instructions:

"I want you to honor the man in front of you—his essence and potential as a father."

The woman in front of me was clearly disturbed. She looked intensely at me. She was about to cry.

"Kneel down at his feet and praise him," the facilitator said, "praise your father."

My partner tensed up, then shuddered.

"You don't have to do this," I said.

"No," she said stoically, "I'll do it."

She knelt down and prayed at my feet. When she returned to eye level she said:

"Your eyes are like my father's." She was going to cry.

We moved around the circle clockwise, and I was face-to-face with the woman who opened the door for me when I arrived. We were instructed to find a space, take some pillows and sheepskins, and make a nest. I did not really like where this was leading.

The voice came over the speaker again: "Look at the woman in front of you—she is a goddess—worship her inner goddess—worship her inner Shakti. What will you offer to your Shakti?"

I surprised myself by saying:

"Shakti, can I dance for you?"

"Yes," she purred.

I stood up and started doing my impression of Indian erotic dancing.

"Can I lie down?" Shakti said.

"Yes, Shakti," I replied.

She lay there as if she was in bed on a summer afternoon about to switch from reading erotic fiction to having a session with her vibrator. As I waved my arms around, she seemed to get more and more pleasure. I started to stroke my hands across her legs and shoulders.

The voice came onto the speaker:

"Now reverse roles. Shakti, praise your Shiva."

"Can I stroke you?" she said.

"Yes," I responded.

She stroked my face and then my shoulders. She stroked my chest, my legs, my feet, my thighs. Then she started purring. She got more and more into the role and began pawing at me. She hissed at me and we moved around vigorously. Now I had a hard-on.

"It would be great to do this every week," she whispered in my ear. I didn't respond, I just continued to yield to her swipes.

Soon it was over. Most people sat around talking. I put on my shoes and headed directly for the door. Shakti stood at the door and bade me farewell.

"Maybe I will see you at another one of these events," she said.

"Mmm, maybe," I said.

Walking toward the tube station, I had the overwhelming feeling that I had been having sex all afternoon. I felt that pleasant sense of postcoital relaxation. It seemed that acting out the role of Shiva or being attacked by a sexual panther had done something for me that hours of porn, multiple sessions of sexercise, and the arts of the pick-up could not.

I'm not sure whether I had discovered my inner sacred masculine essence, but I had realized that maybe I should stop taking sex so seriously.

CARL, JUNE 30

As the month was coming to an end, I had to admit my failure. Sexual kung fu was not for me. My attempts to become multi-orgasmic had failed. All I had experienced was embarrassment and shame. But instead of simply giving up I decided to do one last thing. I was going to confront my shame and fully embrace it.

I was back on the same street where I had started my sexual experiments exactly one month earlier. It was hot and humid. I slowed down as I neared the sex shop. I felt awkward. Wearing long linen shorts and a blue-and-white striped Oxford shirt didn't help. A man in his fifties walked past me on the street. He looked like an insurance salesman, with thin-framed glasses and short blond hair, his white shirt tucked tightly into a pair of khakis. He looked like me, in twenty years' time.

He nervously glanced over his shoulder, and then he snuck into the sex shop.

In 1716, the anonymous pamphlet *Onania* described masturbation as a heinous sin of self-pollution. Even though most people admit to masturbating today—in the US, 94 percent of young men and 85 percent of young women—it isn't much less taboo in modern times. In an article published in *Aeon* called "A Handy History," a historian explained that while we like to talk about casual sex with strangers, we remain silent on the topic of solitary sex with ourselves. "Belief in the evils of masturbation has resurfaced," the historian explained. Today, it appears "in the figure of the sex addict and in the obsession with the impact of Internet pornography."

I followed my future double down the steep flight of stairs, through a narrow corridor, and into one of the booths. It was small and cramped like an aircraft lavatory. There were no lights apart from the screen and the blinking dashboard. A soft leather chair, like a truck seat, sat in the corner. Above the seat was a small shelf with a box of Kleenex.

Still standing, I took a few deep breaths to fill my lungs. I concentrated on my chest as it expanded and then I blew out the air. *Do you feel any particular emotions right now?* I imagined the soft-voiced man from my mindfulness app saying, "Whatever you feel, it's okay." I closed my eyes and repeated the lessons I'd learned from practicing mindfulness. Forgive yourself. Be open-minded. No emotions are wrong.

I sat down and put a couple of coins in the slot. A video came on the screen, just an inch away from my face. I took out my phone and put on a timer. This time I didn't plan to stay longer than necessary. This wasn't going to be a twenty-minute-long act of self-love.

Four-and-a-half minutes later, I was running up the stairs, sweat pouring down my back. I hurried down the street, half-crying, then burst into a café and locked myself in the toilet. I washed my hands for what seemed like ten minutes, breathing heavily, looking into the mirror at my twisted, sunburnt face, feeling like a creep.

JULY

PLEASURE

CARL, JULY 1

I was going to meet a friend at a bar across town. On the way, I bought a pack of cigarettes and a lighter. He was running late. I sat down and ordered a beer and started reading *Cigarettes Are Sublime* by Richard Klein, a professor of literature at Cornell University. On the back cover was a quote from Oscar Wilde: "A cigarette is the perfect type of perfect pleasure. It is exquisite, and it leaves one unsatisfied. What more can one want?" I flicked through the pages with old black-and-white pictures of Marguerite Duras, Coco Chanel, Pablo Picasso, Humphrey Bogart, Jean-Paul Sartre—all accompanied by glowing cigarettes.

Twenty minutes later, my friend arrived. I lit up my first cigarette in four-and-a-half years and asked him to film me. The first few drags were hard. My throat was not used to the smoke and tried to protest.

Cigarettes didn't taste good in the way sugar tastes good to children, Klein explained. They made you sick. They were poisonous. They killed. But it was not in spite of their harmfulness, Klein continued, "but because of it that people profusely and hungrily smoke." The pleasure was negative, or sublime, in the Kantian sense. Pleasure and pain were mixed together, in a lethal way.

Few things in my life had been more difficult than stopping smoking. I had been a committed smoker from the age of fifteen and was not able to kick the habit until I was thirty-two. Smoking had caused me a lot of harm. I was constantly coughing and feeling sick. But I loved it all the same.

Later that evening, as I walked back home from a nightclub, I had finished my first pack. I could feel the nicotine circling through my body, awakening my brain, removing all anxiety, sending out signals of reward. Truly, this was enjoyable. I could think of no other thing that gave me a more intense and immediate sense of pleasure.

ANDRÉ, JULY 1

This morning I didn't follow my well-honed morning ritual, leaping out of bed at daybreak. Instead I lounged comfortably for a while, before reaching for my copy of *The Hedonist Manifesto*. The history of Western philosophy since Plato had been disastrous, I read. It punished "anyone who sought to celebrate the drive to life." Fortunately, there was a hidden history of hedonistic thinkers who saw pleasure as the ultimate aim in life. "They refuse to turn pain and suffering into paths to knowledge and personal redemption." Instead, "they propose pleasure, enjoyment, the common good." To become a hedonist, I had to master the art of pursuing pleasure.

Putting the manifesto aside, I wondered what the first step might be. For me, pleasure meant food and drink, so I would start there. I headed out to our local corner store and bought the ingredients for a bacon sandwich and a Bloody Mary. Purchasing booze and bacon from a Muslim shopkeeper didn't feel great. To make matters worse, it was near the end of Ramadan, and it was still only eight o'clock in the morning.

Back home, I went into the kitchen and mixed myself a drink. As I fried the bacon, Mel came down the stairs.

"What are you doing?" she asked.

"Making a bacon sandwich," I replied.

"Why?" She looked mystified.

"Well, according to a recent poll, a bacon sandwich is the favorite food of one in ten British people. So, I thought I'd start with that."

She shook her head and left.

Her confusion was understandable. I had been a vegetarian for over sixteen years. My decision to stop eating meat was probably the only New Year's resolution I ever kept.

When I'd finished my bacon sandwich, I started to wonder what all the fuss was about. Why did so many people describe this as their favorite food? I hadn't enjoyed it at all. In fact I'd rather have plugged Carl's vibrator up my ass than eat those fried strips of bacon.

A few hours later, I walked into my local pub. A man in his late seventies was already halfway through his first pint. I still had a taste of swine grease in my mouth from breakfast. But nevertheless, I sat down at a table and ordered a burger and a beer.

My peace was interrupted when Carl called me on Skype. In a few days, we would present a TEDx talk in Bratislava. Carl had taken control, as usual, and written an entire script for us. I had read through it a few times, and now he wanted me to memorize it.

Carl sounded manic. For the next thirty minutes he wanted to run through the script. I took out my laptop, opened the document, and read it out. It was the start of July, and we were supposed to be enjoying ourselves. Reading through a script a hundred times and trying to memorize every line wasn't my idea of hedonism. Besides, I was just digging into my first burger in sixteen years, and I didn't want Carl's fussing to get in the way of that.

CARL, JULY 2

Early next morning I met up with André at Vienna International Airport, and we went together in a cab to Bratislava. Our hotel was located on a small street with green trees, and we sat down in the courtyard to have a beer, although it was only 11:00 a.m.

"Let's practice the talk," I suggested. André was reluctant. It was only now that I realized that he hadn't memorized it. We had gone through it the previous day, over the phone, but he had cheated. He'd been reading from the script while getting drunk in the pub.

I freaked out. He really didn't take this seriously. Despite the therapy, we were back to square one.

"I'm just your little actor in your personal theatre performance," André said.

Fuck you, I thought. *I'm the one doing all the work, and all you do is whine.*

Bratislava was hot. Almost forty degrees Celsius. We walked through the old part of the city, the sun overhead. We had lunch in a nice Slovak pub. André said he was tired and put his head down on the table, entirely unconcerned about the other guests. He closed his eyes and went to sleep. I left the restaurant to smoke.

An hour later we arrived at the Slovak National Theatre for the rehearsal. We weren't far into our talk when André fucked up—he went completely blank and couldn't remember his lines. Tomorrow we were supposed to speak to 700 people.

ANDRÉ, JULY 3

"Let's do some mindfulness," I whispered in Carl's ear. We were sitting at the front of the theatre, feeling anxious. We were up next.

The speaker before us was a young Norwegian, talking about his experience of narrowly escaping the bullets of Anders Behring Breivik's machine gun during the 2011 attacks in Oslo and Utøya. The audience gave him a standing ovation. It was hard to imagine a harder act to follow. I put on my Jawbone, my Muse, and my running watch, and we ran out on stage.

As soon as we were finished, Carl ran off. I thought the speech went fairly well. Clearly, he didn't. I saw him sitting by himself outside, smoking morosely. My sense of achievement instantly evaporated.

Later in the afternoon, Carl calmed down, and we sat outside on big, comfortable cushions looking up into the blue sky, smoking cigars and drinking red wine. For the first time this year, I was feeling happy. This was what we should be doing. I vowed to let my inner hedonist loose that night.

CARL, JULY 3

It was all over very quickly. It didn't go as planned. André danced onto the stage, moving like a drugged robot, flipping his head back and forth. Was I surprised? Of course not.

The previous night I had dreamed that he was going to do just this: ditch the plan and do his own thing. In the dream, I had become so angry that I had banged his head against a concrete wall. The blow was harder than planned. He fell down on the ground, like a bag of potatoes. Blood flooded from his mouth. I tried to shake him back to life, but it was too late. He was dead. Did I actually want to kill him?

During the speech, André fucked up, missing his lines twice. I felt empty and uneasy as we walked off the stage. I realized that I wasn't comfortable yet speaking publicly about the project. Without properly contextualizing it, André mentioned my visit to the masturbation booth. I started to think about my daughter and wife, and suddenly I felt as if this whole project was a stupid mistake. For the first time, I regretted having started it.

André was happy though. We were outside the theatre, on a terrace, basking in the sun. He downed an admirable number of glasses of wine in quick succession, then borrowed a bike and started riding around a fountain in a never-ending loop, cigar in his mouth. Hundreds of people were standing on the stairs watching him in disbelief.

Later in the evening, we followed the organizers and some of the speakers to a small bar. André was completely out of it by this time. He was showing off his man camp techniques: shouting and screaming, falling on his knees, then falling onto the floor, crawling around, kissing people's feet.

"Is he always like this?" one of the organizers asked.

"It's not the first time," I replied and changed the topic.

ANDRÉ, JULY 8

After a brief stop at home in London, I was in Naples. It was noon, and I was having my first beer of the day. It felt like I was making great progress in becoming a hedonist. By the time Carl arrived at 3:00 p.m., I was already quite drunk. The waitress was looking at me disapprovingly, and it was time to move on.

We found a bar in the Spanish Quarter where you could buy an Aperol spritz for one Euro. They were lethal. After I'd drunk about ten of them, I did a hundred squats outside the bar. Why? I had no idea. A neighboring restaurant owner was so impressed he convinced me to do the same outside his establishment. It was too much, and I ended up vomiting in a nearby alleyway. Afterward, Carl dragged me off home. I was clearly still in the mood to party, because when we came back to our flat I ended up dancing around the apartment naked. Carl sat down by the kitchen table, filming me, like some kind of pervert. It was after midnight, and I felt I had completed my assignment for the day.

CARL, JULY 9

Sitting in a shady piazza in Naples, smoking the first cigarette of the day, drinking a café fredo, discussing philosophy—it should have been perfect, but André spoiled the moment with his groaning.

"If this is pleasure, I don't want it," he said. I could tell he was suffering from a vicious hangover.

"I don't know if the ancient Epicureans would have approved of drinking ten Aperol spritzes, then doing a hundred squats. That wasn't what they meant by the pleasurable life," I said.

"No, what was it then?" he inquired.

"For Epicurus, pleasure was about the tranquility of the soul and absence of bodily pain. Not getting pissed, vomiting, and dancing naked."

I took another drag on my cigarette. The smoke vanished in the hot sun.

"So, what did they do?" André asked.

"Three things," I said, before taking the final puff on my cigarette. "Pursued knowledge, cultivated friendship, and led a temperate life."

"A temperate life? That doesn't sound very hedonistic."

"They were dedicated to the simple and natural pleasures in life. They avoided excesses."

"Right," André said, and ordered two more café fredos.

ANDRÉ, JULY 9

Halfway through my third café fredo, as I listened to Carl describing Epicurus's theory of pleasure, it dawned on me: I had been thinking about pleasure all wrong. From now on, I should be a proper hedonist and spend my days savoring simple pleasures like knowledge and friendship.

When it was getting close to lunchtime, we strolled through the city, toward a well-known restaurant near Piazza Bellini. A perfect little place, the exterior was draped in lush greenery. The food was delicious. For dessert I had a beeramisu—tiramisu, made with beer.

As the afternoon wore on, we talked about our fantasies. If I was really honest with myself, I had very few fantasies. Carl, however, had tons. This whole year was an excuse for Carl to live them out. Learning French, memorizing things, writing a book—these were things Carl wanted to do anyway. I bet CrossFit was a secret fantasy, too. I didn't mind Carl doing all these things. I just didn't get why I had to be dragged along in the process. It was like *Fight Club*, I pointed out—a normal guy gets absorbed into the life of a crazed individual.

"Exactly," Carl said. "It's exactly like *Fight Club*. You're Edward Norton. What's his name in the film? Jack? And I'm Brad Pitt. Tyler Durden."

Carl looked as if he'd had an epiphany.

"That's it," he continued. "This means I don't exist. All of this is about you. I'm just an imaginary double you have to invoke to get things done. I'm the one you can blame everything on. And then you'll have to kill me."

I wanted to dismiss Carl's theory, but I remembered that Chuck Palahniuk wrote *Fight Club* after he had attended a Landmark training session. And hadn't it been Carl who had forced me to attend Landmark back in January? Who even paid? Was it him or me? Things were getting confused.

CARL, JULY 10

We jumped on a ferry out to Capri, then we took a convertible limousine up the mountain, where we had a wonderful lunch on a quiet piazza, drank more wine, and smoked more cigarettes. We went for a walk, visited a beautiful villa that was once owned by a famous Swedish doctor, and then we took another taxi down to the shore. We climbed down the cliff, leapt into the green water, swam into a dark cave and then out again, floating in the salty water. *What could be more pleasurable than this?* I thought as I dried in the sun, smoking another cigarette.

When we got back to the flat, it was dark. I asked André if he wanted to watch the film I had recorded a few nights ago, when he had danced around the room naked. He said okay, but his face twisted in shame as he observed his nocturnal moves. Then we put on the video I had recorded of myself masturbating. It wasn't graphic. Nor erotic. Just a close-up of my face. But the effect of watching those facial expressions and the way I had my mouth half-open and my eyes half-closed—it was really too much to handle. We threw ourselves on the floor, rolling around, laughing and crying.

I still didn't know who we were, or why we were doing all of these things. I didn't know if I was Tyler Durden or Jack, or someone else, or just no one.

I woke up this morning with a hangover from hell, caused by ten days of hedonistic excess. Perhaps I should have followed the ideas of Epicurus more closely.

To address this dire situation, I began searching for hangover cures. I read about Roman vomiting recipes, Scottish people who drank Irn-Bru (which according to the article tasted like melted plastic), and a declassified Soviet-era compound used by KGB agents to combat the effects of alcohol. Reading about these disgusting remedies was only making me feel worse. Maybe I was thinking about this all wrong. Perhaps the point of overindulgence is the pain that follows. If treated right, a hangover could be pleasurable. There was something undeniably appealing about lying prostrate all day: taking it easy, gorging on junk food, and watching box sets. For me, the license to be lazy was more attractive than the permission to drink. I made up my mind to have a protracted hangover, throwing myself into a slothful and pleasurable existence.

First stop: McDonald's.

Going to the world's largest hamburger joint might sound like an ordinary thing to do, but not for me. I had not eaten at McDonald's in the past decade. The menu made me confused at first, but I spotted some classic items from my youth: an Egg McMuffin and a hash brown. I ordered both along with an extra-large Coke for good measure.

After two bites of the hash brown, my entire mouth was slathered with grease. I took a few liberal sips of Coke, which stripped all the fat from my mouth. The McMuffin was bland, but it was saved by a mysterious salty taste. I added ketchup and finished it. I then sat there for a moment, staring blankly at the empty food wrappers. As I got up to leave, I bumped into my kick-boxing trainer.

"André! Where have you been, man? Coming in today?"

"Ah, I was away, giving a TED talk," I replied. He seemed impressed.

"So today?"

"Ah, well, I just wanted to spend it chilling out."

"Okay," he replied, "but you need to train. Next week then?"
"Maybe," I said.

CARL, JULY 12

I smoked my last fag at Naples's airport and left the remaining cigarettes with André. What made these thin rolls of tobacco so delightful, I learned from *The Compass of Pleasure*, was that they hijacked the intrinsic pleasure circuit that is apparently located in the forebrain.

But cigarettes were a troubling, menacing pleasure. By the end of my two weeks as a chain smoker, I was smoking close to three packs each day, and it was no longer very pleasant.

At the airport, on my way back from Naples, I went to a restaurant and ordered a carbonara and a glass of red wine. As I delighted in the food, I read *The Decadent Cookbook*, with recipes of *Cat in Tomato* (when skinning the cat, "remember there are more ways than one!"), *Dog á la Beti* ("Prior to being killed, the dog should first be tied to a post for a day and hit with small sticks to 'shift' the fat in the adipose tissue"), and *Entrecote á La Bordelaise* ("skin and de-gut your rat"). I learned that the Roman Emperor Heliogabalus "ordered elephant trunk and roast camel from his kitchens," and that Caligula once "gave dinner guests an entire banquet made of gold."

Inspired by these stories, I decided that food and wine were going to be the next areas of focus as I continued my hedonistic pursuits. I was going to spend the next few weeks at the seaside, so why not use that time cooking perfect classic dishes and sipping good wine? That should be a life worthy of the pleasure-seeking decadent.

When I landed in Stockholm, I phoned up my brother-in-law. He loved food and wine more than anyone I knew. It was his life. He got enthusiastic as I told him about my idea. I asked him to buy some expensive wine, and I said I'd pay.

Later in the evening, at the Stockholm seaside, my brother-in-law and I cooked some delicious steaks that he had bought from the market.

He had also bought two bottles of shamelessly expensive wine. I opened one of them, a Pomerol from 2009, and let it air while preparing the meal.

The meat was done to perfection. The wine was extraordinary. After I had finished my plate, I poured some more wine and took a sip. I closed my eyes and savored the taste as it filled my mouth. The terrace was bathed in the evening sun. Slowly, the sky grew reddish. I looked at the kids as they played in the garden, casting long shadows over the deep green lawn.

It was a moment of joy. Almost perfect. I say almost because one crucial thing was missing: a cigarette. It was the secret ingredient, which had to be added to reach that sublime level of enjoyment. I was reminded of Sartre's reflection on cigarettes as he was trying to quit. He was afraid that, without cigarettes, all other experiences would become impoverished. Watching a theatre performance would no longer have the same charm. Working in the morning would not be the same as before. And dinner would no longer taste as good as it used to.

Smoking seventy cigarettes a day was not sustainable. It would be my death. But I had to agree with Sartre. I sorely missed them. Especially now, at this particular moment. It had been two days since I had my last cigarette. And I craved it.

ANDRÉ, JULY 13

A few weeks earlier I had asked my Finnish friend what pleasure meant to him. We talked about drinking, eating, and fucking. But then we got into the pleasures of sloth: staying at home and doing nothing. This sounded a bit like Epicurus' idea of pursuing a state of perfect tranquility.

"What do you do when you're doing nothing?" I asked.

"I play video games," my friend told me. Later, I discovered how widely shared this pleasure was. Forty-nine percent of Americans regularly play video games, and on average every citizen of the US spends 1,737 minutes a month on them.

Determined to test this theory of pleasure, I walked into a shop called "Game." Not having played computer games since the age of thirteen, I felt like an illiterate person walking into a library. I had been advised to buy *Battlefield 4*, a first-person shooter game that had sold over 7 million copies. I also bought *Grand Theft Auto*, a driving game that was part of a series that had sold over 235 million copies. When I asked the pallid woman behind the counter for advice, she looked at me with pity.

I carried my new Xbox and games home and then began what turned into quite a lengthy process of loading it all up.

After two hours, I was playing.

My character appeared in a dark hallway of a flooded school. Children's paintings on the walls were marked with bullet holes. I didn't know where I was or what I was doing. I moved around the building in an uncoordinated way. I got a gun and had a shoot-out with two terrorists across the road. But I got killed, again and again. Eventually I succeeded in killing the two gunmen outside. Then I moved on to the next scene which was a courtyard in a school. After a long day of playing, I was feeling no joy or pleasure. All I could feel was emptiness.

Why was I not experiencing the joys of video games that my friend had described? Searching through the neuroscientific research, I found that video games triggered the release of dopamine in the brain. The same hormone released by drinking, drugs, sex, and gambling. This stimulation of dopamine meant that video games could become addictive. To get this hormone hit, some gamers would sit playing games for days on end. In Simon Parkin's *Death by Video Game*, I found the story of Chen Rong-Yu, a twenty-three-year-old Taiwanese man, who was found slumped over dead in front of the screen after playing *League of Legends* for twenty-three hours straight in an Internet café.

For me, it was impossible to understand why someone would play video games until they died. What made these games so alluring, Parkin explained, was the sense of control they offered to people who otherwise felt they had very little control over their real lives.

I suppose I was lucky not to get the same sense of pleasure as my gamer friends. Perhaps if I played games for months, I too could become addicted. But that didn't seem to be a very pleasurable prospect.

CARL, JULY 14

My nicotine cravings grew weaker day by day. I wasn't too worried about a relapse. Besides, I had my Pavlok wristband in case I slipped.

Focusing on food helped, too. I was cooking things I had never made. I started with arancinis—deep-fried rice balls. I had eaten some on Capri. They were delicious and suitably decadent. I started off making a plain risotto. While waiting for the rice to cool down, I sipped on an Aperol spritz. I rolled the sticky rice into balls, made a hole in the middle, stuffed them with buffalo mozzarella and prosciutto. I covered them first in flour, then whisked eggs, and finally rolled them in bread crumbs. I then immersed the balls into the deep fryer. A few minutes later they resurfaced, perfectly golden. I served them as starters, and they had a wonderful taste.

Meanwhile, we had prepared a slow-cooked osso buco. It was not made of cat or dog, nor flamingo, which was also popular amongst the truly decadent. Instead we used veal shanks.

As we finished our food, it was time to think about dessert. Out on the terrace, the deep fryer was still going, and in the kitchen cupboard I knew there were some old chocolate bars. Deep-fried Mars bars were the ultimate expression of shameless decadence. I covered the chocolate bars in batter, and lowered them into the boiling oil. I was thinking about Caligula as I consumed my third Mars bar.

Before walking home that evening, my brother-in-law opened the fridge.

"I wouldn't give this to anyone," he said, and handed me a piece of meat, wrapped in plastic. It was guanciale—pork cheeks—which is the main ingredient in an authentic carbonara. Pancetta and bacon were only poor substitutes, he explained. They had brought the guanciale with them from a recent trip to Italy.

"We'll come over for lunch tomorrow. Don't mess it up," he said, giving me a brotherly pat on the shoulder.

ANDRÉ, JULY 21

The idea of a Master Cleanse came to me about a week ago. I met with a friend for lunch. While chewing my way through a burger, she asked if I had ever thought about going on a juice detox. I had not, but it seemed like a good idea. I had been drunk almost every day of the month, and, for the last week, I had been eating only junk food. My menu for a typical day had been cake for breakfast, a burger for lunch, crisps as an afternoon snack followed by a large pizza for dinner. All washed down with plenty of Coke. Now I was wheezing and feeling apathetic. I was ready for a change. I had to heed the advice of Epicurus and pursue pleasure differently.

I went back home and read about juice and juicers online. The authors of these blog posts seemed to have a near religious belief in the power of liquidized fruit and vegetables. The most extreme juicers recommended the "Master Cleanse." This diet was developed by Stanley Burroughs during the 1940s. In the 1970s, he published *The Master Cleanser*, a book that described the method and its benefits in great detail. Later I found out that Burroughs had been charged—but not eventually convicted— with unlawfully selling drugs, practicing medicine without a license, and second-degree murder. This happened after he treated a twenty-four-year-old leukemia sufferer with a thirty-day course of lemonade mixture, herbal teas, colored light, and therapeutic massage.

The Master Cleanse was simple. For ten days you would mainly live off lemonade. But to properly induce bowel movements you drank laxative tea in the evening and saltwater flushes in the morning.

So, for three days I had been only drinking a lemonade mixture during the day, followed by a cup of herbal tea in the evening. Each morning, I woke up and prepared a saltwater drink: two teaspoons of salt mixed into one liter of water. To get all that salty water down my throat, I imagined being a teenager in a beer-drinking competition.

It took a day for the full effects of the Master Cleanse to set in, which happened to be during my daughter's annual sports day. I had entered the father's running race, and, in my weakened state, I came last. I ambled home, mixed up a lemonade, then lay down on the couch. Any intention of doing something productive dissolved as I fell into a deep sleep. I dreamed I was eating. As I emerged from my slumber, not yet fully awake, I felt guilty. It took me another thirty minutes to return to reality and realize I had not broken my Master Cleanse.

After two days, I looked forward to my salt flush in the morning. It became the major event of the day. But I was starting to feel weak and tired. When I drank a lemonade mixture, it would temporarily lift my mood, but then I'd crash again. I would retreat to bed and sleep for two hours. When I woke, I felt dizzy. I had another lemonade. That didn't help, either.

My legs were aching. It felt like I had been running a marathon. As I closed my eyes, psychedelic visions appeared—dragons mixed with paisley patterns.

A proper Master Cleanse is supposed to last for ten days, but I only managed three. I would have continued, had the month been dedicated to losing weight or boosting suffering. But I was supposed to be pursuing pleasure, not pain.

CARL, JULY 21

Over the last ten days, I had made carbonara with guanciale, and slow-cooked ragù bolognese with chicken liver and pancetta. Then I made Heston Blumenthal's roast chicken, which took two days to prepare. On the first day, the chicken had to be soaked in salty water for six hours, then quickly dipped into boiling water and ice water, wrapped up in a towel, and put in the fridge. On the second day, I cooked it in the oven on low temperature for six hours before frying it in a pan, making the skin golden.

Then I made fresh pasta. I studied dozens of recipes, from classic ones to optimized life-hack versions, before attempting the perfect dough. I mixed it all together: the eggs, the extra egg yolks, the two types of flour, the salt, and the oil. I worked it with my hands for ten minutes, wrapped it in plastic and put it in the fridge. An hour later I took it out and started working with the rolling pin to make it really thin. I left the long pasta plates to dry on the kitchen table, then rolled them up, and cut them into pieces. When I rolled them out again, I had long strips of pappardelle. I cooked the pasta for a couple of minutes and served it with a slow-cooked beef stew.

For the grand finale, I made tortellini with two different fillings: one with porcini, and one with peas, ricotta, and parmigiano. I made the pasta dough and put together the small, filled flowers of pasta. I made a tomato sauce, grilled some kale in the oven, and melted butter with sage, herbs, and white wine. Five hours later, I served it. I was exhausted, but satisfied.

I had spent the last ten days drinking wine, swimming in the sea, reading novels, and cooking elaborate meals. The days had been warm and beautiful.

I felt as though I could go on like this forever. Day in, day out. Living my whole life on an island, cooking and eating, reading and writing, swimming and sleeping.

ANDRÉ, JULY 23

For as long as I could remember, one of the first things I did in the morning was to check my email. Earlier in the year, when trying to improve my productivity, I had kept this to a minimum. Now, there were no limits. As soon as I got bored, I found myself mindlessly scrolling through Facebook. It was supposed to be a small pleasurable break to get me through the day. But now it *was* the day. And it wasn't pleasurable.

Searching through the academic research, I came across a study of the impact of technology on 661 professionals published in *MIS Quarterly*. The authors concluded that ever-present technology made the professionals more stressed. Perhaps the constant hail of digital interruptions was what got in my way of living a pleasurable life?

As I continued my search, I read about digital detoxing. By putting my devices away, I could become more mindful, less anxious, improve my relationships and begin to truly appreciate the world around me more. Maybe what I needed to do was to truly disconnect? One week without email, social media, computers, and the internet.

I had activated an out of office email message. I had only done this once before, ages ago, but I had continued to compulsively check my email during the two weeks I was supposed to be "out of office."

I placed my computer and iPad on a shelf and removed social media and email apps from my phone. I was going to be out of office for real this time.

When I sat down to enjoy my digitally detoxified life, my eyes fell on the physical clutter around me: stacks of papers, piles of books, mountains of clothes, shoes thrown on the floor, toys everywhere. I felt like I was floating in that huge pool of plastic that circles the middle of the Pacific Ocean.

It suddenly became clear to me: if I wanted to find true pleasure, I needed to declutter my entire life.

CARL, JULY 25

I loved eating good food, but cooking was too exhausting to be altogether pleasant. Instead I decided to do nothing.

Remembering my conversation with André in Naples, I began re-reading the letters of Epicurus, who preached a philosophy of pleasure: not the excessive and luxurious pleasures of the decadents, but what Epicurus called natural and simple pleasures. "Thus when I say that pleasure is the goal of living," Epicurus wrote in a letter to Menoeceus, "I do not mean the pleasures of libertines or the pleasures inherent in positive enjoyment." The key point was to do very little. It suited me fine, as I was already spending most of my days swimming, reading, and overlooking the sea. But being an Epicurean was not altogether easy. There were two main barriers: expectations from other people, and my own sense of guilt.

When I made the decision to stop doing things, I was staying on an island with my parents-in-law. I had spent hours each day cooking for them, which had been my contribution to the household. Now, all of a sudden, I stopped cooking. I didn't say why. I just didn't do it any longer. Instead of withdrawing into the kitchen at about five in the afternoon, as I would normally do, I just remained on the terrace, staring into the sun, sipping on a glass of white wine. I just sat there, doing nothing, calm as an Epicurean. And sure enough, after an hour or so, someone else would take over the responsibility and make sure dinner was served.

And then there was a football cup, between different islands. I was supposed to play. But I didn't. According to the Epicureans, it was much more dignified to stay away from that sort of frenzied activity, and just observe calmly. So I went up to watch a match, and stood by the sideline. I ignored the angry looks from my teammates.

I had also learned from Tom Hodgkinson's terrific book *How to Be Idle* that I should throw away my alarm clock. The idler Jerome K. Jerome called these pitiful inventions "artful contrivances that go off at the wrong time and alarm the wrong people." I was ashamed to admit I had set the alarm every morning since the start of the year, including weekends, and even this month, when I was supposed to be optimizing pleasure. The book convinced me that lying in bed was a noble and pleasurable activity. So I placed my phone in a different room, and tried to sleep as long as I could. Yet during the first few days, I still woke up at about seven, far earlier than the rest of my family. I tried to remain in bed, but after about half an hour I grew bored and got up.

I also had to avoid all forms of duties. Skiving, I learned, was a revolt against the work-obsessed ideology of "suffering now, pleasure later." Swedes loved to remain active during the holiday, either by working out or working in the garden or building something or planning meaningless excursions. And they loved to make idle people feel guilty.

To remain completely inactive in the face of these demands was not easy. It required hard mental work. My model was Oblomov, the protagonist of the nineteenth-century novel of the same name. He was the ultimate idler, regarding himself as "constitutionally incapable of exertion" and unapologetically free from ambition.

Reading these stories helped me overcome the sense of guilt I would otherwise feel when not contributing to anyone or anything. As an idler, I was free from anxiety and worry. I was free to live as I pleased. "Being idle," Hodgkinson explained, was "about fun, pleasure, and joy." Besides, I was in good company: Walt Whitman, Oscar Wilde, and Jerome K. Jerome all celebrated idleness as the most noble form of life. Whitman wrote: "Of all human beings, none equals your genuine, inbred, unvarying loafer." The moment I was able to push my guilt aside, I started to love this way of life. It was like mindfulness, but for real.

ANDRÉ, JULY 29

Living without technology was easy. Cleaning up the house was a lot harder. I recalled having read about a best-selling self-help book, *The Life-Changing Magic of Tidying Up*. At the time, I wondered: what kind of hysterical person would buy that sort of book? Now I was desperately searching for it myself.

I found the book in the self-help section of a shopping mall bookstore, between sewing and military history.

Marie Kondo, or KonMari as she preferred to be called, explained that, one night, she had a miraculous breakthough. Cleaning was not about putting things away. It was about identifying the objects that genuinely brought her joy and then getting rid of everything else. Out of this realization, she had built up an entire system that she was convinced would change people's lives. I would no longer be anxious, I would never need to tidy up again, I would be able to move on with my life, and I would start taking pleasure in the things around me. I might even lose some weight.

During the night, I dreamed about cleaning. KonMari appeared in my dream, and talked with me in an innocent Japanese accent. The following morning, I woke with a single goal in mind—to declutter my life.

I started, as KonMari advised, with my clothes. I took them all out from my overstuffed wardrobe and from under the bed and nearly every other place in the house. I put them all on my bed. There were hundreds of items. I sorted them into categories—suits, shirts, trousers, underwear. Next, I went through them, one by one, asking the simple question—did this bring me joy? If yes, it was placed into a pile to keep. Everything else was tossed into a pile for the charity shop. I was surprised how fast I got rid of about half my wardrobe. Whole eras of my life were eliminated. Out went my floral shirt collection from my late twenties, the t-shirts from my years as a university student, the denim jackets from my teenage years. This was my intimate sartorial history, and it was going to a charity shop.

Then came the folding. I perched the book on the edge of a messy set of drawers and followed the method as closely as possible. I folded up my t-shirts, my running clothes, my socks. My overflowing set of drawers was suddenly relatively empty. And when I was finished, I stepped back. Surveying my wardrobe, I felt a strange pleasure. I suddenly felt unburdened, like a spiritual seeker who had just renounced their worldly concerns. Was this the kind of sense of tranquility Epicurus had written about?

As I pushed all these bags of clothes into the hallway, I considered moving to the next task—the kitchen. Just then, our cleaner arrived. I could tell she did not approve of the results of my decluttering. Nor did she want me to take the next step and empty out the kitchen cupboards.

Over the course of the last ten days, I had trained myself to do nothing, and I loved it. Following the art of idleness had proved much more effective in bringing peace of mind than all the meditation and yoga and mindfulness I had tried in May.

For my last day, in an attempt to optimize idle pleasure, I was going to design the perfect day. I had made a schedule in advance, based on Hodgkinson's book *How to Be Idle*. I woke up at about nine, without the help of an alarm, and slowly walked from the smaller guesthouse into the main house, where I wrote for an hour. Writing was the one "productive" activity that the idler approved of. At around ten, my wife and daughter came up and we had a long and delightful breakfast together, out on the terrace, listening to Art Pepper, staring into the sun. It was beginning to get hot now, and we walked the few hundred meters down to the small beach and swam and read. At noon, we drove to a nice restaurant by the sea for a long lunch.

When we came back home, I sat down on the terrace to read in the shade. I was getting tired now. My mother shouted from the other house, asking if I wanted a cup of coffee. I said no, because I had learned that coffee in the afternoon was an abomination to the true idler. I retreated into the bedroom for an afternoon nap. "You must sleep sometime between lunch and dinner," Hodgkinson advised, "and no halfway measures."

It was three o'clock, and I was pleased to note that I had kept to my carefully designed "pleasure schedule." My daughter woke me up a few moments later. I was feeling refreshed and we walked down to the sea for another swim. It was warm and peaceful and we stayed there for a long time. I checked my schedule again. It was five o'clock and time for an afternoon walk. "The pedestrian is the highest and most mighty of beings," I had learned, "he walks for pleasure, he observes but does not interfere, he is not in a hurry, he is happy in the company of his own mind, he wanders detached, wise and merry, godlike."

Godlike, I strolled along the gravel roads. The birch trees whistled in the wind, and a few birds were singing in the distance. I turned onto a smaller path, walked down to the sea, and sat on a rock.

Forty minutes later, I passed my sister's house. From the road, I could see her husband in the kitchen preparing dinner. It was my turn to cook, but I had masterfully shirked that responsibility. I sped up a tiny bit, hoping they would not see me. Which was when I heard a bicycle behind me, and someone clearing his throat. I twisted around and saw my neighbor. *Shit!* He was there to pick up a crib from my sister, and he probably needed help to carry it back home. I sped up some more, pretending I had not seen him. He was one of the model citizens out here. His lawn was always perfectly mowed, and he painted his house regularly. As the road turned and I disappeared from his sight, I could relax again.

At six o'clock, I was back at my sister's place, still on schedule and having my first drink, followed by a wonderful dinner and more drinks.

The month had been terrific, from start to end. I had cherished the smoking and the drinking and the life of the decadent. I had enjoyed the days spent cooking. And I had loved the lazy days of noble inactivity. It dawned on me that being idle was really my type of spirituality. I made a note to myself to discontinue my expensive subscription to the mindfulness app and to start integrating the philosophical principles of idleness into my life.

AUGUST

CREATIVITY

CARL, AUGUST 1

Since the final days of June, I had sneaked out of bed in the early morning to sit down and write. But I wasn't writing the old academic stuff. This time it was *real* writing. Fiction. I was writing a thriller.

Sure, I was getting ahead of myself, but I needed more than a month to write a novel. Besides, it had not disturbed my quest for enjoyment too much. Writing fiction with a cigarette hanging out of my mouth felt pretty damn good.

I didn't aspire to write a fancy literary novel. That seemed too difficult. Instead I wanted to write a Nordic noir thriller. It seemed less pretentious and, if it was going to work out, I could possibly sell it in September as a way of making money.

Back in March, I met up with Lee Child and Andy Martin at a coffee shop in New York. Andy Martin was an old friend of mine. He was a lecturer in French at Cambridge and had written books about surfing, Brigitte Bardot, Napoleon, and the rivalry between Sartre and Camus. During his last project, he had spent one whole year shadowing Lee Child, watching over his shoulder as he composed his latest adventure with Jack Reacher. Lee Child was a giant in the world of crime fiction, with more than 100 million books sold.

I told Lee that I was considering writing a thriller.

"Why write your own thriller, when you could just steal an old one, and claim it as your own?" Lee said.

"Isn't that illegal?" I asked.

"I don't think so. Not if it's part of a prank."

"Brilliant, that should save me a lot of work." I said.

"I'm sure Lee could find a great rare title," Andy Martin added, knowing I was clueless about crime fiction.

"Sure," Lee said.

A few months later I emailed Lee and asked if he had come up with a suitable book.

"I'm tempted to suggest *No Highway* by Nevil Shute," he wrote back. "Timeless story, easily updated for details."

I ordered the book from a second-hand bookshop and read it. Lee was right. This was a perfect book to adapt.

But there were things I still had to resolve. If I was going to steal a novel and claim it as my own, would I have to fool everyone else, too? Would I need to lie to agents and publishers? I sent an email to a friend in publishing, asking for advice. He said it was going to be difficult to find an agent who would go along with the deception. I had to fool them, too. He said it was a risky plan, and that I'd probably get into serious trouble once I revealed the prank. Moreover, Nevil Shute's book was from the 1940s, and still protected by copyright law.

At this point I realized the plan wasn't going to work. I was back to square one.

I phoned Andy Martin, who was back in England, and asked for advice. I explained I might have to write a book of my own, unless he'd be keen to write the book with me. I remembered Andy once telling me he wanted to write a thriller himself. He had studied the craft so closely, and for so long, that he should be capable of doing it himself.

"Yeah, sure, let's give it a shot," he said.

"Fantastic!" I replied.

After calming down, I added: "You know, we could still take stuff from other books, as long as it is out of copyright."

"Hmm. Good point. How about Camus's *The Outsider*? Should be out of copyright. Maybe we could use that as a model?"

The moment he said *The Outsider* I knew it was going to happen.

ANDRÉ, AUGUST 4

I was feeling optimistic as I laid out the small packet of inks and painting brushes on the table. But when I looked down at the blank piece of paper, my enthusiasm waned. *What the hell was I going to paint?*

It was the first week of the month, and I was on vacation with my family on the Isle of Wight. Over the last week or so, I had been blissfully disconnected from the world, doing nothing. I was supposed to be creative, but I much preferred to take it easy, watching my daughter play on the windswept beach. Eventually I decided to do some paintings. In high school, while the other boys were playing rugby, I remained in the art room, painting. My artistic self was long forgotten, but maybe now was the time to reclaim it.

We stayed in a quaint cottage in a small seaside village famed for its watercolorists in the nineteenth century. It should have been the perfect place to spark my creative ambition. And yet, I couldn't find anything to paint. I glanced over the newspapers I had been reading. My eyes stopped on a photograph, which I tried to reproduce. Then I tried another.

When I had finished, I lined up my paintings. There were ten in all.

CARL, AUGUST 6

The idea was to use Camus's classic book and transpose it to Nordic noir. When we started writing, we tried to use some of the original text, but soon we found it was easier to write ourselves. Some of the scenes and characters could be recycled. We had replaced the emotionally detached Monsieur Meursault with a young ex-Muslim, Nada, who at the outset of the book was taken away in a car by her father and uncle. They would try to kill her in an attempted honor killing, but she kicked her uncle out of the speeding car and killed her father with four shots from his gun. Nada was our outsider.

I knew very little about how to write fiction, let alone thrillers, but there was no shortage of advice to be found online. An article in *Writer's Digest* listed the ten basic ingredients of a successful thriller. First you needed a good story, such as a "hero slaying a dragon," which was kind of what Nada was going to do at the end, although we had yet to work out who that dragon was. Second, you should write about the underdog, which Nada, as an ex-Muslim living in the north of Sweden, indisputably was. Third, you had to provide multiple perspectives. Nada's boyfriend Björn, a cautious PhD student in corduroy, did that work. The fourth requirement was a good action scene at the start, which we had with the attempted honor killing in the car. The fifth point: make clear what your protagonist wants, and what she fears. This was more difficult since Nada, as a modern version of Meursault, did not really want anything and she certainly had no fears. Sixth was to make bad stuff happen to your protagonist. No problem there. Nada would be spending most of the book in prison where she would wake up one night, tied to her bed, with a sleazy guard on top of her, unbuttoning his trousers. Point seven was to make your character change, which was not really possible because, like her precursor Meursault, she remained existentially detached and unwilling to change. Point eight was to make the pacing quick. This was tricky, because Nada's days in prison were sometimes slow, but we did what we could to speed it up. Point nine: show—don't tell. This was the part I was finding most difficult. Creating a convincing sensory reality for the reader was really fucking hard. The tenth and final point was that the reader should learn something, whether about crafts or jobs or social issues. The book was set in both affluent and poorer areas of Sweden, with Björn hailing from an upper-class family from a posh area of Stockholm, whereas Nada was from an immigrant family from the poor suburbs. These details were meant to be educational—they would explain to the reader what was rotten in the state of Sweden.

I had spent the last couple of days reading Stephen King's *On Writing*. He said any novel consisted of only three parts: narration, description, and dialogue. Don't focus on plot, he said. It would unfold organically as you brought your characters to life and let them influence the direction of the story. Nada and Björn had been with me for a month now, although they were currently apart. After killing her father, Nada was in prison fighting for her life. Meanwhile, Björn was fumbling around in the Stockholm suburbs, trying to figure out who the hell was behind this.

ANDRÉ, AUGUST 7

We were making our way through the botanical gardens in Ventnor on the Isle of Wight. At a distance, I could see a group of women in their seventies or eighties sitting behind tables. We walked closer, and I saw that they were selling their own paintings. This was the Isle of Wight Watercolor Association. I studied their work and began talking with one of the more talented members. She told me about her technique.

Even though her paintings were far from brilliant, they were nevertheless more than I could ever achieve. I realized that my plan to become an artist in one month was hopeless. I would have to try something else.

CARL, AUGUST 8

Whatever Carl writes, it's never any good.

I couldn't remember whether it was my Swedish teacher in high school who said it, or if it was my Swedish teacher in secondary school. It could have been both. Neither thought very much of me. My parents were there when the blow was dealt, so I asked if they still remembered it. They did. It was my high school teacher who said it, during one of those yearly appraisal meetings, when the teachers could take revenge on their pupils. My art teacher was too drunk to recall my name, but my Swedish teacher remembered me. I was the boy who couldn't write.

Yet now, decades later, as a middle-aged man, I was trying to write a novel. Was it all revenge? Was I trying to prove my teachers wrong?

Either way, I still found it hard to write, especially a thriller, which had to be fast and direct and written with a distinctive voice. On the recommendation of Stephen King, I had killed the passive voice I usually hid behind in my academic writing. I also tried keeping the writing free from pretentious adverbs. It had to be clean and simple, crisp and sharp. I read out loud to myself to try out the characters' voices, and I spent hours on end googling images of prison cells and courtrooms. Andy Martin kept sending me his chapters, which often reinforced my self-doubt as a writer.

Perhaps what I needed was a creative writing course?

After searching through dozens of online courses, I came across one that appealed to me: "Write Like a Pro." It was designed for those who had a book in mind but were struggling to weave it together. It was cheap, only $149, but it didn't start until August 17. That was too late, so I continued my search. Most universities seemed to offer courses, but they were expensive. A two-year MFA in writing could cost up to $70,000.

Feeling disheartened, I took comfort in the advice of Stephen King: "You learn best by reading a lot and writing a lot, and the most valuable lessons of all are the ones you teach yourself."

ANDRÉ, AUGUST 12

It was a hot summer's day in London, and I was at home searching the web for tips on how to "boost creativity." Soon I had a long list of techniques: making yourself very tired, meditating, drinking booze, lying down, spending time alone, surrounding yourself with blue or green, doing a brain dump.

As I went back through the list, I noticed that I was already doing many of these things, but I just couldn't see how they were helping me to become any more creative. Besides, I didn't even know what I wanted to create.

Feeling disheartened, I queued up Tim Ferriss's list of music he recommended as the ideal background tracks for creativity: Faith No More, Rammstein, and Slayer. I then opened up my notebook, poised my pen, and waited for inspiration to strike. When the music was over I had three ideas written down:

Create a luxury brand targeted at the homeless
Begin a new political movement called "The Brexistentialists"
Launch a middle-aged boy band
Looking back over them, each idea seemed as stupid as the next.

CARL, AUGUST 14

"If you're a bad writer, no one can help you become a good one," Stephen King wrote. I was in the seaside house struggling with a particularly difficult chapter. Nada was still in prison and Björn ended up having sex with a journalist who was also covering Nada's case. They were dancing in a kitchen late at night, holding each other, but the scene didn't feel right. It felt cheesy. Stephen King was probably right. Some people, like myself, will just never cut it.

I was reminded of a homeless guy I used to see ages ago. He was always standing outside the same convenience store in central Stockholm, playing the harmonica with a radio pressed against his ear. He'd been there for years, playing and dancing. Despite all those hours of practice, he couldn't get a single tune out of his instrument. One day, the homeless guy was gone. No one had seen him, and I presumed him dead. But only a few days ago, as I was passing that same convenience store, he was there, back again after years of silence. And he sounded just as bad now as he always had.

When I asked Andy Martin if he had some advice on how I might boost my creativity, he sent back a podcast interview with K. Anders Ericsson, a Swedish psychologist, who had done research on what he called deliberate practice. As I listened to his encouraging thesis, my mood improved. Geniuses were not qualitatively different than the rest of us, he claimed. But unlike that homeless harmonica player, they had found a way of improving their skills in a deliberate fashion, constantly pushing themselves outside their comfort zone.

In a 1993 article in *Psychological Review*, Ericsson and his two co-authors claimed that "expert performance" was not due to innate talent, but the result of "prolonged efforts to improve performance while negotiating motivational and external constraints." To become an expert, it was necessary to have access to teachers and facilities. One also had to practice in a deliberate manner for at least ten years. To avoid exhaustion, the actual practice should be sustained only for a limited time each day.

Was this the technique that great authors used, too? I remembered from Mason Currey's *Daily Rituals* that most authors only wrote for a few hours each day. Those were probably the intense bursts of deliberate practice that Ericsson had in mind. Philip Roth had described writing as a nightmare because a "writer is locked in a battle with his work."

I spent the rest of the day trying to get the scene right. Like Roth, I was locked in a long nightmarish battle with my writing, but just before dinner I finished my first ever sex scene.

ANDRÉ, AUGUST 16

Half the month was gone, and all I had was a page of ludicrous ideas. Looking back at my list was depressing. But I remembered that some time ago, Carl had suggested trying out stand-up comedy. *Why not?* I thought. It was as good of an idea as any. After all, comedy was all about failure, and failure was what had defined this month—perhaps the entire year. At least if it all went to shit, I could try to make a joke out of it. I started toying with titles for my imaginary comedy show: *How to Waste a Year of Your Life and Learn Nothing in the Process.*

Being funny was alien to me. When I tried to crack a joke, it always fell flat. My sense of comic timing was nonexistent. I clearly needed to go back to basics, so I started reading.

Humor, I learned, was all about structure. Jokes had two parts: a set-up and a punch line. The set-up must be short and snappy. The punch line should deliver a twist. The funniest point had to come at the very end, ideally in the last word. It should all be delivered with a straight face. A comic must never talk when the audience was laughing. Once you had a punch line, you added another on top of it. Then another. And you always had to save the best for last.

One blogger I read suggested a stand-up comic should aim for four to six laughs per minute. That meant an entire routine of five minutes needed twenty to thirty punch lines.

I was ready to start trying to construct my own jokes. I went outside into the garden at the back of our house, sat down in the shade, and started randomly writing down topics—academic life, children, my own childhood, thrillers, Boris Johnson. Yes, Boris was a good one.

Later in the evening, I heard Ricky Gervais being interviewed on the radio. In an offhand remark, he told the interviewer that good comedy was about an average person trying to do something that they did not have the ability or resources to do. I started wondering whether this entire project was precisely about that.

CARL, AUGUST 17

Choosing the right word processing program was a crucial part of the creative process, I discovered, as I continued my quest to become a professional writer. Microsoft Word, the software package I used, was described as "the worst possible option." I went on to read about other programs I had already used, like Pages and Scrivener, as well as some I had not used like iA Writer and Bywords. There were also meditative text editors like Ommwriter and ZenWriter, which focused on relaxation and played meditation music.

Then there were programs like Flowstate, which promised to help overcome writer's block. The program was similar to many of the others I had tested, but it had one significant difference. You had to keep writing. Or else everything would disappear.

The method was simple. First, you had to choose how long you were planning to write. If you didn't press a key for five seconds, everything would disappear. After only two or three seconds, you could see the text beginning to fade, and you could not save the text until you had reached your target of five, or ten, or thirty minutes. Only then could you relax, and carry on writing at the speed you desired.

I started off with fifteen minutes. I was going to write a diary entry, summarizing the previous day, but as soon as I started to write, my brain shut down, and I couldn't remember a single thing that had happened that day, or even what day it was. I just kept typing.

When I had reached my goal of fifteen minutes I stopped and read through the text. Page after page of complete nonsense.

The next day, I gave Flowstate another go. This time I had to write a new scene for the thriller. Björn was visiting Nada in prison and had some important news to tell her. Five minutes into my thirty-minute session, my phone rang. It was Sally.

"Hi, darling, I'm afraid I can't talk right now."

"Why is that?" she asked.

"I'm writing."

"But you can take a one-minute break, no?"

"No, only five seconds." I was pressing the space tab every five seconds, preventing the words from dissolving.

"Five seconds?"

"Well, you see, I'm doing this thing where I have to keep writing because otherwise it will all disappear."

"Disappear? Surely you can save it?"

"Fuck it," I said and stopped pressing the key. The words got weaker, before finally disappearing into the white screen, never to be found again. It didn't matter. They were useless anyway. I wrote slowly by nature, and this was not the technology for me.

After a week of experiments, I felt a strange gravitational force pulling me back to Word. It had caused me a lot of pain in the past. But like all abusive relationships, it was hard to get out.

ANDRÉ, AUGUST 17

From what I had learned, the foundation of joke writing was to get as many topics on the page as possible and then to start to freely associate. Picking funny words seemed to be important, as was timing, but I should not get ahead of myself. The crucial point now was just to get lots of ideas down on paper.

After everyone had gone to bed, I watched some stand-up comedy on YouTube. From one video by Stewart Lee, I learned there were two ways to be funny: hit the audience directly with a punchline, or slowly tickle them with a shaggy dog story. His conclusion: you can say almost anything as long as there was a bomb underneath it. I asked myself, what's the bomb lurking underneath all of my attempts to become a stand-up comic?

CARL, AUGUST 18

"You should have an agent, and if your work is saleable, you will have only a moderate amount of trouble finding one," Stephen King wrote. "You'll probably be able to find one even if your work isn't saleable, as long as it shows promise."

When we started writing *Nada* about a month ago, I sent an email to a Swedish agent, representing the famous stars of Nordic noir, explaining that I was working on an existential thriller loosely based on Camus's *Outsider.* I received a short but encouraging answer. They told me that they would be happy to read it once we had something to show. But according to *The Writer's Digest Guide to Literary Agents*, I should approach multiple agents at the same time. On their user forum I found a long discussion on "How Many Query Letters Should You Have Out There." Three or four, one writer suggested. Not more than ten, another one chimed in.

"Let me check with Lee's agent, Darley Anderson," Andy said when I spoke to him over the phone. By now, we had 150 solid pages and we were eager to see if it was saleable.

While waiting for a response, I read an interview with Darley Anderson. He explained that they received 1,200 proposals each month, close to 15,000 a year. They accepted five. He said there were more hopeful writers today than ever before, but that most of them were simply dreamers. Perhaps I belonged to that category, too.

Later in the afternoon, we received a response from an agent at Darley Anderson's, saying she had spoken to some colleagues and that our book, with its existential twist and Camus's influence, wasn't right for them. She offered, however, to write a list of other agents who might be interested. We said yes, thanks, and soon received a list of ten agents with names and addresses. Andy seemed to know who they were and picked out two from the list who we then emailed.

ANDRÉ, AUGUST 19

I was in Helsinki for a PhD defense. Events like these were normally very formal and boring. But today the audience was laughing. This was all because of the opponent, a Danish professor. I noticed he was using all the techniques of a great comic. Fumbling to give the audience time to laugh, bringing about the ridiculous in the sublime, and always ending with a bomb.

Later that night, I had to give a speech at the formal dinner. I was expected to say nice things about the PhD candidate to make his family proud. But I thought this would be the perfect opportunity to try out my stand-up comedy routine, so after a few warm speeches, I took to the stage.

The crowd was in a good mood and already on their third glass. I opened with a story about a professor who made his assistant rub out underlined text in second-hand books. That got some laughs. Then it went downhill as I told stories about how awful it was to be a junior academic. I wasn't really thinking about the implication of this story—that life after receiving a PhD was miserable. I could see the audience, one by one, turning away from the stage and making for the bar. I ended the speech with a few warm words and merged back into the crowd.

What the hell was I doing?

Rule number one of these kind of events is that you should speak about the person in whose honor it was being held. I had just spent five minutes talking about myself. And what's more, I was trying to be funny, and I just wasn't.

CARL, AUGUST 19

I wrote a short note to the Swedish agent, saying we would send them the first 200 pages within the next few days.

While waiting for their response, I read some more about the agency. They had sold a television show for $48 million. They represented Jo Nesbø, Anne Holt, and Leif G. W. Persson—who were all multi-millionaires now. The most recent success story was Fredrik Backman and his book *A Man Called Ove*, which had been on the *New York Times* best-seller list for months.

ANDRÉ, AUGUST 22

There were five ways you could write jokes. Today I was going to try all of them. I sat down at the desk in my office looking out on a summer morning in London. I opened my notebook and started jotting down some words that I could redefine. Most of the definitions didn't work. The best I came up with was *Life Coach: someone to outsource your self-hatred to.* Next, I moved on to the word clouds and double word clouds. This proved to be more interesting. I came up with a couple of good ones, I thought.

I then began searching the newspapers for funny words. I found a handful of phrases that were potentially interesting. But I was more intrigued by stories that were so surreal you didn't need any wordplay to draw out their comedic aspects. Like the story about a recent brawl between real estate agents and Class War protestors outside Boris Johnson's house.

The final strategy was to make surreal connections by doing a mental reversal, whereby you investigated how objects would see the world if they were subjects. I was blank. I couldn't come up with a single surreal connection. The entire exercise took me hours, and by the end of it I was feeling defeated. After all that hard work, I only had two new jokes.

Later in the evening, we were sitting in the garden. My parents were visiting from New Zealand. As we made polite conversation, they asked what I was doing at work at the moment. I normally avoided giving too much detail, but this time I told them I had decided to learn stand-up comedy. They fell silent.

"Our family is not particularly funny," my father said.

I had to agree with him there. We quickly changed the topic and began talking about the best time to prune the trees in the garden.

CARL, AUGUST 22

I was sitting in our seaside house, staring at the sea. Sally and Esther were in the garden. I had just sent off the first 200 pages of *Nada* to the literary agent.

"Many thanks for this. I will come back with my thoughts soon," she responded straight away.

I was paralyzed. I was just going to sit here now, at the desk, looking at the sea and listening to my heart pounding.

ANDRÉ, AUGUST 24

Yesterday evening, Mel and I went to a comedy club for an open-mic night. The club was located on a busy street full of bars serving craft beer and hot dogs to hipsters. According to *Time Out*, "getting a spot at the open-mic night of this long running Shoreditch club is a big deal for newcomers." It was where future stars came to perform.

There were at least a hundred people in the audience. The stage was a typical stand-up venue—black curtain, brick wall, a single mic. Big groups of drunk office workers sat around the stage. Mel and I sat off to the side.

The MC came on stage. He was a young guy with the swagger of Eddie Murphy in his prime. After warming up the audience, he introduced the first act: a Norwegian talking about how depressed he was. Two laughs. Then a PhD student tried to crack jokes about architecture and psychoanalysis. Silence. Fortunately, the acts started to improve. A Lebanese woman talked about her father, an English guy abused the audience, an African man pretended to be a dictator. Waves of laughter rolled in.

Back home after the show, I thought now would be a good opportunity to try some of my jokes out on Mel. I read through a routine I had written earlier that day. It was a long political joke based around austerity, infrastructure spending, and childcare. After one paragraph she was asleep.

But when I woke up this morning, I nonetheless felt convinced I should try to perform on that stage. It was probably a stupid idea, but I rushed to my computer and sent an email to the host of last night's show. I told him that I had been on TV, written for newspapers, and that it was now time for me to develop a stand-up routine. Could I have a slot, I asked?

An hour later, he replied, saying he had booked me in. I was in shock. Now I would have to take this seriously.

When Mel came down the stairs, I told her the good news.

"That's a terrible idea," she said.

"Why?"

"I'm not trying to be mean," she said, looking at me sternly, "but you're just not that funny. That stuff you read to me last night. It just wasn't, you know, funny. In fact, I can't recall the last time you told me a joke that made me laugh. You're just going to be embarrassing and ruin that poor host's show. There is no way I can come along and be part of this."

I stopped listening to her and stared out the window. I knew she was right. But I also knew I had to do it. I sent an email back to the host saying that I'd be there next week.

I now had a new urgency. I spent the rest of the day trying to write out a new routine about Phil Collins.

CARL, AUGUST 27

For his latest three-book deal, Lee Child had received around $30 million. John Grisham had a net worth of $200 million. Second to romance, crime was the most lucrative genre, selling about $782.2 million each year.

But this, of course, was not the reality for most of us. On a website for aspiring writers I learned that "a typical first-timer advance might be anywhere from $5,000 to $15,000."

As I waited to hear back from the agent I could not help dreaming about an astronomical first-timer advance—perhaps something in the vicinity of Stephen King's debut, *Carrie*, for which he was offered $400,000.

ANDRÉ, AUGUST 28

It was the last night of the Edinburgh Fringe Festival, the world's largest arts festival, and the natural meeting place for amateur and professional stand-up comedians.

Together with ten other aspiring comedians, I had spent the last couple of days trying to learn the art of stand-up. The tutor was a tall English guy wearing a Spider-Man hoodie, a Spider-Man cap, and matching shoes in Spider-Man red. His attention wandered the moment someone else started speaking. Come to think of it, I don't think he was even that interested in his own voice.

Our first exercise was to write down a long list of things we felt passionate about. I was struck that, among all the stuff I scribbled down, nothing was associated with the comic material I had painstakingly worked on over the last two weeks.

When it came time to share our personal stories, I was taken aback by the passions of my fellow comics. One of them said he was passionate about "eating pie" (which, he explained, was another expression for cunnilingus). A guy said he passionately hated "smelly pussies." The atmosphere was like a locker room, and despite my extensive efforts to confront my manhood, I was feeling distinctly uncomfortable. Besides, I wondered what the Danish drama student—the only woman here—was thinking.

After talking about our passions, we had to pick out topics to work on. One guy would talk about working at a Spanish resort that hosted drunk English tourists. Another talked about working as a UPS driver.

Over the next two days, we developed our material, cutting it down, making it as focused as possible. We tried our routines out on our fellow comedians. Some people dropped out, but those who remained seemed committed.

And so, after days of intense work, it was time to take to the stage. The Danish woman went first. She was followed by the Italian guy, but he lost his nerve as he was about to walk on stage. "I'm not doing this," he told the MC. "Take me off the list." The tutor didn't care, and nor did the MC. The show went on without him.

Soon it was my turn. I walked up from the back of the room, got up on stage, and introduced myself. An audience of about fifty people looked at me, passively, as if saying *make me laugh*. As I began to talk about my impending midlife crisis, I saw the stony faces of older men looking at me. *What fucking midlife crisis, pal*, they seemed to be thinking.

The audience was silent. I only got one laugh for an offhand comment about using YouTube to do parenting. Time seemed to pass quickly—at least for me—because all of a sudden it was over. I shuffled off the stage. I got a few scattered polite claps. The kind you give to a friend's tone-deaf child after a musical recital.

I returned backstage and a couple of my fellow aspiring comics gave me some weak pats on the back. I knew it had been a disaster. I felt empty. Mel was right—I wasn't funny, and I shouldn't even try to be. I was supposed to stick around to get feedback from the tutor, but I just wanted to get out of there as quickly as possible.

Later that night, I asked myself whether I should do it again. My immediate reaction was "no." But then I thought about the theory of deliberate practice that Carl had told me about. The only way to actually learn something was to try, fail, get feedback, and then try again.

CARL, AUGUST 29

I had written my first novel. Or the first 200 pages of my first novel. And now, as I was looking back at the process, I was struggling to make any sense out of it. I had spent the month reading *Writer's Digest* and books about writing. I had searched for suitable online courses in creative writing. But the more I had read about the process, the more disconnected it seemed to become from the actual practice of writing. The creative process just seemed to happen, without conscious thought.

How do you find your ideas? When the Swedish comedian Hans Alfredson was asked this question, he always used to say that he got them from a small factory in Germany. Stephen King said there was "no Idea Dump, no Story Central, no Island of the Buried Bestsellers." Ideas just seemed to come from nowhere, "sailing at you right out of the empty sky."

Had I become more creative over the course of the month? Had I become a better writer? Maybe. But all I could say with certainty was that I had certainly enjoyed being so deeply immersed in creating something. For the first time during this whole year, I had actually been able to realize one of my own fantasies rather than living out the fantasy of someone else.

ANDRÉ, AUGUST 29

As I sat eating breakfast, I typed out my script from the evening before. I could immediately see what went wrong. It was more of a short story than a stand-up routine. I had no clear punch lines and too much material.

Most stand-up comics worked according to a formula. First a few quick jokes, usually one-liners, to warm up the audience. Then three to four larger chunks, each of which should prompt a quick laugh. The best chunk always came last. In my routine, I had no warm ups and only two chunks. The laughs didn't come at the points where I had expected them. If I was going to do this again, I had to delete most of my material and start over.

CARL, AUGUST 30

Hi Carl,

Me and a colleague have now read NADA and we've discussed it at the office with the rest of our colleagues.

My heart was pounding. My mouth was dry. They had read it. They had discussed it. This was what I had been working toward for two months. My literary debut. And now I was going to receive the verdict.

I think this is an exciting project and much of what we've read so far is good and original. There's potential in what you've written and I'm excited to see where the story goes.

I kept reading, waiting for the *but* or *however*, followed by a gentle rejection. *Sorry, but this is not for us.* But there were no buts or howevers. No rejection. They said there was room for improvement, and they offered some detailed suggestions. They didn't actually promise anything, but they said they liked what they had read and were keen to read it again, when the whole book was finished.

I read the email again. The agent spoke about our characters and the plot in an engaging way—as though we had actually created something real.

ANDRÉ, AUGUST 31

I headed into a bar that specialized in foosball. It must have been a popular business concept, because the place was packed. Simon and Peter were already there, and they both said they were looking forward to the show. After ordering beers, they asked me to go through my routine. They looked on expectantly as I began. I got a few laughs from this sympathetic audience, but only a few.

After finishing our beers, we walked around the corner to the comedy club and milled around downstairs. I found the list of performers and noticed that my name was not there. I was devastated. I had gone to all this trouble for nothing.

When the host arrived, I introduced myself and said that I was missing on the list. He seemed nonchalant.

"Yeah, you were here last week, right?" he said.

I nodded. "I emailed you."

"Okay, no worries, I'll slot you in."

He then pointed to a small area in the corner, beside the stage.

"Hang here," he said.

There were about six comics waiting. I joined them and poured a glass of water—the drink of choice for most comics when they were waiting to go on stage.

During the first break, I spoke to one of the other performers. He was clearly one of the least skilled in the group. Still, it turned out he had been doing this for three years. When I asked him how recent his newest material was, he told me it was six months old. I was feeling really nervous now.

At the beginning of the second set, the MC came up and shouted in my ear, "You'll be up soon." He looked at me intently. Anxiety was bubbling up in my stomach. The last two performers had got the audience laughing. When the last one finished the crowd clapped, and I ran out on stage.

I launched into my opening jokes. Three laughs. People looked at me in expectation, as if to say, *Come on, you're a comic, so say something funny*. When I moved into my first chunk, the crowd went quiet. It didn't work. Clearly it wasn't funny, it was just awkward. Then I launched into a story about kids pretending to be grown-ups. People laughed a little this time. And then, at a distance, I saw a light flashing. It meant I had to get off stage. I wrapped up quickly.

I had missed my two favorite parts, but that didn't matter. I was happy. Or rather, I was elated. People had laughed, if only a little. That was all I wanted.

When I was off stage, Peter and Simon rushed over and hugged me. I started to feel really good. I had done it! I could not remember when I last felt such strong sense of achievement.

We walked around the corner into a fashionable bar and ordered whiskey. It was time to celebrate. As I took my first few sips, I relaxed. I forgot about my anxiety. I now held the firm delusion that I could legitimately call myself a stand-up comedian.

SEPTEMBER

MONEY

CARL, SEPTEMBER 1

I knew it was a hideous thing to say, but I hated money. I really did. From the bottom of my heart.

Still, I paid all our bills. I thought of it as clearing a clogged drain. It had to be done, right? I opened the envelopes, took out the bills, paid them, then threw them in the garbage. I tried not to look at them for too long. As a consequence, I only had a vague idea about what we paid in insurance, electricity, Internet, phone. I normally glanced over my credit card statement, never going through the items in detail. I knew I was spending too much money on food and wine and restaurants, but I could see no point in reminding myself of my sins.

Just thinking about these things made my heart sink. I got anxious and was filled with self-hatred. I wasn't expecting people to have sympathy for me. Why should they? I didn't. I was spoiled and lazy. After all, I had the money to pay the bills, which was a pretty damn good position to be in—much better than a lot of other people who were struggling to make ends meet. I knew I was lucky. But that only made me feel more ashamed.

I was from a relatively well-to-do family where everyone except me was good with money. When we had dinner together, they often spoke about loans and mortgages and interest rates. It always made my heart race and my palms sweat, and I would try to change the topic as quickly as possible.

So it was time to do something about my financial situation. I opened my computer and sent an email to my bank manager and my accountant. Then I emailed a guy at a speaker's agency who had gotten in touch with me about a year ago asking if I could come to their offices for an audition. When I didn't reply, they sent another message asking if we could meet to discuss an appropriate price that they could sell me for. At the time, I felt ill at ease with this expression—*a price we could sell you for*—but now, as I was assessing my market value, that was exactly what I wanted to find out.

I was planning to spend the coming month thinking of myself as a commodity, a product that had to be branded and sold on the market.

So the next email was to my mother. As it happened, she used to work as a career counselor, and I thought she could help me venture into a new, well-paid career. I had the solid but unimpressive salary of an academic. If I wanted to make serious money, I had to leave the safe space of academia behind and fly into the corporate world of glass and steel. How hard could it be?

My goal was to get a job that paid twice as much as my current one.

ANDRÉ, SEPTEMBER 2

I thought I knew a thing or two about how markets worked. After all, I'm a professor in a business school and I had spent years studying how financial institutions malfunctioned. I wasn't an expert in finance, but I thought that I knew enough.

After reading Steve Siebold's book *How Rich People Think*, I realized I was wrong. According to Siebold, I was trapped in a typical "middle class" way of thinking about money. "The middle-class approaches money with the mind of an overanalytical academic," I read. "The world class approaches money like a child who doesn't understand lack and limitation and honestly believes he can do anything."

If I wanted to be part of the "world class," I had to give up my idiotic middle-class values of hard work, modesty, and financial prudence. To grow rich, I must realize that any limitations were just a creation of my faulty thinking.

After closing the book, I was determined to kill off my middle-class risk aversion and spend the month hunting out possibilities. What better way to do that, I thought, than becoming a trader on the financial markets?

CARL, SEPTEMBER 2

I had sat in this armchair a thousand times before, but this time it was different.

When I was in my early twenties, and occasionally staying in my parents' house, I sometimes ran into my mother's candidates. They would sit in the armchair, and my mother would sit on the couch. They were elegantly dressed executive types. They had recently lost their jobs. But since they were important people, they weren't kicked out on the street like ordinary workers, but instead offered the opportunity to meet an experienced career counselor, who happened to be my mom. She helped them process what had happened so they could move on to their new lives and new careers.

I was one of these candidates now, sitting in the armchair, ready to receive help from my mom. She had retired a few months back, but when I called her to ask if she could take my case, as her last candidate, she agreed.

She took out a paper from a plastic folder. "Here," she said, "Let's begin with your present situation." I had to reflect on my current work and write down what I wanted to make of my professional life.

"I actually have a pretty clear idea already," I said.

"Mm-hm, and what's that?"

"I'm looking for a job with as high a salary as possible." I paused. "I want to find out how much I'm worth on the market."

"Hm, okay," she said, and took off her glasses. "You would be looking for an executive job then."

"Yes, that sounds about right," I said.

"We need to find out which area first."

"Communications?" I said. "I mean, my job now is basically writing and talking, and that's the basis of communications, right?"

"Yes, maybe."

"Or human resources?" I tried. "After all, I'm teaching a course in HR."

My mother took out another paper from the folder.

"We can decide on that later," she said. "We first need to write down your competencies."

I looked at the paper she had given me. "What exactly is a competency?" I asked.

"Things you are good at." She began reading out examples of competencies from another paper. "Leading teams. Executing meetings. Planning collaborative agreements. Securing resources. Planning and executing project management."

"I don't really know if I have any competencies," I said.

"Of course you do. Go home and think about it, and we can speak again tomorrow."

ANDRÉ, SEPTEMBER 5

I had a small stack of books sitting next to my bed, with titles like *Trade Your Way to Financial Freedom*. They all seemed to agree on one thing—you don't want that evil taxman taking a cut of your hard-earned profits. Your investments should be "tax efficient." Reading on, I found that one-way traders with a shorter time horizon could avoid taxes on their earnings was by spread betting.

I often saw huge adverts for spread-betting in the tube. One featured a young man in a fine suit stretching his hand out toward a vicious dog. Presumably the dog was the market and the young man was the brave trader prepared to take a risk.

Aside from these macho images, I still had no idea what spread betting actually was. I logged on to one of the largest spread betting sites and watched a video titled "Is Spread Betting for Me?" It had upbeat music, slick corporate production values, and was all held together by the deep, confident male voice of the narrator.

Soon I got the drift: spread betting allowed you to bet on whether a financial market would move up or down. If the market went your way, you gained. If it moved against you, you lost. The big difference between spread betting and normal trading was that you did not actually buy or sell an asset. All you did was put money on the direction a market would move in. To me it looked like betting. But you were gambling on shares and currencies rather than horse races or football games.

CARL, SEPTEMBER 7

My mom flicked through the paper I had sent her.

"I'm sorry, but I had to be honest," I said.

"That's the point." She looked at the analysis I had made of my current situation. The first question was about my goals. "To leave academia and get a well-paid job in industry," I had written.

When did I last make an active choice? the next question read. I didn't know. *Was this project an active choice? What made me feel joy in my work?* I thought back to the sex month and the stark absence of joy it involved. *When did I work at my best?* Probably when I was using Pomodoros and smart drugs.

And then the billion-dollar question: *What is your dream job?* Retirement, I wrote as number one. Then being financially independent. Maybe that wasn't a job, in the strict sense, but I guess being retired didn't qualify, either. *How close are you to your dream job today?* "Pretty close, actually," I wrote. I was lucky to do what I really liked: teaching, writing, and reading.

"What's next?" I asked, once we had finished going through the questions together. My mom took out the paper with my competence profile and the short story I had written about myself. I presented myself as an academic with great expertise in the field of HR who now wanted to test his wings in the corporate world. My mom suggested some changes, then we opened my computer and found a couple of head-hunting firms. They were specialized, as they put it, in matching talent with challenges. Just like the aspiring best-selling author couldn't get by without an agent, the aspiring top executive couldn't survive without a headhunting agency.

"You will have to follow up with a phone call in a few days and try to arrange a meeting," she said, as I had registered my CV on three sites. "And you should add a profile on LinkedIn."

As I walked back home, I was feeling more hopeful than ever.

ANDRÉ, SEPTEMBER 8

I had Rickard on the phone, the only friend I had who did spread-betting.

"Have you tried trading CFDs?" he asked.

"What?"

"Contracts for Difference."

"No, what are they?"

"A financial tool. They allow you to bet on prices going up or down."

"Okay."

"You can buy them on spread-betting sites."

"I checked one out the other day, called IG. To be honest, I found the experience a bit overwhelming," I said.

"Why's that?"

"Well, there were all these flashing numbers moving up and down every second. I had no idea what they meant. And those warnings about losing money. They didn't exactly inspire confidence."

"It's not so scary," he said, and went on to explain how the trading site worked. He asked me to log on.

"Can you see that list starting with FTSE?"

I looked at the screen covered with blinking numbers.

"Yes."

"Okay. Those are the main financial markets. Share markets, bond markets, commodity markets."

"Right," I said, still dazed.

"Let's just pick one. Take FTSE 100. That's the 100 largest companies listed on the London stock exchange."

I clicked on FTSE 100.

"Now you see that graph?"

"Yeah." A new page appeared with a big graph in the middle.

"So that's the price of the overall market," he explained.

"Okay."

"Can you see those tools at the top of the screen? They help you decide where the market may go next. Click on that button where it says 'technical.'"

I clicked on the button, and suddenly two parallel lines appeared above and below the long skinny rectangular boxes that indicated the actual market price.

"What are those lines?" I asked.

"They're the trading channels."

"Trading channels?"

"Statistical predictions of the highest and lowest possible price over a period of time."

"Oh, okay."

"The idea is, when the market reaches the top line, it'll probably go back down. When it reaches the bottom line, it'll probably go back up."

"Okay, so I should sell when it reaches the top line and buy when it reaches the bottom line of the channel."

"Exactly."

After this explanation, I felt a little less confused. But he added a warning.

"You need time to trade this stuff. It can be quite immersive. And always close your positions before collecting the kids."

CARL, SEPTEMBER 8

The walls were covered with photographs of best-selling authors. Fredrik Backman was there, the author of *A Man Called Ove*, which had sold close to 3 million copies.

"We like your book. It has a distinctive voice. But it's a bit slow in the middle," the agent said. Her assistant was nodding in agreement.

"Yes, we could change that," I said, and took a sip of coffee.

"And as a reader I'd like to get to know the lead character better."

"Mm-hmm," I said, writing this down in my notebook.

"And I'm interested to see what you will do with the ending."

The meeting drew to a close.

"Do you think the book has potential?" I asked.

"Yes, I think so," she said.

I promised to send the completed 300 pages the next month. As I cycled across town for a meeting with my accountant, I imagined my portrait on that wall of best-selling authors.

My accountant had an elegant yet sporty look: he was wearing red jeans, a green jacket, and loafers. "If you make $23,000 a year," he said, "you can pay yourself a dividend of $18,000." He drew the figures on a white board.

I didn't understand much of what he was saying, but I loved sitting there, listening to how I should avoid paying too much taxes, imagining that I was going to sell millions of copies of my thriller.

"But all of this could change," he said. "If the leftist government gets their way they'll put a stop to this method." I shook my head in feigned disbelief, pretending to be on his side. I didn't tell him that I voted for the left. I preferred my accountant to be a pro-business market fundamentalist. Honestly, who wanted a socialist accountant to take care of their company?

I signed a bunch of papers to set up a new company, disconnected from my legal person, which was the kind of company I was going to need now that I was planning to make a lot of money.

When I came back home, Sally was lying in bed.

"I feel pregnant," she said, resting her palms on her stomach.

"You think you *are* pregnant?"

"Feels like it. I can check?"

Five minutes later she came back into the bedroom with a pregnancy stick showing the positive result.

"Wow, that's wonderful!" I said, and we kissed.

"Are you sure?"

"Absolutely," I said. "Now I really need to sell that thriller. We need to move somewhere bigger."

ANDRÉ, SEPTEMBER 13

I logged on to the IG spread-betting site and set up an account. From what I could tell, IG was the most popular spread-betting site in the UK. It had a large share of the 90,000 regular spread betters in the UK. I could now trade on anything from Facebook and gold, to the Swedish krona and US government bonds. I could even bet on the outcome of the upcoming US presidential election.

I started with the most familiar market: the FTSE 100. From what I had learned from Rickard, markets zig-zagged between relatively predictable extremes. I should click "buy" when the market hit the bottom of the trading channel, and "sell" when it hit the top of the trading channel.

I watched the FTSE 100 track upward to the top of the line, then abruptly fall back. When it reached the bottom line of the graph, it went back up again. This seemed easy enough. I jumped in with a bet of 50 pence per point, which meant that, for each point the FTSE 100 fell, I would gain 50 pence. I also set a stop loss. If the market went beyond a preset point, my bet would be closed. A stop loss was like a guardrail, preventing me from losing more money than I could afford.

Once I had placed my bet, the market almost immediately went against me. I was expecting it to fall because it had reached the top of the band, but it kept rising. I panicked and raised the level of the stop loss.

This was exactly the kind of irrational thing a real trader would never do. But I so dearly wanted to make my money back, I did it anyway. I remained fixed to the screen, watching the price of the FTSE go up and my trading account go down.

I was now down a few pounds. Objectively, it was nothing. But the costs in my mind were huge. I wanted to prove I was not a loser. I was determined to win it back. So, I placed another bet that the market would go down. And sure enough, it began to fall. When I closed the bet and a few pounds were added to my account, I felt like a skilled trader.

The afternoon disappeared as I placed one trade after another. Before heading out to pick up my daughter, I heeded Rickard's advice and closed all my positions.

CARL, SEPTEMBER 14

I learned from listening to a job coach on YouTube that I shouldn't chase after companies. Instead I should make companies chase after me. The only problem was that the companies weren't chasing me. Since I had sent my CV to three headhunting agencies a week ago, my phone had not yet rung. It was time to act.

I browsed through the website of one of the headhunting agencies. They said they offered sustainable recruitment services. I wasn't entirely sure what that meant. Recruitment that would help save the polar ice caps?

I looked at the pictures of their consultants. They all looked the same. Blond, good-looking women in black power suits and white blouses with white smiling teeth, blue eyes, and perfect skin. The men were in suits and white shirts, smiling, blue eyes.

I rehearsed a formal presentation of myself, and called the man who was responsible for communications.

"Hi, my name is Carl and I work at Stockholm University."

"Yes," the consultant said.

"I sent my CV to you last week. I'd be interested in changing careers. I'd like to try something new, in the private sector."

"What's your field? Communications? Economics?"

"Er, yes, communications. I think. Well, I've been teaching human resources, not just HR. I mean, er, I've taught other subjects, too. You know, like, management and that type of thing." I was stammering. "And also, you know, I've written for magazines and newspapers and I'm, you know, used to talking to media and stuff like that."

"What's your name?" he asked. "Your surname."

"Cederström," I said. "Carl Cederström. I can send my CV again."

"No, that's all right. I found it here."

"Okay."

"Can I call you back in a minute, when I've had the chance to look at this?"

An hour later the consultant called back. "I've looked at your CV now," he said. "You've done a lot."

"Yes, er, thanks."

"But I'm not sure communications is your field."

"No?" I said.

"Do you have any previous experience in communications?"

"Experience? Well, you know, I've been writing and, also, you know, teaching. It's all about communications, right?"

I was losing him.

"You know what, maybe it's better if you try HR," he said.

ANDRÉ, SEPTEMBER 14

I woke up, made myself a cup of Earl Grey tea, went upstairs, and logged on. I was waiting for the London market to open. As soon as the clock flipped over to 8:00 a.m., the FTSE started to jag downward. Based on statistical trends, I had bet the market would go down. In trader speak, I was shorting the market. And sure enough, the market continued to fall. There must have been some bad news. But bad news for someone else was good news for me. My trading account was going up. And that was all that mattered.

I had to go out for a meeting. Some of my trades were still open, so I downloaded the IG mobile trading app, which allowed me to keep an eye on the market as I moved through the city. When I went down into the tube station, I found myself cut off from the Internet, which meant I was also cut off from the market. A wave of anxiety hit me. What was going on? Where was Wall Street heading? All these thoughts went through my mind as I traveled under London. When I got off the train, I rushed out of the station to get some reception. I was relieved to find my trades were still doing okay.

CARL, SEPTEMBER 15

"In whatever circumstance we may find ourselves in life, attitude is everything." I was reading Richard Nelson Bolles's 1970 best-seller *What Color is Your Parachute?* Mastering job-hunting techniques was only a small part of getting a job, he said. Cultivating the right attitude was at least as important. When looking for a job, I should focus on that which I could actually change, constantly re-assessing my situation and accepting that whatever might happen in my life had a meaning, including those things that may look bad on the face of it, such as losing my job.

I also had to keep making phone calls. I should make at least twenty calls every morning, Bolles suggested.

I phoned the next headhunting company. I knew from their website that they worked with top executives and young talent. Objectively, I was neither a top executive nor a young talent. I wasn't even young. Young in the game, yes, but that was hardly an advantage. Still, I had learned to think optimistically. A negative attitude was the last thing I should bring to the phone conversation.

"I was wondering if we could meet and sit down to discuss future opportunities," I said, hoping I could arrange a face-to-face meeting. This was the next step, my mom said.

"You look like an interesting person, and we always like to meet interesting people," she said, while glancing through my CV. "But we are really busy now."

"I see, but maybe later?"

"You see, we're hiring top executives. To be honest, I'm looking at your CV here. You seem to be lacking the necessary qualifications."

"Mm-hm."

"You would compete against people with *years* of experience from HR in practice."

"Yes, of course."

"Look, it's unrealistic that you could go from your present position to a job as an executive," she continued.

"You think so?"

"Yes, you'd have to rethink your options. Maybe you could start lower down in the corporate hierarchy, to gain experience."

"Okay," I said, feeling beaten down.

"Are we on the same page here? You do understand what I'm saying?"

"Yes, I understand," I said.

"It is simply too large a leap. Okay?"

"Yes. Too large a leap. Of course," I repeated.

After we hung up, I felt despondent. I had clearly made a wrong assessment of my market value. But I knew I mustn't give up. I was repeating Bolles's words to myself: *In whatever circumstances we may find ourselves in life, attitude is everything. We must never shrink from doing the hard work of rethinking our whole strategy.*

ANDRÉ, SEPTEMBER 15

Logging on to my account and trading was not good enough. To be a real trader, I had to develop a trading philosophy. And that was what I hoped to gain from the book I had up on my screen: *Zen in the Markets*, by a Chicago futures trader named Edward Allen Toppel. Flicking through images of Japanese temple gardens, yin-yang symbols, and quotations from Zen masters, I began reading about how the greatest enemy in trading was the ego. To be a successful trader, you had to follow a set of simple rules: buying low and selling high, letting profits run while cutting losses quickly, adding to winning positions, not losing positions, and going with the trend. The problem was that your ego often got in the way of seeing the ultimate reality. To be a great trader, you needed to totally immerse yourself in the ultimate reality, which was the market. I had to become like a monk who, instead of contemplating a rock, focused his entire being on the market.

Reading on, I discovered some techniques to become an egoless Zen trading master. Each day before trading, I should do a course of meditation, followed by five minutes of visualizing the undulating flow of the market. During the day, I should periodically chant a personal affirmation. It sounded like an excellent idea, but what would my affirmation be?

The answer came on the next page. A Zen trader should try their hand at writing haiku. I followed his advice. I got out a pen and paper and opened my trading screen. I sat there, pen hovering over the page, contemplating the instantly changing seasons of the market. Then it came to me:

FTSE is up, Dow is down
A trader breathes out
The Nikkei will be open soon

CARL, SEPTEMBER 16

Before you can reach success, I learned from Napoleon Hill, you could be sure to meet defeat and failure. Since it was published in 1937, Hill's self-help classic *Think and Grow Rich* has sold more than 20 million copies. It was based on interviews with five hundred successful men. What they all had in common was that they never gave up. Their greatest success, Hill explained, "came just one step beyond the point at which defeat had overtaken them."

I was on the phone again with another recruitment consultant, determined not to be overtaken by defeat.

"Surely, there must be a way to migrate from academia to industry," I said. I was more strident this time, trying to speak with a new sense of entitlement.

"Yes, of course," she said.

"And I would only leave academia if I was offered a better salary."

"What do you make now?" she asked.

I told her my salary. "Oh yes. You'd certainly make more than that as an HR executive."

I breathed a sigh of relief.

"Look, I need to ponder this," she continued. "Let me get back to you next week. Okay?"

ANDRÉ, SEPTEMBER 16

Sitting at my desk, I closed my eyes and tried to visualize the peaks and troughs of the market, rising and falling like waves. I saw myself like an insignificant surfer bobbing on each wave, waiting for the right swell to come in. After five minutes of contemplating this pleasant scene, I opened my eyes and pulled up my trading screen.

The day disappeared like I was in a trance, as I placed one trade after another. My ego crept in every now and then, but I beat it back by reciting my haiku.

Soon it was evening, and everything went quiet. It was Friday. All the markets around the world were closing for the weekend. A sense of calm came over me. As I sat there, watching the flat line of the market tick away, I felt like a Zen monk contemplating a limpid moonlit pool after everyone else in the temple had fallen asleep.

CARL, SEPTEMBER 20

The speaker's agency did not have time to see me this month, but a consulting firm had approached me, asking if I could give an inspirational seminar for HR executives. They had offered me $1,700, which was more money than I had ever been offered for speaking in the past.

It was nothing compared to Bill and Hillary Clinton, who, from 2001 onward, had made $153 million in paid speeches, receiving an average of $210,795 for each address. The former Swedish prime minister was on the market too, but he was charging no more than $12,000.

According to a report from Bharat Book Bureau, the market for motivational speakers was worth around $1 billion, but despite the thousands of aspiring motivational gurus, there were only about twenty that made good money out of it.

On my way back home from the workshop, I read an email from the recruitment agency. It was another consultant, who said he had read my CV. He wanted to know what kind of job I was looking for exactly, and what would make me stand out among other candidates. I hit reply and wrote: "I want to become an HR executive, and what makes me stand out from the other candidates is that. . . ." Then I froze, unable to come up with anything. I had to think positively. I needed to demonstrate my superiority and visualize success. Yet nothing came to me. I was blank.

ANDRÉ, SEPTEMBER 20

I would sit for hours staring at the screen, watching the markets flashing red and green. If I was eating lunch with a friend or teaching students, I would find any excuse to dash off and check where the markets had moved in the last five minutes. I would wake at 3:00 a.m. and check on the global currency markets. The only way I knew something was going on in the real world was if it appeared in the markets section of the business news. When Mel asked what I was doing in my office late at night, I gave a one-word answer and returned to staring into the screen. Was I becoming addicted to the market?

I opened a new screen and searched for stock market trading and addiction. Soon I was reading a letter from three Italian doctors published in a recent issue of *Addict Health*. A clear sign of addiction, they explained, was when "Trading activity becomes the main activity in daily life." I moved uncomfortably in my chair, then forced myself to run through a checklist included in the article:

Am involved in compulsive daily trading. Yes.
Needs to spend increasing amounts of time trading and/or looking for new financial instruments to invest in. Yes.
Altered sleep-wake rhythm (e.g. waking at night to be connected for the opening of foreign financial markets). Yes.

All in all, I had seven out of twelve symptoms. Five or more, they said, and I was at risk of trading addiction.

As I opened my trading screen again, my feelings of discomfort seemed to dissolve. I was reminded of the words of a man who Natasha Dow Shüll spoke with in her study of gambling machine addicts in Las Vegas: "You erase it all at the machines—you can even erase yourself." By spending hours staring at the movements of financial markets on my screen, had I been erasing the rest of the world, and even myself? Had my ego finally dissolved?

CARL, SEPTEMBER 21

In his 1952 book, *The Power of Positive Thinking*, Norman Vincent Peale suggested that in order to reach success, I had to envision myself as successful. Always picture success, he said, "no matter how badly things seem to be going at the moment." I needed to believe in my own capacities and show how I stood out from the crowd. "Make a true estimate of your own ability, then raise it 10 percent," Peale said.

Determined to make an impression, I sent a response to the recruitment consultant, saying I stood out among the crowd by being a world-leading expert in HR. This was more than a 10 percent exaggeration, but I had to come up with something spectacular to stand out. Norman

Vincent Peale's recommendation seemed to work. The recruitment consultant wrote back. He wanted to speak to me.

"So here's my question," I said when he called. "Is it absolutely impossible for an academic like myself to move into industry?"

"Not impossible, but without experience you'll be struggling."

I contemplated his words. They were pretty definite. It was hard to envision success now. Things were not going badly. They were going appallingly.

"You know what?" I eventually said in a tone of defeat. "I'll stop trying now. I'll get back to my job as an academic."

"Well, if something comes around we could always be in touch."

"Fine," I said.

How many recruitment consultants had I spoken to? I was losing count. It didn't matter. They had all come to the same conclusion. I was worth nothing out there, on the market, at least in the area of HR. Not even the power of positive thinking could change that. I was lucky to have a job that I liked. Chasing after corporations, seeking to sell yourself on the job market, was more humiliating than I had expected. I couldn't help thinking that this was the experience of my students. Even before graduating, they were competing for jobs, constantly working on their personal brand, always expected to find new ways of making themselves saleable.

ANDRÉ, SEPTEMBER 21

All day I was trapped in meetings, but when I got my chance, I snuck off to the toilet and logged in to my trading account. *Yes!* I called out as I hunkered down in a cubicle. The US dollar had fallen and the yen was up. All my losses from trading the yen and the US dollar had turned into gains in less than an hour. Take the profits now before something changes, I told myself. So, as I sat on the toilet with my trousers around my feet, I clicked a button and made a healthy profit.

What made this any different from gambling? In my office, I found a copy of *Something for Nothing*, written by the historian Jackson Lears.

What had made America great, he wrote, was not just the Protestant work ethic, but also its chance ethic. Risk-taking was seen as a way of escaping the grind of hard work. It was only through chance that your life could be transformed in an instant. Flicking through the book, I found a passage where he described day traders "sitting entranced at their computer consoles, dodging bullets, riding momentum, selling out just in time (they hoped), and feeling drawn inexorably to the frisson of danger. Their solitary, obsessive existence bore a striking resemblance to the life of the compulsive gambler."

Was that me—a compulsive gambler? While pondering this question, I found myself drifting into a Marks & Spencer in the middle of the financial district. I bought a bottle of Burgundy and some French cheese to round off the day. As I queued up to pay, I noticed I was surrounded by bankers, many of whom had probably spent the day trading in the same markets as me. They were buying ready-made meals for one and a few cans of lager. If this was the life of a trader, I was starting to live it.

CARL, SEPTEMBER 27

As it had become clear to me that I did not have the required qualifications to become a well-paid executive, I returned to my unresolved project of personal finances.

I was sitting in my office going through piles of receipts. I had promised to return these to my accountants a long time ago, but I had kept putting it off, and now I was feeling too embarrassed to get in touch with them. Besides, I seemed to have lost receipts and couldn't locate important documents. My heart was racing again.

According to Cambridge University researchers, one in five of all Brits suffers from financial phobia. Like me, they felt sick at the sight of bank statements. In an article published in the *Journal of Neuroscience, Psychology and Economics*, called "Measuring Financial Anxiety," two authors had developed a Financial Anxiety Scale. As I went through the questions, it was clear I was one of those afflicted.

I find monitoring my bank or credit card accounts very boring.
Yes, you could say that.
I prefer not to think about the state of my personal finances.
Mm-hmm.
Thinking about my personal finances can make me feel guilty.
Yes, that's why I try not to think about it.
Discussing my finances can make my heart race or make me feel stressed. Yes, and I start sweating.

Nearly half of those suffering from financial phobia would experience increased heart rate from just thinking about dealing with money. 15 percent felt frozen and immobilized, 12 percent felt ill, and 11 percent experienced dizziness. The only way through this fear was to confront it.

To avoid feeling stressed all the time, I should set aside one day each month to deal with my finances, and I should try to become interested in money.

ANDRÉ, SEPTEMBER 28

It was 2:00 a.m. when my alarm went off. I rushed downstairs, turned on the television, and logged on to my trading account. Donald Trump appeared on the screen. Late last night I had opened a short position on the USD/JPY pair. I was betting the US dollar would go down against the yen. According to financial commentators, this would happen if Trump performed well in the presidential debate.

I was rooting for Trump. Personally, I hoped he would lose the debate as well as the election. But for the purposes of speculation, I was now on Trump's side. Each time he opened his mouth I hoped that he would land a blow on Hillary, and that she would wobble. *Come on Trump! Show her.*

As they got into the swing of the debate, the US dollar started rising. With each strange digression or angry outburst from Trump, the dollar kept going up. I was losing, £20, £40, £60, £100 and more. Hillary laughed off his attacks and answered questions with calm confidence. The US dollar kept going up. I was screwed.

When it was over, Trump ran off stage. Hillary stood around waving. But more important, I was down £200. The polls showed Hillary had triumphed. Donald and I had lost. I switched off the TV and closed my trading account, feeling deflated.

CARL, SEPTEMBER 29

Today was my finance day. I had learned from the blog *Mixed Up Money* that "dedicating 1 day a month to your finances is so rock n' roll." I emptied my drawers of envelopes and papers and spread them out on the kitchen table. Determined to do this properly, I systematically followed a guide I had found on lifehacker.org.

Immediately after breakfast, I phoned my telephone provider to update my contract. I phoned my credit card company and asked to get an itemized list of all my spending since the start of the year. I set up a new account with my bank. I spoke with my bank manager, and then to a woman at the tax authority. I reviewed my contracts with insurance, electricity, and Internet companies. I set up automatic payments, downloaded budget apps, payment apps, and a mobile banking app. By the end of the afternoon, as I gave up for the day, I was feeling anxious and empty. I was certainly not feeling rock n' roll.

ANDRÉ, SEPTEMBER 29

For weeks, I had been glued to every turn of the financial markets. I had traded on the share market, the currency market, and the commodities market, and I was fed up. Why had I been so unsuccessful? I found a research paper with the dry title: "An Evaluation of Alternative Weighted Indices" written by some of my colleagues. In their research they had taken a group of very experienced fund managers and got them to pick some shares. Then they set up a computer to randomly select stocks in the way that a monkey would. It turned out that the monkey algorithm did just as well as the fund managers. Making random selections was just as good as spending hours doing research and making educated trades. So, I decided I would make myself into a monkey and just trade randomly.

I opened the trading platform on my phone. *Wall Street?* I'll bet on that. *Up or down?* I randomly picked down. I opened a position then switched off my phone. How much would I lose or make by the time I got home, I wondered?

As I walked through the door, I rushed upstairs and logged on to my trading platform. The familiar rush returned. *Fuck yes*, I had made about £70 from an unexpected fall on Wall Street.

When I started making dinner, I opened my trading platform again and randomly let my finger fall on a market. *Oil?* Okay. *Up or down?* I was feeling good, so up. I placed the trade then made a deal with myself to leave the position open until I had finished cooking. When the food was ready, I logged on to my trading platform again. I had made £30.

This random approach worked perfectly.

I sent an email to Carl. He was clueless when it came to trading. I asked him to pick a market and suggest which direction it would go. *Meat*, he replied. I scrolled through the markets and found Chicago Mercantile exchange where they traded livestock. *Cattle or hogs? Up or down?* I asked Carl. *Hogs down, cattle up*, he replied.

I placed a position on lean hogs delivered in October to go up and live cattle available now to go down. I should have known better than to ask Carl. When the markets closed a few minutes later, I had lost about £25 on the cattle and £10 on the hogs.

CARL, SEPTEMBER 30

It was the last day of the month, and it was time to review my personal finances.

To prepare myself for the humiliation, I watched a clip on YouTube from the sadistic television series, *The Luxury Trap*, about a young couple with enormous credit card debts. As the experts reviewed their finances, explaining how irresponsible they were, the couple stood side by side with their heads lowered, feeling ashamed. The man was forced to sell his car. He cried.

I was going to do the same thing now, although I would act as both victim and judge.

I logged on to my bank account and went through every single expenditure since the start of the year, organizing them according to the same categories used in *The Luxury Trap*: housing, food, transport, clothes, mortgage, and other costs.

As I had suspected, the majority of my money was going to food, wine, and restaurants. Transportation costs were low, because we had no car, and housing costs and mortgage were relatively low, too. My budget for clothes was close to zero.

I then moved on to calculate what this project had cost me. I had tried not to think about it, because it made my heart race, but I sat down and added it all up.

TOTAL: $8,200
COURSES ($5,600)
TECHNOLOGY ($1,350)
BOOKS ($500)
LUNCH / DINNERS ($750)

ANDRÉ, SEPTEMBER 30

I wasn't alone in my random approach to trading. Marcel Proust apparently invested in a random way, picking shares on the basis of how appealing he found their names. He added the Tanganyika Railway and Ural Oil Fields to his portfolio because they sounded like places he might like to visit. Unsurprisingly, Proust's strategy did not work very well. It nearly bankrupted him.

But in the vain hope I would not be as unlucky as Proust, I continued to trade randomly. Now I was making decisions on the basis of what I was doing at any particular moment. So, while drinking my morning coffee, I traded coffee on the London Coffee market. Since it was nice, I bet it would go up. I kept the position open until I had my next coffee.

A few moments later, a knock came at the door. It was the grocery delivery. I helped him move the bags into the kitchen, then I opened my computer, searched for the delivery company, and bet the shares would go up as well. After all, the delivery guy seemed nice enough.

When it was time for lunch, I searched the kitchen for food. All I could find was gluten-free pasta, so while waiting for the water to boil, I ate some bread and placed a long position on both corn, the main ingredient of the pasta, and wheat, the main ingredient of the bread.

As I drank my second cup of coffee after lunch, I closed my coffee position. I had made £30. It was nearly two thirty now, and the Chicago livestock market would be open soon.

Two twenty-eight, two twenty-nine, two thirty. Bang!

The numbers began blinking, moving up and down. After only a few minutes, the cattle price had plunged and I had lost nearly £200. I was rushing off for a meeting, but I wasn't ready to let go of the cattle yet.

A few hours later, when the meeting was over, I checked on my platform.

Fuck no! I had lost about £350 on the cattle, about £60 on the wheat, and £90 on the corn.

The markets were closing for the day, and I walked down the street feeling dejected. But I realized the currency markets were still open. A group of tipsy office workers flooded out of an office building, followed by a Mariachi band. I opened my trading account, and tried to place an order to go long on the Mexican peso. "Sorry," it pinged back. "You need more funds in your account." I started the process of loading up more funds, but then stopped myself. *This was nuts.* I looked wistfully at the numbers flashing red and green one last time, then closed my trading platform, deciding never to try this again. My month as a trader was over, and all I had to show for it was a loss of about 500 quid in my bank balance.

OCTOBER

MORALITY

ANDRÉ, OCTOBER 1

I sat in a large conference room with 400 other people. We had our thumbs stretched out in front of us, shouting at our thumbs: "You're not good enough!"

A man with rectangular glasses took the stage: "Imagine your thumb is dressed like Ronald McDonald." He laughed at his thumb. Soon 400 people were also laughing at their thumbs. "Tell yourself 'all is good, I feel better.'"

"All is good," I said to my thumb. "I feel better."

Giving positive affirmations to my thumb seemed like a strange start to a month that was focused on doing good. But a few weeks earlier, I had decided that if I was going to make it through the rest of the year, I needed to do something drastic. And attending a weekend seminar on Neuro Linguistic Programming (NLP) should be drastic enough.

NLP had kept popping up during the course of the year. Pick-up artists loved it, and attendees at Landmark talked about it constantly. NLP promised that we could take full control over our lives. By rewiring our thoughts, we could achieve the goals we had set ourselves. NLP was "invented" in California during the 1970s by Richard Bandler and John Grinder. Since then, hundreds of thousands of people had attended

NLP training. In the UK alone, there were over 30,000 "licensed NLP practitioners." While I had met people who were evangelical about the "powerful tools" offered by NLP, I also knew that anthropologists had studied NLP and described it as "folk magic." Nevertheless, I was intrigued, so I signed up for a weekend seminar led by two well-known NLP experts.

One of those experts came up on stage. He looked like a senior executive about to present a refresher course on a marketing strategy. His belly swelled under his gray suit. I knew his face. Wasn't he a television hypnotist?

"Let's try to develop a better you," he said. "Close your eyes and start stroking your arms. Imagine the best you. Yes, that's right. Make the image stronger."

I was struggling, but no image appeared in my head.

"Stretch your arms out, John Travolta style."

I flung out my arms.

"Now smile and say 'eeeeeeee.'"

The room filled with long eeeees.

"Imagine there's a bell in front of you. Ring it. Ding!"

Four hundred dings rang out. *Eeeee! Ding! Eeeee! Ding! Eeeee! Ding!*

"Now, ring your neighbor's bell." I reached over and pretended to ring a bell in front of the man sitting next to me. *Ding!* I felt ridiculous.

After a short break, I returned to my seat. "Purple Haze" by Jimi Hendrix was flooding out of the speakers. A sturdy old man lumbered onto the stage. He wore a shirt-suit-and-tie combo that only a Texan could dream up. "This man has done more than any person to improve human existence," the hypnotist said. He must be the guru who "invented" NLP, I thought.

Within minutes, he got onto his favorite topic: himself. He had not taken a holiday in eight years; he could kill anyone with his bare hands; he was an accomplished physicist and computer programmer; he built top-secret weapons for the US defense department. It felt like I had chanced upon an unhinged military contractor in a hotel bar.

"You know all those people who go searching for enlightenment by climbing up a mountain to visit a guru?" he said, baring his white teeth. "I hired a helicopter to take me up the mountain. I found the guru and asked him to tell me his secrets. The guru said it would take years for me to learn them. So, I grabbed him by the throat and held him over the cliff. He soon started talking." He looked around at the excited crowd with bloodlust in his eyes.

Before we had a moment to process what he was saying, he was off on another chain of random associations. "There are ghosts in the hallway of the hotel. It's fucking haunted. But don't worry," he said. "I've performed exorcisms. I know a lot about demons."

What the hell was this? Had I paid £450 to listen to this crazy old man all weekend!

Following another break, the hypnotist was back on stage. "Think of a person who makes you feel good," he said.

My daughter came to mind.

"Now what color does that person make you feel?"

Pink?

"Where is that color?"

In my chest?

"Now imagine that color spreading across your entire body."

Pink was creeping over my entire body.

"Open your eyes, and tell the person next to you what you saw."

I turned to face a sad-looking salesman.

"Well, I thought about my daughter," I told the salesman. "She was pink."

"Your face just changed," the salesman said. "See, it really works!"

The salesman went on to tell me how he had found solace in NLP after being diagnosed with cancer. His story jolted me out of my comfortable pink haze. Clearly there were desperate people who found something in NLP. If I was suffering from cancer, perhaps I would have found NLP attractive too.

CARL, OCTOBER 1

I woke up with a sense of guilt this morning. Last night, I bought food and wine for $150, and now it was all gone. Such stupid behavior would have to come to an end right now.

After breakfast, I remained in the kitchen and began reading a book called *Doing Good Better*. It was written by a young Oxford philosopher who was explaining how to do the most good, in the most effective way possible. If we wanted to help, we should look at facts, not emotions. In the same manner as investing in a company, we should "look at the best available evidence in order to work out where you will get the most bang for your buck." When they had started investigating charities, they found that the "best" ones were hundreds of times more effective than "good ones." The most effective charities, I learned, were often rather unsexy, like deworming kids in Africa or buying malaria nets.

Later in the afternoon, as we were having dinner at my parents' place, I was asked what I wanted for a birthday present.

"I already have everything I need, so you could donate the money you'd otherwise spend on gifts to the malaria foundation."

"Well, that's just not going to happen," my mother said. "I want to buy presents for you."

"In that case, I'll have to sell all of the stuff you give me, and then donate the money myself."

"That sounds like a lot of fun," my wife said.

I was just getting into my new role as moral Carl, and I had already alienated my family.

As I went to bed, I was relieved to notice I had spent no money during my first day of being good.

ANDRÉ, OCTOBER 2

As the second day of the NLP seminar began, a trim young man with spiky hair walked onto the stage.

"What's your name?" the hypnotist asked.

"Pedro."

"What do you do, Pedro?"

"I'm a sales trainer . . . but my real passion is organizing yoga retreats."

"Do you want to learn how to be successful, Pedro?"

"Absolutely!"

"Okay, you need to imagine you're stepping into the body of someone who is really successful in your field. For instance, when I wanted to be a successful TV presenter, I would imagine stepping into the body of Noel Edmonds."

Noel Edmonds, I thought. Wasn't he a British daytime TV game show host? I remember Carl writing an angry op-ed article about him, after Edmonds claimed that people got cancer due to their bad attitudes.

"So, Pablo, who's your role model?"

"Tony Robbins!"

Tony Robbins, I thought, who else? The most successful motivational speaker in the world.

"Great! Now imagine Tony's posture. Imagine how he stands, how he holds his chest, how he holds his head. Step into Tony."

Pedro pushed out his chest proudly and looked around the audience like a minor dictator who had just seized power. He began bouncing up and down.

"How do you feel, Pedro?"

"I feel good!"

"Now, step out of Tony."

A scared, boyish look came over Pedro's face.

A few hours later, the seminar was finally over. The hypnotist lingered at the door looking to sign autographs.

"What a great weekend," he said.

"Yeah, fantastic," a woman in the crowd said. As I walked back I was wondering whose body I should step into. Maybe I should be Mahatma Gandhi for the month. Or Mother Teresa. Or Nelson Mandela. Suddenly, the options seemed unlimited.

CARL, OCTOBER 2

I signed up to "Giving What You Can," an organization set up by "effective altruists," encouraging people like myself to donate a minimum of 10 percent of my salary to the most effective charities. But I had a more ambitious goal in mind: to save a life in the developing world. The cost was about $3,400, which was not 10 percent of my monthly salary, but close to 100 percent. But I had saved $1,700 from the previous month. Now I had to save $1,700 more. I was looking at a month of frugality.

I had promised to take my daughter and her friend to the cinema. When I met up with her parents, I explained to them that the kids would have to go alone. They looked worried. "I'll sit right outside and wait, in case they get scared or something," I explained. It was the first time their daughter would go to the cinema unaccompanied. I didn't say the reason was that I was saving money to donate to the world's poor. I was tempted to lecture them on the topic and point out that 18,000 children died from preventable diseases each day. But I didn't have to. They accepted my proposal without complaints.

ANDRÉ, OCTOBER 3

At around 11:00 a.m., I received a call from Carl.

"I'm going to set up a refugee camp," he explained.

Even by Carl's standards, that sounded extreme.

"What are your plans?" he asked.

"During my NLP course, I learned how to change my thoughts and behaviors."

"How?"

"You imagine stepping into the body of someone you admire. You adopt their posture. You see the world through their eyes."

"Okay."

"So my plan is to step into the body of a different ethicist each week."

"Oh, okay," Carl said. He sounded a little confused.

"Yeah, the first week I will become an Aristotelian. The next week Kantian. Then I'd spend a week as a Utilitarian. The final week I will live as a Libertarian."

I think Carl was a bit surprised by my immediate resolve. Usually, I would be hesitant in the face of any new challenge. Not today. Maybe the NLP was working.

CARL, OCTOBER 3

According to the effective altruists, there were two ways of being good. Either you got into a well-paid job and gave as much money as you could to charity, which they called "earning to give." Or, you could do good via your job, typically by acquiring a powerful position in politics and making sure that resources were distributed to those who really needed them.

I knew from last month that I wasn't going to find a better paid job than the one I already had, and reinventing myself as a politician seemed like a long shot.

Volunteering was an obvious option, but the effective altruists said the benefits were negligible, especially if I was planning to do it during a limited time period, in which case I would do more harm than good since I would be taking up the valuable time of professional charity workers.

As I was running out of options, I could only think of one thing: writing.

To get some guidance, I met an old friend who worked in public relations. I explained that I wanted to do something good, perhaps investigative journalism. I could write about unscrupulous private companies looting the welfare system. Some individuals had set up refugee homes for vulnerable people where the living conditions were inhumane. One such company had made a 4,000 percent profit, which they had proceeded to invest in a golf course. Maybe I could try to set up my own refugee home to reveal how scandalously easy it was to do. For maximum impact, my friend advised, I should collect information and leak it to media. If successful, it could help influence a law banning companies from looting the welfare system.

Based on the principles of effective altruism, I began to assess the plan according to a series of criteria. How many people would benefit? Was this the most effective thing I could do? What would happen if I did not do this? Would someone else do it? What were the chances of success?

Unfortunately, I did not get very far, because I found that the process of setting up homes for refugees was more complicated than I had first expected. The application form was long, and it would take several weeks to receive a response. I was back to square one: frugality.

ANDRÉ, OCTOBER 4.

In the evening, I lay back on the couch and opened up my old copy of Aristotle's *Nicomachean Ethics*. Following the technique I had learned during my NLP seminar, I tried to imagine myself as Aristotle, lecturing half-naked young boys about the good life.

Toward the end of the book, Aristotle wrote about what he thought was the greatest virtue: contemplation. He described contemplation as "the highest form of activity . . . since the intellect is the highest thing in us." If I was going to be an Aristotelian for a week, why not spend my days contemplating? I could follow Aristotle's example by hanging around the city and engaging in philosophical discussions. Perhaps I could take a chair out to public places, sit there, and just think. I thought it appropriate to use a deck chair—the only piece of furniture that Ludwig Wittgenstein had in his rooms in Cambridge.

CARL, OCTOBER 4

Was this what virtue felt like? Slowly walking up and down the aisles of a cut-price supermarket looking for the cheapest food?

On my way home, I listened to another podcast about effective altruism. One of its most vocal defenders explained that, if you happened to be inside a house that was on fire, and you could either save a child or a painting by Picasso, you would have to save the painting. Once you sold the painting, the money could be used to save thousands of children's lives.

Later in the evening, as I was making a bland potato soup, I told my wife about the dilemma of the burning child.

"But that's just sick," she said.

I later read a wry response to this utilitarian line of thinking by the philosopher Kwame Anthony Appiah. If you would see a child drowning in a shallow pond, he said, you should not save him but let him die, take his clothes, sell them, and use the money to donate to charity.

ANDRÉ, OCTOBER 6

Emerging from the tube at Bank Station, I chose a spot directly outside the stock exchange. I unfolded my two white deck chairs, propped up a small whiteboard, and wrote on it with a black marker pen: *Pop-up philosophy. Stop, sit down, and just think.* Trying to step into the body of Aristotle, I sat down on my deck chair and tried to contemplate.

It was lunchtime. Office workers sat around me munching sandwiches, stabbing at their phones, and puffing on cigarettes. Their indifference was offset by an occasional smile from a passing tourist. As time wore on, I wondered what I should think about. Given I was sitting at the heart of one of the largest financial centers in the world, capitalism would have been the perfect topic. But my mind wandered. After a couple of hours, I folded up my two chairs, cleaned off my sign, and headed home. I wondered whether I had inspired the virtue of contemplation in the people who saw my sign.

CARL, OCTOBER 7

Since my last visit to the supermarket, I had not spent a dime. Yesterday, when I was meeting a friend for coffee, I said I didn't want to spend any money. Eventually he offered to buy me a coffee, which I reluctantly accepted, and then drank while quietly telling him that the money could have been spent more effectively. I had just read an essay by the utilitarian philosopher Peter Singer who argued that it was morally unjustifiable to indulge in luxuries when the money could be donated to international aid.

Back home, I emailed one of the more famous effective altruists, hoping he could help me find something meaningful to do, but he wrote back saying he did not have the time to speak to me. Instead I found a website, called "80,000 Hours," designed for young people who wanted to do good but were not sure how to do it. I filled in a career quiz. *Was I good at math and science?* No. *Could I write?* Yes. *How far through your career are you?* Late, it turned out, because the target group was people aged twenty to thirty. After answering more questions, the website spat out a recommendation: I should go into party politics or become a grant-maker for a foundation.

ANDRÉ, OCTOBER 7

I unfolded my chairs outside the headquarters of a large bank that had been bailed out by the government during the 2007–8 financial crisis. As soon as I was set up, a security guard came over.

"You need to be outside this line," he said, pointing to a mark on the pavement.

I shifted my chair outside the line, then sat down again.

When he was gone, a homeless woman zig-zagged my way.

"Are you selling deck chairs?" she asked.

"No, I'm promoting contemplative thinking," I replied.

"I haven't got time for that," she said, and then promptly disappeared.

After she left, two security officials approached. As they came closer, I could hear the words "reputational risk."

"What are you doing?" one of the suited officials asked.

"Pop-up philosophy," I replied.

"What's that?"

"We encourage people to take some time out of their day to think."

I was not sure where the "we" came from. I seemed to speak in a new tone of confidence when imagining myself as Aristotle.

"How long will you be here?"

"I'll be gone in an hour."

They seemed pleased with my answers and left me alone. During the next hour I met a hedge fund manager, two technology entrepreneurs, and a few others who preferred to remain anonymous. All of them sat in the chair next to me and joined my quiet contemplation for a few minutes. It seemed that thinking was more popular in the City of London than I had expected.

CARL, OCTOBER 8

A close friend was visiting, and he didn't know I was on a zero-based spending scheme. I suggested we go for a long walk.

"You know about effective altruism?" I asked.

"Yes, I read an article recently. They want us to give away ten percent of our income, right?"

"As a minimum, yes. You should give as much as possible. The more the merrier."

"But where do you draw the line?"

"That's what I've asked too."

"I mean, in terms of cutting down on your expenses, should you sell your house and live in the forest? Stop buying food?"

"Or just die?" I said.

I recalled the end of *Love and Death*, when Woody Allen explained that we shouldn't think of death as an end, but as a very effective means of cutting down our expenses.

We paused outside a restaurant. It was late now.

"And in terms of doing good," my friend continued. "Should you work in an investment bank, or maybe rob one?"

We sat at a table and ordered a bottle of red wine and some tapas. As the plates arrived, I was looking around the table. Where there was food, I just saw money. The meal was going to cost me more than I had spent for the whole month thus far. When the check came, I was secretly praying he would volunteer to cover the costs, but he didn't.

"Shall we go for another drink?" my friend asked.

"Could do," I responded, "but let me first check something."

I had downloaded a new app, which listed all the bars in Stockholm that sold cheap beer. It turned out that one of the recommended places was just down the road. We went there for one last drink. This time, my friend paid.

ANDRÉ, OCTOBER 9

I unfolded my chairs and propped up my sign outside St. Paul's Cathedral. After about ten minutes, a little girl ran over to me.

"Why are you sunbathing in the rain?" she asked. I had no answer.

After about twenty minutes, I stood up, leaving the seat unmanned. Soon tourists began sitting down, taking photos of themselves and presumably posting them on Facebook and Instagram.

An hour later I moved on to Oxford Street, where I found a spot directly outside the entrance to H&M. Hundreds of people walked by every minute.

After about an hour on Oxford Street, I moved on to the BBC. No one was around, so I packed up after about thirty minutes. As I sat on the tube on the way home, I wondered whether Aristotle would have been proud of me. Had I really been able to step into his body as the NLP experts had advised?

CARL, OCTOBER 12

"Of all the stupid things you've done this year, this is by far the most provocative."

Sally wasn't in a good mood. I had returned back home from the supermarket where I had bought more flour and potatoes, but no deodorant.

"It's too expensive," I said, "and not really that important."

"So you want to walk around stinking like a pig."

I said nothing.

"Honestly, I don't think there's anything worse than pretending to be poor."

"But I'm trying to do something good here. I'll give all the money away to those who really need it."

Living according to the doctrine of effective altruism was not easy. The most difficult principle to maintain was to care about everyone equally. My wife and daughter were, in theory, no more important than people on the other side of the planet. They had no more right to deodorants than poor men in Burkina Faso.

And yet, as much as I tried to accept these ideas, I was ashamed to admit that I would rather save my wife and daughter from drowning than those two unknown men in Burkina Faso.

ANDRÉ, OCTOBER 12.

Walking up the stairs of a converted textile sweatshop in East London, I tried to imagine I was Immanuel Kant. This week, my mission was to embody this Prussian philosopher for whom ethics was about following rules, what Kant called the categorical imperative, which could be applied to everyone. One of the most famous examples of Kant's imperatives was to always tell the truth. For him, it was a universal duty. So I decided to spend the week being scrupulously truthful.

It was late in the evening, and I was chairing a panel with four well-known technology entrepreneurs. When the discussion began, one started waxing lyrical about her passion for cloud-based solutions.

"How can anyone be passionate about cloud-based solutions?" I asked. She looked a little ruffled. Surely, the words "cloud-based solutions" and "passion" belonged in separate sentences. Ignoring the question, she continued talking about the exciting world of SAP platforms. I could tell that being a Kantian was not going to be easy.

CARL, OCTOBER 14

Yesterday evening, as I watched the news, there was a story about the alarming shortage of kidneys. Why had I not thought of this?

I found a pamphlet online for people interested in donating their kidneys. It was rare, it said, that people other than relatives gave away their kidneys. I then found a thread on an Internet forum. A young guy said he wanted to donate his kidney. Everyone said he was stupid. He proceeded nonetheless, but when he got in touch with the hospital to offer his organs, they had declined the offer. They deemed that he wasn't psychologically stable.

I read through the information, then sent Sally a text. She was out having drinks with some doctors from the hospital where she worked.

"How long does it take to donate a kidney?" I wrote.

"Who's doing it? You need to be family, I think," she replied.

"No, you can be anonymous."

"But you can't sell your kidney!"

"Not sell. Give away for free."

"To whom? For your project? Idiot!"

I was well aware that this was a drastic decision, but I desperately felt I needed to do something.

After breakfast this morning, I called the clinic and asked if they were interested in my kidney. They seemed surprised by my offer, and said they'd get back to me.

Then I sent an email to another hospital asking if they were keen on my sperm. A reply came: they had enough sperm. I phoned another hospital in Uppsala to ask if they were interested. They were, so we scheduled a time for me to come and give a test. I also signed up to give blood.

I phoned André, delighted to have found a way to move forward.

"You should give your shit away, too."

"My shit?" I asked.

"Yes, for fecal transplants."

I searched the web and found that there were only two cities in Sweden where they performed fecal transplants: Örebro and Jönköping. It seemed fitting because, having lived in one of them and visited the other, I was of the view that they were both shitholes.

ANDRÉ, OCTOBER 14

What good had I done in my life? I was still asking myself this question when I woke up this morning. The previous evening, I had realized just how pathetic my do-gooding had been.

I took part in a debate about "eudaimonia" held at the central London YMCA. Afterward, a group of people took to the stage who had actually done something good with their lives. There was a doctor who had developed a new type of surgery, two people who had started a fencing group for Muslim girls, and a guy who was working for a design agency that was trying to stop poor people from eating so much unhealthy food. Hearing their stories made me feel ashamed. This month, I was trying to do good, but all I had been able to muster was sitting around in deck chairs pretending to think.

CARL, OCTOBER 15

It was my mom's birthday, so I decided to take a break from my life of frugality and invited her for lunch. I had bought her a book instead of a donation for malaria nets. On the way out of the mall, I told her about the money I made from the talk I gave the previous month, and that I was now going to donate it all to the malaria foundation.

"Are you kidding?"

"No."

"Have you really thought this through? It's a lot of money."

"Yes, I have thought this through very carefully."

"So this isn't one of those charities where everything goes to the leaders?"

I found myself giving her a lecture on the principles of effective altruism, explaining that this was by far the most effective way to spend the money.

ANDRÉ, OCTOBER 17

Today I was going to bring Kant to the City of London. Speaking the truth was an obvious thing to do, but what else did it mean to be a Kantian? While thinking about this question, I kept coming back to a remark one of my students had made in my ethics class: *everyone thinks picking up litter is a duty, yet we leave the job to someone else.* So my Kantian task was to become a rubbish collector.

When I reached the now-familiar spot directly outside the stock exchange, I tried to imagine I was Immanuel Kant going on one of his meticulously timed daily strolls. But instead of planning my next philosophical work, I would do a universally revered good of collecting garbage. I pulled out a black trash sack and began searching for rubbish. There were cigarette butts in every crevice and corner. Once I had cleaned up the small square, I looked around the garden beds. There were hundreds of cigarette butts, crisp packets, and coffee cups ground into the dirt. These were only a tiny proportion of the 6 million cigarette butts dropped in this tiny part of London each year. I didn't want to pick them up, but I forced myself. After all, I was doing my duty. Once I had gotten most of the cigarette butts around the edge of the garden, I extended my sweep.

Every few feet, I found more cigarette butts. Smokers glared at me as I stooped down to pick up the cigarette butts they had just thrown on the ground. I was learning that doing your duty did not necessarily make you popular.

As I reached Liverpool Street, the thing I had been dreading happened: I met two real street cleaners. I tried to keep my head down to avoid their gaze, but it was difficult. I had no idea what Kant would have done in this kind of situation. They looked at me like I was a bad street juggler. I sped up to get away from them as quickly as possible.

A few hundred meters later, I reached the border of the City of London. I was finished with clean-up duty for the day. I certainly didn't feel more moral. But the point with Kant's philosophy was not to *feel* good, but to *do* good. Washing my hands, however, did feel good.

CARL, OCTOBER 17

I was at home reading *Strangers Drowning* by Larissa MacFarquhar. Her book recounted stories about people who had given everything away, sacrificed their lives for the poor, protested against injustice, and been thrown into jail for their trouble. One woman began crying when she received a second-hand DVD player from her partner because it reminded her of the suffering of the workers in Chinese factories. One man was devoted to animal rights, especially the animals that no one else seemed to care about, such as worms. I was particularly moved by the story of Dorothy, an American woman who had relocated to Nicaragua in the mid-1980s to set up a clinic for women. Ten years later, she was under threat. A band of guerilla soldiers wanted her dead because she treated everyone who needed help, including their enemies. Each night, she prepared coffee in case the soldiers showed up. When they finally did, they first tried to rob her. But she had no money. Then they threatened to rape her. But in the end, they didn't. Just as they had left, she remembered the pot of coffee. She ran after them, shouting that she had prepared coffee for them. They thought she was crazy and kept walking.

Inspired by her story, I thought I should go back to basics and become kind. I searched the web and came across a movement called Random Acts of Kindness. As I read through their web forums, I noted down some of their ideas:

Today you are going to treat yourself and talk to yourself with kind-ness and love. Take the time to think of someone who could use your well-wishes and offer them. Try saying "Thank You" at least ten times a day—direct five to yourself and five toward the world.

I was sitting in the kitchen reading through their advice when I looked out the window. A construction worker was in the courtyard of my apartment complex, sawing. I put on my shoes and went down to ask if he wanted some coffee.

"What, me? Thanks so much, but that's not necessary."

"It'd be my pleasure," I said.

He looked stunned.

"Thanks a lot. But no."

I went back up to our flat and read more advice. *Talk to people I've not been in touch with for a long time. Smile at strangers. Pick up someone else's tab in a restaurant.*

I could really do with some practice. Yesterday, my wife had sent a picture from our wedding. What a nice picture, I thought, not con-necting the dots. When she came home from work later that evening, she was disappointed to find out I had missed our wedding anniversary. I was such an idiot.

To rectify my ignorance, I started cleaning the whole house, I did the laundry, then sat down and drew a picture of our wedding photo. It took me a couple of hours. I then went out to buy flowers and a cake, which I left on the table for Sally to find when she came home.

ANDRÉ, OCTOBER 19

As I was looking at my watch, wondering whether I would make it to my lecture on time, a passenger on my train carriage started screaming. "I can't breathe! I can't breathe!" she gasped. She was about seven meters from me on a packed train. At the time, I thought that the distance was great enough to absolve me of any responsibility. But when the people standing closest to her did nothing, my inner Kantian kicked in.

"Is there a doctor on the train?" I yelled.

"I'm a nurse," a woman farther down the carriage replied.

Then a doctor joined her. They took the suffocating woman to the platform, laid her down and called the station staff.

As the train moved away from the platform I felt guilty for not doing enough. What would Kant think of me now?

CARL, OCTOBER 20

I arrived in Uppsala just before nine. It was a crisp autumn morning. The sun was just cutting through the mist. The smell of rotten leaves was all around.

I walked into the clinic. At the end of a long corridor, in a small lab, I found a man in blue medical scrubs.

"Are you Carl?"

"Yes, that's right."

"Here you go," he said and gave me a small plastic cup with a lid. "You may have to wait, because I think all the toilets are occupied." He stood up and walked out the corridor with me. "Check the handicapped toilet," he said.

I went down the corridor. The door was open, and I went in. This was like returning to the masturbation booth. Only this room was brightly lit. It was clean but certainly not very erotic. I took out my cell phone and watched the same short porn film that I had used when first trying out the prostate vibrator. Sitting on the toilet, it took some time to get into the right mood. After finally filling the cup, I walked back and gave it to the doctor.

"You didn't spill anything?"

"No, don't think so."

We sat down and he explained the process. It turned out that, in the event of my sperm making the cut (only 20 percent did), I had to come back thirty times, over the course of one year. He explained that they gave the sperm to lesbian couples and women who wanted to have kids without a man.

As I walked out into the sunlight again, I sent a photo of the toilet to André. "What a beautiful place for a life to start," he responded.

Later in the evening, back in Stockholm, I had dinner with an old friend. I looked around for a table whose tab I could cover. I couldn't bring myself to do it. No one looked like they were worthy. Instead I thought of giving a huge tip—a classic act of random kindness. I ended up paying for the dinner and adding a 50 percent tip. This was not what an effective altruist would do. But I was focusing on kindness now. At first, the waitress looked surprised. Then she said thanks ten times, spinning around, as though she was a figure skater.

The act was meant to make me feel good. But I only felt strange. Was this what it meant to be kind?

ANDRÉ, OCTOBER 21

I woke up this morning relieved that I could step out of the body of Immanuel Kant. I planned to spend the coming week as a utilitarian. That meant trying to do the greatest good for the greatest number. But how should I do that? Give money away to the world's poor? Carl was already doing that. End cruelty to animals? I was already a vegetarian. Maybe I could try comedy? It was meant to increase happiness, and that was what utilitarianism was all about. I knew my own stand-up routine was not good enough to create a surefire utility boost, so I would have to look elsewhere. Maybe I could use someone else's routine? I started looking through lists of the favorite comedy routines in Britain. Monty Python's "Ministry of Silly Walks" popped up. Yes! This is what I should do to increase happiness: restage the "Ministry of Silly Walks."

When I emerged from the tube station at Bank, I pushed my nervousness aside, crossed the street and slowly started the routine outside the austere gray stone entrance to the Bank of England. I flung my legs more wildly with each step as I began the loop around the bank. While my body shuddered along, I kept a deadly serious face. Most passersby looked away. A few laughed. One or two took photos of me from a safe distance.

As I rounded the corner, I focused on my technique. The perfect fling of the leg upward, the ideal crouch, the well-timed lunge. Financiers streamed past. When I came to the far side of the Bank, I passed a fashion shoot. A woman wearing heels and a trench coat walked backward and forward while a photographer snapped photos. Ten people stood behind the photographer laughing at me. One of the assistants took a video on her phone.

When I had completed my loop, I crossed the road and sat down on the bench where I had begun. The whole thing had only taken about fifteen minutes. I was not sure how much happiness I had created in others, but I was overjoyed.

CARL, OCTOBER 21

Last year, almost 163,000 people applied for asylum in Sweden. 50,000 were from Syria; 35,000 of them were unaccompanied children.

Many Swedes had helped out in one way or another. I had done nothing. I remembered a friend had invited two young men from Syria for dinner. He said there was a website called the Invitation Department where you could sign up to do so.

Our guests arrived on time. It was a father and his young son, the same age as Esther. They were not from Syria, it turned out, but from Chile. And they were not refugees. They were not even poor. The man had brought a tasteful bouquet of flowers. He worked as an engineer. His wife was a medical researcher, but couldn't come because she was busy that evening, playing the piano with their daughter. The boy politely said no to dessert, explaining he had already had too much sugar in school.

They were sophisticated intellectuals dressed in Ralph Lauren, who wanted to practice their Swedish. They had no clue they had been invited to dinner as part of my morality project.

I was starting to hate myself.

ANDRÉ, OCTOBER 26.

Tonight, I attended a book launch. There was a long line of people waiting to order drinks at the bar. This was a perfect opportunity to explore the libertarian principles I would live by this week. I jumped right to the front of the line. People in the queue seethed but said nothing. Once I had my drinks, I turned to the people who were actually first in line. "Do you want me to buy you a drink?" I asked. This only made them more annoyed. "I've committed to live as a libertarian for a week," I explained. "Part of my moral code is to offer side payments when I violate other individuals' rights. The drinks would be a side payment for me taking away your right to buy a drink first by being at the front of the line." They accepted my offer. They seemed to find the whole thing rather funny. My week as a libertarian was getting off to a great start.

CARL, OCTOBER 27

This had been the worst month since June. Living as an effective altruist had made me depressed. All I had managed to do was to save up money to give to charity. Maybe that was an effective way to do good, but it sure wasn't exciting. I was also struggling to accept the philosophical principles behind utilitarianism. Privileging the needs of family and friends was seen as a pernicious impulse. But without my family and friends, I'd have little else to live for.

Trying to be kind was not much easier. I downloaded several apps, such as Good Deeds and the Kindness Challenge, offering advice on how to be kind. But I hated the tone and vocabulary. It was hideous—like being trapped in an endless Oprah Winfrey show.

A close friend of my family was dying, and last week I had visited her for the final time. When I bought flowers, I was thinking that this was precisely what the kindness apps had suggested. But I was sickened by the thought that I had gone to see my dying friend as part of a kindness project. Death was not a fucking project. Nor was morality.

ANDRÉ, OCTOBER 30

My plan was to try to walk from one end of Oxford Street to the other in a straight line. Like a good libertarian, I would assert my individual rights by not getting out of the way for anyone. I knew this would be hard, so I tried the NLP technique again and imagined stepping into the body of a libertarian. I was wearing a business suit on a Sunday. That certainly helped.

After taking my first steps, I crashed into a few shoulders. Maintaining my straight line got harder when I came to a large group of Italian teenagers. They refused to move. I stood in front of their circle as they talked. Soon they stared at me, impassively. I tried to move them aside using only a parting gesture made with my hands. They stared back at me. Eventually they parted, looking at me with a mixture of anger and confusion. I continued on my way, shouldering aside other groups of people. Then, directly in front of me, loomed a family who were out shopping. I couldn't bring myself to charge directly through them. I stepped around them and then returned to the straight line. Being selfish was harder than I had imagined.

When I got to the end of Oxford Street, I felt relieved. Then I realized that Speakers' Corner was close by. I hadn't been there since delivering my asshole speech back at the beginning of April. I decided to stop by again. The place hadn't changed. A crowd of 200 people stood around listening to religious and political nutters. I headed straight for the closest speaker: a large African evangelical Christian.

"Can I pay you to stop talking?" I asked him.

"You cannot use money to stop the word of the Lord," he bellowed back. "But I bless you, my brother," he added, holding out his hand for me to shake.

I moved on to the speaker with the largest crowd surrounding him. His topic was some indecipherable conspiracy theory.

"Can I pay you to stop speaking?" I asked, holding out a handful of cash.

"How much?" he asked.

"Name your price," I replied.

"Ten quid."

I handed him a crumpled note and he stood down. The crowd applauded. I felt like my libertarian cash was well spent.

Following this minor triumph, I headed back to Oxford Street. I cut a straight line down the pavement. This led me directly into a group of insecure teenagers and through a group of old men who instantly moved aside. As long as I didn't accelerate into people, they would move. If I bumped into someone, they usually thought it was their fault. During these small confrontations, I saw people's dignity crushed.

CARL, OCTOBER 31

I read about a couple that regularly performed random acts of kindness. One of them was to hide wallets for people to find. When the stranger opened the wallet, they'd find a ten-dollar note along with an inspiring message instructing them to pass on the good deed.

I decided to replicate the act, but instead of wallets, I bought two glittery gift boxes and put a five-hundred-krona bill ($57) inside each of them along with handwritten notes. I couldn't bring myself to write anything "inspirational." Instead, I just wrote "here's some money for you to do what you want with."

I went down to a big square and left one of the boxes on top of a garbage bin. I hung around, watching to see if someone would pick it up. Fifteen minutes later, feeling bored, I went off to the university, where I left another box on top of a garbage bin. Everyone passed the box by. After a while I picked it up myself, and placed it, half open, on a café table. I stayed within sight but no one picked it up. Twenty minutes later I had grown tired of waiting. I left the box where it was and headed back home. It felt like a suitable ending to a month that had felt like a failure from start to end. Sure, I had saved a lot of money—enough to save a person's life, according to the equations devised by the effective altruists. But I had not donated the money yet. It was still just resting in my account.

After I got back home I noticed that I had a voice message from the sperm clinic. My sperm had not passed the test. I put away my phone and threw myself on the couch, feeling defeated.

ANDRÉ, OCTOBER 31

It was approaching rush hour when I boarded a tube train heading for central London. I looked around the carriage, spotted a woman in her twenties, and walked up to her.

"Excuse me," I said. "How much would it cost to buy your seat?"

She looked at me, shocked.

"You can have it for free," she said.

"But I want to pay for your inconvenience."

She shook her head.

"I insist," I said, as I pulled a wad of cash out of my pocket.

Eventually she took two pounds. "It's okay," she said, pocketing the coins. "I'm getting off at the next stop."

At the next stop, I moved carriages. When the train was moving again, I approached a kind-looking man and asked to buy his seat. "You can have it for free," he said, "I'm getting off at the next stop anyway."

I repeated this same procedure for ten stops, all the way to Tottenham Court Road, right in the center of London. Most people took a few pounds, particularly when I was especially forceful. Two people simply insisted on giving me their seats for free.

On the way back, the carriages were packed. I looked for difficult targets: angry-looking businessmen who had just finished a grueling day in the office. When I proposed my offer to one, he snapped back "I want my seat." Another angry businessman wanted to bargain. When the price was over £30, he told me he would keep his seat. "You're the only person who has tried haggling over the price," I said. A hint of happiness appeared on his sour face.

Later that evening, I walked into the BBC to do a radio interview When I was sitting in the studio, I pulled out a cigar, a bottle of whiskey, and a glass. Fortunately, the interviewer was not in the same studio, so I lit up my cigar and sipped my whiskey as I talked. It was probably the most pleasant radio interview I had ever done.

When I got on the tube to head home, there were plenty of seats. But I thought I should give my libertarian experiment one last try. A young man sat opposite me.

"Can I buy your seat?" I asked.

"Sure," he replied without blinking.

"How much do you want?"

"A tenner."

I handed over the cash and we began to talk. He was a musician from Poland, he told me. He'd come to London to be a rock star, but at the moment he worked as a waiter. I gave him some of my remaining whiskey and we started swapping stories. It seems that life as a libertarian was fun. It was certainly more amusing than picking up bankers' cigarette butts.

NOVEMBER

ATTENTION

ANDRÉ, NOVEMBER 1

According to Christopher Lasch's classic book, *The Culture of Narcissism*, self-improvement is part of our desperate search for attention. It seemed the project would not be complete without exploring this aspect of self-improvement culture. As I ran around the park this morning, I wondered how this might be possible. The obvious answer was to work on my existing public profile by gaining more Twitter followers and more exposure in the news. But it seemed boring. I wanted a greater challenge. Maybe I should create a new identity and see if I could become famous with it.

By the end of my run, I had come up with the outlines of a new me. He would be an image-obsessed self-help junkie with no self-awareness or impulse control. I gave my new character the name Lucian Luper.

When I texted Carl to introduce him to Lucian, it turned out that Carl was looking for a new identity too. As we sent messages back and forth, I started using emojis. I had always hated these symbols. But Lucian loved them. My screen filled up with smiley faces and sushi symbols.

When I returned home, I began setting up Lucian's digital identity. The first step was creating a new email account: lucian.luper@gmail.com. I could then use my new email address to set up Twitter (@lucian_luper), Facebook, Instagram accounts, and a YouTube channel.

I even registered a new website for Lucian—www.lucianluper.com. The entire process of creating a new digital identity took me less than an hour.

CARL, NOVEMBER 1

Even though I lived in a society obsessed with appearances, I rarely thought about my own. This would change now, as I set out to attract attention through improving my looks. My mission was to become a hunk by the time this month was finished.

I had done some preparatory work. A month back, I started another training plan designed to put on as much muscle mass as possible. My personal trainers had recommended a program called Max Overload Training, which, according to the AST Sport Science website, "will accelerate muscle growth and strength faster than any other training method." The website offered a day-by-day training schedule, which I had followed religiously.

The training had paid off. I was eighty-three kilograms when I started the program in October, and now I was eighty-eight kilograms.

On my way back from the gym, I stopped by an electronics shop and bought a selfie stick with Bluetooth connectivity. I then went home, undressed, and started to take photos of myself. I tried different positions, rooms, and lighting, but the results weren't great. My abs were still hard to discern, and despite all the training, my chest muscles were not noticeably larger.

I downloaded an app called Selfie Gym Photo Editor, but adding fake abs to my shirtless selfies turned out to be difficult. They looked anything but real.

I signed up to Instagram with my new name: James Shelley. I had found a research article called "The Attractiveness of Names" that explained why some names were perceived as more attractive than others. Attractive names, I learned, combined common first names, such as James and John, with relatively rare surnames, such as Shelley, Cassel, or Burton.

I uploaded my profile picture and began adding people to follow: Kim Kardashian (about 90 million followers), Nicki Minaj (70 million), Katy Perry (60 million), Justin Timberlake (40 million), Justin Bieber (80 million) and Cristiano Ronaldo (90 million). I was hypnotized when flicking through the half-nude pictures of Cristiano Ronaldo. This was what I wanted to look like. He would be my aesthetic role model for the month.

Feeling inspired, I selected one of the fifty selfies I had taken earlier in the day, adjusted the contrast and light, and uploaded my first shirtless selfie onto Instagram. I didn't look much like Cristiano Ronaldo, but there was still plenty of time to do something about that.

ANDRÉ, NOVEMBER 3

I had always felt embarrassed about taking selfies. But it seemed that I was in the minority. There are 250 million photos tagged #selfie on Instagram. Every year, over 240 billion selfies are posted onto Google's servers. And that was only a fraction of the actual number of selfies that are uploaded annually.

But maybe my hesitance was well-founded. A study published in *Social Psychological and Personality Science* found that selfie takers tended to overestimate their attractiveness and likability. Selfie snapping could even endanger your life. In recent years, more people had been killed taking selfies than in shark attacks. But if I wanted to become Lucian Luper, I needed to take these risks.

I began my journey into digital narcissism by taking a photo of my breakfast, or rather Lucian's breakfast, and uploaded it to Facebook. I then walked out the door with the aim of taking as many selfies as possible. A phone booth became a selfie booth, passersby looking on with pity as I snapped away.

After about twenty minutes of my selfie-stroll, I witnessed the aftermath of a road accident. A man had been hit by an SUV. He lay on the road, convulsing. The emergency services had just arrived. Lucian wanted to take a selfie with the accident in the background, so as the ambulance crew rushed in, Lucian got into position. But as much as NLP had taught me about how to step into another character, I just couldn't take things this far. There were some boundaries I couldn't cross, even as Lucian.

CARL, NOVEMBER 4

At the start of this year, I was absent from all social media. Now I was on Facebook, Twitter, LinkedIn, and Instagram. I learned that among the 400 million active Instagram users, I belonged to the marginal category of people who were over thirty-five years old, who made up only 10 percent of Instagram users. I quickly started following more than five hundred people but only a handful of them followed me back. I found a guide on *Forbes* explaining that, to gain followers, I needed to use the right hashtags, such as #instafollow, #likeforlike, #follow4follow, and I had to like other people's profiles.

I browsed through #gymselfies, #abs, and #crossfit and liked all the people who offered to like me back. I scrolled through thousands of pictures of shirtless men in the gym and women taking photos of their butts. The line between porn and exercise seemed rather blurry. Flicking down the list of photos, I clicked like on all of them, except the photos of undernourished teenage girls in small sports bras, which made my heart sink.

This was the culture of narcissism I often worried about as my daughter was getting older. Now I was part of it myself, mindlessly showering likes on insecure people who craved attention. But I was determined to fully immerse myself in this world, if only to experience the effects myself.

The first thing I wanted to do was to examine my own appearance closely. I uploaded a selfie on prettyscale.com, which promised to assess my face using artificial intelligence. It rated me as 78 percent pretty and listed my prominent features: long face, small forehead, good interlocutor distance, and good nose for face. I went through the same procedure, using another site. This time I was rated only 47 percent attractive.

But I was more interested in what real people had to say about my appearance. I found many sites, such as ratemybody.com, ratemyface.com, and hotornot.com, but they all seemed to have closed down in the last few years. Maybe they had all gone out of business after Instagram was launched in 2010 and cornered the narcissism market. The only rating site that still seemed to be active was a subcategory on Reddit called rate-my-appearance. I posted a series of selfies and asked the users to offer honest feedback and constructive ideas about how I could improve my looks.

Later that evening, I had received a few comments.

Average to cute 6/10
5.5 Average, I don't think you need to change anything for looks, but if you just want a change up for yourself try a diff hairstyle, but once again imo not needed.

7.5/10 You're kinda my type
What you could change is maybe try a modern haircut with short sides and long top? and maybe in addition to that try a short beard? that's just my suggestion though - the possibilities are infinite, just try out what can be tried out and stick with what you like the most

ANDRÉ, NOVEMBER 4

"You should create a media scandal," Carl suggested as we spoke on the phone. "Maybe Lucian could die."

Carl was starting to get excited.

"Oh, now I've got it," he continued. "Cancer! Lucian is dying of cancer. And then he blogs about it."

I went silent.

"That's what Belle Gibson did."

"Who?"

"Belle Gibson. The wellness blogger. She faked cancer, then wrote a book about how to cure it with alternative medicine."

"Carl, I'm not going to fake cancer."

"Okay, but you should create some kind of scandal. Have you read Laura Kipnis's book?"

"No. Which one?"

"*How to Become a Scandal.* You should find some inspiration there."

After we hung up I found a review of the book in the *New York Times.* I read about Lisa Nowak, an "astronaut who put on a wig and pepper-sprayed her ex-boyfriend's new lover." I could tell that all Carl wanted was for Lucian to go mad and create a scandal, but I felt ill at ease about that. I'd had enough of humiliation.

CARL, NOVEMBER 7

"Fuck yes!" I screamed.

"What?" my PT shouted from the other side of the room. He came up to me, coffee in hand.

"Look!" I said, pointing at my computer. He leaned over the screen.

"90.7. Shit! What did you start at?"

"77.6," I said.

"Wow, that's thirteen kilograms then."

Since the start of the year, I had gained more than ten kilograms of muscles. But the sacrifices had been considerable. During the last five weeks, I had eaten an excess of 5,000 calories a day. I was using a weight-gaining powder called Mutant, which contained 2,900 calories and 114 grams of protein. On the back of the package it read: *LEAVE HUMANITY BEHIND.* I drank two liters of this sludge every day. Every time I drank it, I was on the brink of throwing up. But now, having broken the ninety-kilogram barrier, I felt it was totally worth it.

ANDRÉ, NOVEMBER 9

Trump had won the election. Even Lucian was devastated. On my way into work I lay down on the pavement and pretended to be dead. I took a selfie, and uploaded it to Facebook under the cover of Lucian Luper.

CARL, NOVEMBER 9

As I was doing my second set of bench presses, I thought about Christopher Lasch's claim that, in the early 1970s, as people lost hope in improving the world politically, they retreated into self-improvement.

It was no small irony that our year of self-improvement was also the year when both Britain and USA had fallen apart politically.

The gym was quiet and empty. It was the perfect place to forget about the troubles of the world. After a long shower, I took a few selfies in the mirror and posted them on Instagram.

ANDRÉ, NOVEMBER 10

Carl's suggestion that I should create a scandal had freaked me out. I was putting Lucian on hold for the time being and going back to my own personal brand.

To help me rebrand myself, I consulted my colleague Tom. He was an expert in using stories to create a brand. His office was just down the hall from mine, but it was much more orderly. "I need help," I said with a slight tone of desperation. "I want to build my personal brand. You're the expert. What should I do?"

Tom pulled up a PowerPoint slide on one of his two large computer screens on his desk. "Here's a list of things you should do to build up your personal brand." He ran down a list of questions. "First, you need to work out what your objective is. Is it click-throughs, likes on Facebook, something else?"

"I have no idea," I said, "I guess I need to work that out."

"Next, who is your audience? What do they want, what are their problems?"

This question was so basic, and yet I had no clue. "I guess I need to think about that, too," I said.

"Once you have figured out who your audience is, you have to define which platforms they use."

"Mm-hm," I said as I wrote this down in my notebook.

"Then what are you going to tell them? What is the gap of information they might have?"

This was going to be hard, I now realized. I had no idea what I wanted to achieve. I didn't know who the audience was or what my message would be. There was work to be done.

CARL, NOVEMBER 10

I was waiting in the clinic. Everything was painted white and had an air of luxury. The two women behind the counter were blond and good looking, wearing white coats. I felt as though I was trapped in a sci-fi movie. Soon the dermatologist came out and led me into her office.

She was probably my age. Her face was perfectly smooth and I could tell her lips had been surgically enhanced.

"So what can I do for you?"

"I was going to ask the same question," I said. "I just wanted to explore the possibilities of improving my appearance. What could I do?"

"Okay, shall we move to the mirror?" she said and left her desk.

I looked at my face in the mirror, feeling detached as always.

"You have a very boyish face," she said.

"Yes, true."

"Maybe we should try and enhance your manly features. Like George Clooney."

I had been thinking about Cristiano Ronaldo as my inspiration, but Clooney sounded good, too.

"Either we could try and enhance your cheekbones."

"Mm-hm. Yes."

"Or, we could try to enhance your chin line. Make it broader, and more distinct."

"How?"

"Fillers. It's called Restylane."

I was nervous now. I had expected to erase a wrinkle or two. Not mess with my basic features. Yet I realized that this was probably going to be much more effective if I was serious about improving my looks.

"How much would it cost?"

"The cheekbone would be between $1,500 and $2,000. The chin line would be $2,800."

"Okay. That's more than I expected," I said.

I had not yet sent the money to the malaria charity, as planned. What if I used it on plastic surgery instead?

"Let's go for the chin line," I heard myself saying.

Five minutes later I was lying in a chair, and the dermatologist rubbed my face with a special cream. I could hear her talking to me, but I had switched off.

Are you doing this because you want to? The words from the yoga instructor came back to me.

As the anesthetic set in, she took out a needle and started injecting the seven milliliters of Restylane. I had no idea what that was or whether seven milliliters was a lot. All I could think about was that I was going to pick up my daughter at school in two hours and I would be walking in with a new chin line, quite possibly looking like a cartoon character.

"This might hurt a bit," she said. I could feel the needle piercing my chin, starting from the ear, and then, step-by-step, with about a centimeter's intervals, moving down to the tip of my chin. I was in some kind of existential shock. What was this project doing to me? I had just agreed to spend $2,800 on a new chin line, instead of saving a human being.

Twenty minutes later, she was done. I looked at myself in the mirror.

"Wow, you look really good," the dermatologist said and took out a camera.

I studied my face in the mirror. My jaw was bigger now. I looked different.

"Can I take your photo?" she asked.

"Sure."

After taking a few snaps, she emerged from behind the camera.

"You will need to come in again in about two weeks, so we can check if everything is okay."

"Sure."

"And don't touch your chin for the first few days. No gym, no drinking."

"Okay."

"And one more thing, you might have some pain during the first two days, and there might be some bruises. But that will disappear."

"Okay," I said as I collected my bag and made for the exit.

Later in the evening, Sally came home from work. She was asking me about my day. I said it had been okay.

"You don't see anything special?" I asked.

"No?"

"I've been to the clinic."

"What have you done?"

"A new chin line. Can't you see?"

"No. What?"

I had just spent a month's salary on a new chin line, and my wife hadn't noticed a thing.

ANDRÉ, NOVEMBER 14

At around 3:00 p.m., I walked into Tom's office again. After exchanging pleasantries, I opened my laptop and began running through a lengthy PowerPoint presentation on my new personal branding story.

"I'm going to become a self-improvement guru on YouTube," I said. "I will make a video blog giving self-help advice to people who would usually not touch self-help culture with a barge pole."

Tom sat in his large office chair, stroking his well-trimmed goatee, listening to my pitch.

"You need to dramatize your brand a little more," he said. "Make it into a gripping story. Maybe you are not the hero of this story. Perhaps you are the guide."

I made a note.

"Also, you need to develop a better account of what the typical self-help vlog looks like. What will yours look like?"

"Well, I've watched a few vlogs of other self-help experts on YouTube who have hundreds of thousands of followers," I explained. "And they followed a pretty standard story line: they had ostensibly great lives but felt that something was missing, so they got into self-help, and after a struggle, they became a better person. Now they wanted to share what they had learned with the world."

"Are you going to tell that kind of story?" Tom asked.

"I'm not sure," I replied.

After walking out of Tom's office, I felt more confused than ever. What was my story? Was it any good? And who was my audience?

CARL, NOVEMBER 14

It was time to start getting ripped. I had gained ten kilos of muscle, but what was the point if they weren't visible? I had to remove the layers of fat.

"Do you think I will ever get decent abs?" I asked my PT.

"Try doing this," he said, as he pulled up his shirt and pulled his skin taut, so that his abs became visible. I did the same. He looked at me.

"Well, maybe. You have to get rid of the fat now."

I had found myself reading more and more men's magazines and blogs. Ripping was a central topic. They all gave the same advice: only eat protein. A fashion model on YouTube described how he did it before every photo shoot. Starting two weeks in advance, he would only eat protein. Fish and meat and chicken. And only green leaves. Especially spinach. This would amount to about 500 calories a day. That meant I was going to cut my calorie intake by 90 percent. It seemed harsh, but I was also happy to finally stop force-feeding myself.

I consulted my personal trainers, and we agreed I should carry on working out as normal, but using lighter weights and putting more focus on my abs and my chest muscles.

After the gym, I went to one of the most expensive hairdressers in town.

"So what can I do?" the stylist asked.

"You can do whatever you want. I want to walk out of here and feel like I'm a new person."

"Okay. Mm-hmm. I think I'd like to make your hair darker."

"Fine. Sounds good to me."

"And then, hmm, cut it down quite a lot, shorter on the sides."

"What about my eyebrows?"

"Yes, I can make them darker, too."

Two hours later, I walked out on the street $300 poorer. It was a big difference though. A complete makeover. I posted before and after pictures on Instagram, then went to do some shopping at our local supermarket. As I was putting some food in the basket, I heard someone giggling behind me. I twisted around and saw Esther and Sally, pointing at me, laughing. Clearly, they found my new look amusing.

ANDRÉ, NOVEMBER 17

Delivery vans and bicycles passed me on the grimy street as I tried to dream up self-help slogans. I stopped at an electrical box on the side of the road, fished my notebook out of my bag, and started taking notes. "Unique Selling Point," I wrote down in capital letters. "Whatever self-help says, I say the opposite." I then added some more lines below:

Self-help says: be yourself. I say: be someone else.

Self-help says: you can change in an instant. I say: it only happens incrementally.

Self-help says: change your mind-set. I say: change your do-set.

During the previous week, I had been preparing myself to become a YouTube self-help guru. The video sharing platform seemed like the perfect medium to get my message out. It was growing fast, with 42 percent of Internet users saying they had watched at least one vlog in the last month. Some popular YouTubers like Zoella (an English woman who filmed herself applying makeup and had 11 million followers) and PewDiePie (a Swedish man who shared videos of himself playing computer games and had 37 million followers) were more well-known among teenagers than mainstream celebrities like Johnny Depp.

Hoping to get a slice of the action, I studied articles with titles "Blogging with Video, How to Go Viral." Following their advice, I had acquired a decent quality camera with a tripod. Equipment in place, I'd been working on my delivery, trying to be personal and tread the fine line between awkward silence and overacting. Heeding the advice that videos worked best when they focused on solving immediate practical problems, I had given each planned episode titles like "How to Be More Productive." I would build up a bank of videos so I could post regularly. Finally, I would limit the length of each of my episodes to below five minutes, trying to grab the audience in the first fifteen seconds.

I had gone on to write ten episodes, each offering tips and techniques for improving the body, personal productivity, the mind, and so on. My newfound slogans would be the cherry on the cake! It was surprising how easily I slipped into my role as a budding self-improvement thought leader.

CARL, NOVEMBER 18

Sally and Esther were in Copenhagen, and I was going on a twenty-four-hour cruise to Finland with my friend Christian.

In the evening, two women in their forties approached us in the bar. They were both single mothers, and they had gone on the cruise to have some "me time."

"Can you see that he's had plastic surgery?" Christian asked them, pointing at my face.

"Really?" one of the mothers said. She had a fringe and long red hair all the way down to her small waist.

"Yes, here," Christian said, and drew a line with his finger along my jaw.

We sat down together by the side of the dance floor with a bottle of prosecco.

"I've also had plastic surgery," one of the women said.

"Really?"

"Yes. Give me your hand."

She guided it under her blouse.

"They're filled with saline. Can you feel?"

"Really?" I said. "How much did they cost?"

"Four thousand dollars."

"Not bad. My chin was $2,800."

We seemed connected somehow. She then started to show her tattoos.

"I have more tattoos."

"Really? Where?" I asked.

"That's for me to know and for you to find out," she said, and gave me a long, meaningful look.

The DJ was playing Chubby Checker: *Come on, let's twist again like we did last summer.* Christian stood up from the table, clapped his hands over his head, and sang along as loud as he could. He was twisting his hips, and we joined him.

The music stopped and the club started emptying out for the night. A few drunk men staggered around the dance floor. We bought another bottle of prosecco and retreated to our cabin.

"Carl is trying to improve his appearance," Christian explained. "Do you think he looks good?"

The woman with the secret tattoos was lying in one of the beds, sizing me up.

"He's fuckable," she said.

They left soon afterward. I wasn't interested in fucking, but I was glad to have received some kind of confirmation.

ANDRÉ, NOVEMBER 18

I set up the tripod, attached the video camera, and switched it on. I was standing in my office against a wall of books, wearing a black turtleneck, black jacket, black trousers, and black boots. This was going to be the classic intellectual money shot. I hit record and spoke straight into the camera, gesticulating like a mash-up of Tony Robbins and Slavoj Žižek.

Meanwhile, across the atrium in my boss's office, a series of meetings ground on. They could all see me from there as I stood alone in my room, waving my arms around in front of the camera. What were they thinking? I would rather not know.

CARL, NOVEMBER 22

I was back at the clinic to take more photos.

When I came here the first time two weeks ago, I knew nothing about plastic surgery. I had now read up on the subject. According to the Plastic Surgery Statistics Report, 15.9 million cosmetic procedures were done in 2015 in the US, a 115 percent increase since 2000. Close to 90 percent were "minimally invasive procedures," such as fillers and Botox. The strongest growing trend was facial rejuvenation, with more than 6.7 million injections of the kind I had received. As a man, I was in the minority, since we accounted for only 8 percent of all cosmetic procedures. I'd also learned that plastic surgery can change more than just your appearance. I was particularly fascinated with one experiment that found that prisoners in Texas who were given plastic surgery while incarcerated were far less likely to a commit a crime once they were released. Would my new look change my behavior as well?

I had also learned that seven milliliters of Restylane was quite a lot. The dermatologist showed me the pictures on her computer. The difference between before and after was undeniable.

"The Restylane will disappear in about six months, so if you want to continue doing this you need to make a new appointment in, let's see . . ."

"I'll get in touch if that's the case," I interrupted.

"Yes, of course."

"But I have to say I'm rather impressed by the work you've done." I pointed at the computer screen. "Maybe you could send me those pictures?"

"Of course," she said, smiling.

In the tube, on my way back, I uploaded the two pictures on Instagram, side by side, with a bunch of hashtags: #restylane #plasticsurgery #beforeandafter #likeme #georgeclooney. Instantly, likes from unknown people started to pour in. *Very good*, one follower said. *Keep going*, added another. Clearly, this was the kind of post that attracted attention on Instagram.

ANDRÉ, NOVEMBER 22

I passed the old insane asylum, which was being converted into upmarket apartments, and walked through the cemetery gates. In front of the first row of graves, I set up the camera and hit record. Halfway through my first take, I forgot my lines. I paused, I took a deep breath, and then I started all over. With each take, the shots were improving. In one, I crouched among four graves. In another, I had a gravestone bearing the words "rest in peace" in the background. In a third, I leaned against a tree, my elbows spread out like an arrogant history professor appearing in his own television series.

Just as I was really hitting my stride, the battery of the camera gave out. I headed home, feeling excited about the prospect of watching the film I had made. After downloading all the material from my camera, I opened iMovie, pieced together each of the clips, then watched it through. The cemetery setting was perfect, and my delivery wasn't too bad.

The phone rang. It was Carl.

"I'm making really good progress with the filming," I told him. "And I've come up with a great title for my channel: Self-Help from the Cemetery."

I could tell something was up. He sounded edgy.

"What's wrong?" I asked.

"Aren't you worried that your self-help show could get confused with our entire book?" he replied. "I mean, we didn't start this whole project to end up offering self-improvement advice ourselves on YouTube."

"What do you mean?"

I was starting to get annoyed.

"I thought this project was supposed to be a critical diagnosis of the self-improvement industry. And now you're becoming a self-help guru yourself."

"But that's not true! I'm saying you should do the opposite of what self-help tells you," I said.

Carl was silent, then replied: "Look, do what you want, but don't attach my name to it."

He hung up.

I was really angry now, but a few hours later I started to wonder whether this whole idea of becoming a self-help guru was an awful mistake.

CARL, NOVEMBER 23

I applied the gel on the two plastic trays and inserted them into my mouth, like a boxer preparing for a match. Last week, I had gone to my dentist and made an imprint of my teeth. I had to sleep with them in for five nights to achieve a significant result. As the trays were in place, I looked at myself in the mirror and smiled. The sight was anything but pleasant.

Sally was already in bed reading. I lay down next to her.

"Do you have any plans for tomorrow?" she asked, her eyes fixed on the book.

I tried to reply, but I couldn't speak.

"What's that?" she asked, and looked my way.

I smiled now, showing her my teeth.

"Fucking hell, Carl!" she said, and turned off the lights. I turned to the side and tried to relax. But it was impossible to ignore the trays in my mouth. This would not be a night of quiet beauty sleep.

ANDRÉ, NOVEMBER 23

I sat on the couch staring at cartoons on TV. After my conversation with Carl yesterday, my attempts to become a self-help vlogger were over. I had nothing to say. Nothing. Then it came to me. Why not make a spectacle out of saying nothing? Almost all YouTube videos had people saying a lot. But what about a film in which I would say nothing? It seemed to fit my mood, and our times. What can you say when you are faced with a year like 2016? All words seem to be clichés. They only added to the rubble of history.

CARL, NOVEMBER 24

I had stopped the Max Overload Training and gone back to CrossFit again. I didn't have enough energy to train by myself. I needed others to help get me through it. I had been on my new 500 calories a day diet of protein and green leaves for ten days. I had already lost four kilos. My energy was gone. I felt drained. Besides, André was angry with me. He wanted to make a series of self-help videos, one for each month of the year, covering the same areas we had covered for the project. When I said people might confuse the project with an ordinary self-help book, he got pissed off. And so did I. I was sick and tired of his complaining. He could do whatever he wanted. I didn't care anymore.

The good news was that my body was finally getting into shape, and I was putting more pictures on Instagram and paying more attention to hashtags and descriptions. After an intense CrossFit session, I took a close-up of sweat pouring down my chest.

I love pure crossfit sweat. Je suis crossfit! #crossfitsweat
#sweat #crossfit
#instabeautiful #aftergym #sweatybetty
#like4like #like4follow #follow4follow
#followforfollow #followback #followme #loveya

Goood mooorning gracious world. Nothing beats the 06:00 Crossfit
#crossfit #motivation #inspiration #belikeme #likeme #you #like4like
#follow4follow #me #awesome

I followed more than 2,000 people. Yet, despite doing so, no more than 300 people followed me. I had to do something about the situation. I found a website from which I bought 10,000 followers for sixty-two dollars. When I received a confirmation of my order, it said it could take up to seven days for the order to be completed. Fuck! At that point, the month might already be over.

ANDRÉ, NOVEMBER 24

This morning, I felt inspired. I was going to make films of myself saying nothing. After all, silence was cool. A book called *Quiet: The Power of Introverts in a World That Can't Stop Talking* had been at the top of the best-seller lists this year. And I often read how mindfulness had lost popularity in favor of retreats where people would spend ten days saying nothing. But ten days seemed like a bit much. For my purposes, five minutes would be enough. Then I was reminded of the most famous use of "silence" in art: John Cage's "4'33"."

I decided to make a film of my own silence, which would last for four minutes and thirty-three seconds. I headed to Embankment Station in central London and set up my camera on a pedestrian bridge that crossed the Thames. The wind ruffled my hair. When a group of school students approached, I heard one of the parents muttering under their breath: "Why is that guy refusing to move for us!" Once I had done my four minutes and thirty-three seconds, I hit stop and moved on. The parents leading the school group said "thank you" in a passive aggressive tone. I spent the whole day recording myself at various places: Trafalgar Square, Piccadilly Circus, Liverpool Street Station.

Back home, I viewed my chunks of silence. I became transfixed. By diving into narcissism, it seemed I had come out the other side. Putting myself front and center made me irrelevant. In every video the background was more important than me. Pedestrians walking through a tunnel, a huge poster with a Caravaggio painting, massive flashing Coke signs, they all said more than I did. I had discovered that a selfie that is four minutes and thirty-three seconds long is no longer about the self.

CARL, NOVEMBER 25

I arrived at the Body Company at noon and waited in their white-painted lobby before entering a small room.

"Do you mind if I take some selfies?" I asked.

"Go ahead," she said, as though she was used to that question. "This won't take long."

"Do you usually get hairier types?"

"Yes."

"Am I the least hairy person you've ever waxed?"

She was silent for a second, thinking, looking at my chest and stomach. "Er, I think so, yes."

Less than ten minutes later my chest and stomach were stripped clean of all hair, and I felt like a baby.

"Now I'm going to tan myself," I said as I was putting on my shirt.

"That may not be a very good idea."

"No?"

"You're supposed to rest for a few days."

"But with this little hair?" I tried.

"Maybe . . ."

I walked down a few blocks to the next beauty salon. I announced my arrival in the reception and was escorted by a woman down a flight of steep stairs into a rough basement and a small room with intense lighting and cracked walls. At the end of the room was a small plastic tent, large enough for a person to stand in. I stripped down to my underwear and stepped into the tent.

"Ready?" asked the woman.

"Just one thing," I said, and went to my bag and took out a selfie stick. "Do you mind if I film myself?"

"As long as I'm not in the film," the woman replied.

The selfie stick failed to connect to my phone, and the woman was getting impatient.

"I could film you instead," she said, and took my phone. She then started spraying my body.

Ten minutes later, she was done My body was golden brown. She set a timer for five minutes and left me in the small basement room. I stood in front of a fan, trying to dry myself. When the timer beeped, I got dressed and went up to pay.

"You mustn't get any water on your face," the woman told me, looking outside. Rain was pouring down.

I hid under my jacket and moved through the crowded street. It was a Friday afternoon, and people were getting off work. I took shelter in the food court of a nearby mall. A new seafood place had just opened. I ordered two oysters and a glass of prosecco, and uploaded a close-up of my meal on Instagram along with the pictures from the tan and waxing salons.

An hour or so later, the rain had eased, and I went to pick up Esther from school. I felt awkward when greeting her teacher. I had a new jaw, new hair color, and now a new bronzed face at the end of November, a time when most Swedes were paler than ever.

ANDRÉ, NOVEMBER 25

I spent the morning editing my selfie films and uploading them onto a channel I had created on YouTube—FourThirtyThreeSelfie.

As I waited, I flicked through my Facebook feed, noticing a story on a British model called Iskra Lawrence. She had boarded a subway train in New York, taken off her clothes and given a speech about positive body image. The film had been shared hundreds of thousands of times on social media. What would happen if I did the same thing? Could that be enough to create the sort of scandal Carl had suggested at the beginning of the month?

CARL, NOVEMBER 26

Esther and I dressed up in our nicest clothes and went to an expensive restaurant. It was Saturday and we wanted to spoil ourselves. I ordered oysters and white wine and Esther had a burger and a Coke. I took photos of our food and posted them on Instagram. When I went to pay the tab, I realized they had not charged us for the drinks. I pointed out the oversight to the bartender. He smiled. It was no mistake. Was this the kind of royal treatment you got when you dressed up, took photos of your food and posted them on Instagram?

ANDRÉ, NOVEMBER 26

At 9:00 p.m., my friend Barbara appeared out of a crowd of drunk football fans at Liverpool Street Station. I explained to her what I intended to do. She was very matter of fact about the logistics. I guess that was the result of years working as a performance artist.

We got onto a Circle Line train. Small groups of people sat quietly along the carriages. After passing through five carriages, we came to a halt in front of a group of four sixty-year-olds who looked like they were on their way to the theatre.

As we left Monument Station, I stepped forward and began: "Hi— you don't know me and I don't know you, but I would like to connect with you today." The audience started to laugh as soon as I dropped my trousers. I repeated word-for-word what Iskra Lawrence had said in the New York subway. As I came to the end of my speech, a young woman began clapping. The other passengers soon followed.

When we jumped off at the next stop, I felt elated. Like I had just pulled off a heist. Barbara played back the video she had shot. I broke into uncontrollable, nervous laughter.

When I got home, Carl called asking how it had gone, and more importantly, what I was going to do with my film. "Let's make it go viral," he suggested.

"Sure."

"I mentioned your plan to a media guru I know. He said you should put it online with the title 'Professor Strips Naked on Subway.'"

"Okay." I said.

I uploaded the film onto YouTube. It was surprisingly easy to make a mad act like this go public.

CARL, NOVEMBER 28

Today was my big day: the photo shoot. I arrived early at the gym. My personal trainer was there. He was in a good mood.

I stepped on the scale and noticed I was down to eighty-five kilograms. I had lost six kilos in two weeks. I was ripped now. You could actually discern my abs and chest muscles. I was still far from the #gymselfies I saw on Instagram, but what I had achieved required two months

DESPERATELY SEEKING SELF-IMPROVEMENT   315

of extremely hard work: first, six weeks of binge-eating 5,000 calories a day and a five-day-a-week Max Overload Training program, and then two weeks of eating no more than 500 calories, focusing on cardio and CrossFit.

The photographer arrived with his equipment and a flash larger than life. We carried on for at least an hour, taking photos, trying different angles and lights to enhance my body. I had sent a photo of Cristiano Ronaldo to the photographer beforehand, for inspiration. I adopted the same pose as the Real Madrid forward, shirtless, with a small towel behind my neck.

Later in the evening, I posted what was going to be my final Instagram picture. I placed my picture next to Ronaldo's. We were standing shoulder-to-shoulder against the same background.

I added a caption: ME & RONALDO

Likes started pouring in.

ANDRÉ, NOVEMBER 28

The previous day I had emailed a link to my stripping video to some contacts in the media. *The Telegraph* was interested in the story and so was the *Huffington Post*.

CARL, NOVEMBER 29

I kept receiving advice from the media strategist. He was one of the most notorious PR gurus in Sweden. He had pulled a series of successful pranks in the past. He had invented a fake political party, run a blog about a fictional suicidal teenage girl, and made the leader of the feminist party burn 1,000 hundred-krona bills on a barbecue.

He said that the phone was going to start ringing in the evening after *The Telegraph* and *Huffington Post* came out with their stories about André's striptease.

ANDRÉ, NOVEMBER 29

In the morning, I waited for my piece to appear on the *Huffington Post*. I refreshed my browser every few minutes. When it finally materialized, I started checking *The Telegraph*. Soon it popped up there too, and I tweeted about both stories.

I sat in a café the entire morning drinking coffee and emailing every editor and journalist I could think of. Carl was in Stockholm doing the same thing. We searched for people who had written about Iskra Lawrence's stunt and sent them messages as well. I would normally be coy about contacting people out of the blue. But today, I was in shameless self-promotion mode. I was forcing people to look at pictures of me on the tube in my underwear, and I didn't care. The mission of the month was to attract attention, and I was determined I was going to make that happen.

By about 3:00 p.m., it became clear that my story wasn't going viral. I couldn't understand why. It had all the characteristics of a shareable story. But people didn't seem interested. Did I need to do something more, or was this the best I could hope for?

CARL, NOVEMBER 30

Had I become better looking? It was time to put another post on Reddit's rate-my-appearance subreddit.

> *Extreme makeover. New chin line (7 ml restylane), new hair cut and color, and new body. I posted my pictures here one month ago. The reception was lukewarm. What do you think now? Any improvements? (note: some shirtless pictures, taken by professional photographer)*

In the evening I had received some feedback

> *Nice hair, eyes, and body overall 7.5/10*
> *Grats on the transformation*

Sexy. 7.5/10
Your jaw looks great.
Before 5, now 6

I was just about to switch off the bedside light on this, the final night of a long month dedicated to seeking attention, when my phone started to flash repeatedly. It was my 10,000 followers order on Instagram that had finally come through. Followers were pouring in, by the hundreds.

I turned the phone upside-down, switched off the vibrate setting, and went to sleep. As November turned into December, all I could see was a muted blinking light, indicating my Instagram presence was finally being boosted.

ANDRÉ, NOVEMBER 30

Carl's guerilla PR guru was right—the story was starting to be shared now. When I woke up, I found an email from someone who worked at ITV, a national TV network. They wanted me to come in for an interview on the evening news. When I switched over to Twitter, I noticed that Iskra Lawrence had retweeted the piece. She had also written a long response. The YouTube views of my video were now up to 7,000.

I searched the web and found a site in the US that had written about my stunt, saying I looked pudgy, like someone who "licks the Cheeto dust" off my fingers. But the author added that I was "the hero we need in an age where people take themselves too seriously." This attention prompted me to start obsessively scouring the web for coverage of my story. All I wanted was more: more likes, more comments, more shares. The attention I was getting was never enough.

In the afternoon, I began preparing for my interview on the evening news. My plan was to act like a serious professor. But Carl had other ideas.

"Why don't you copy FEMEN?" he said.

"FEMEN?"

"You know, the feminists who flash their breasts as a form of protest. You could launch a male version of that and strip on TV. Maybe write something on your chest? I spoke with the guerilla PR guru. He thinks that would be a great idea."

I wasn't sold on the idea of stripping on the evening news, but I guess this was the last act of the year. What the fuck, I'd give it a go.

As I walked through the graffiti-covered backstreets, I tried to picture what would happen next. I'd walk into my office and find someone to write on my chest with a black marker pen. The message: #MenFem. *Every BODY is beautiful.* I'd head over to the ITV studios, mic up, and when I was asked a question by the interviewer, I'd calmly explain why I dropped my trousers on the underground. At the right moment, I would take off my shirt and reveal my hidden message. Who knew what would happen after that?

I was sitting in my office with a marker pen in hand, ready to have the message written on my chest, when the phone rang. "Hiya, is that André Spicer?" a young woman said.

"Yes," I replied.

"It's ITV news. You were booked to do an interview today."

"Yes."

"Well, we don't need you anymore."

"What?"

"Yeah, today's been crazy, hahaha!"

I went silent.

"Anyway, maybe next time. Byeee!"

As the phone clicked, two familiar emotions welled up: disappointment and relief.

DECEMBER

MEANING

CARL, DECEMBER 1

The year was coming to an end, and it was time to figure out what the hell we had been up to. We had deliberately avoided this question. Until now.

I went back to the classic self-help books I had read over the year. What was their purpose? "The object of this book is to help all who seek it," Napoleon Hill wrote in *Think and Grow Rich* from 1937, "to learn the art of changing their minds from failure consciousness to success consciousness."

I found similar advice in Dale Carnegie's *How to Win Friends and Influence People*, published one year earlier, in 1936. "Everybody in the world is seeking happiness—and there is one sure way to find it. That is by controlling your thoughts."

Was I happier now? More successful?

I kept reading. Napoleon Hill explained that the key to becoming successful was to know my purpose, or what he called "Definite Chief Aim." Write it down and repeat it aloud day after day, he instructed, "until these vibrations of sound have reached your subconscious mind."

Did I know what my purpose was?

Napoleon Hill said I needed to know what I wanted to achieve, to get that image into my head, and to keep it there until it was brought to life. If I wanted to become rich, I had to envision myself as rich. If I wanted to become Tim Ferriss, I had to picture myself in his clothes.

The truth was that I still had no clue what I wanted to achieve or who I wanted to be. No images came to mind. Was that my condition? Imageless. Visionless. Purposeless.

ANDRÉ, DECEMBER 2

According to a paper published in the *Review of General Psychology* by two psychology professors, meaning in life (or MIL, as they called it) was made up of a sense of purpose, understanding, and a sense that one's life matters.

The two psychologists had also developed a scale to measure your MIL score. After putting a number between 1 and 7 next to questions like "My life makes sense," "I have certain aims which are worth striving for," and "I am certain my life is important," I added up the score. Mine was 64 out of 105. Not that high. I had a good level of understanding (26/35) and purpose (28/35), but I didn't seem to think that any of it really mattered (10/35).

After I put down my pen and reviewed my scores again, I wondered what this test might have to say about this year. On a scale from 1–7, how much did I comprehend what had happened? 3. Did this year have a purpose? 7. Final question: Did this year matter in the broad scheme of things? 2.

So there was my answer. I knew the purpose of this year, but I had little idea about what actually happened and even less of an idea about why it mattered.

CARL, DECEMBER 3

Today, I received an email from the literary agent we sent our thriller to.

My "failure consciousness" proved right. They said they liked it, but that it wasn't right for them—not at this particular time. A polite dismissal.

I didn't feel disappointed. I didn't feel anything. Just one more failure to add to the list. Now I had two unpublished books on my hard drive.

It felt like a Beckett play. Beckett's classic phrase ("Try again. Fail again. Fail better.") came to mind. But I should not despair. According to an article published in *Slate*, this had become a new catchphrase in Silicon Valley.

I was confused now.

Had the self-improvement industry replaced the ideals of success with failure? And when did Beckett become a self-help guru? Was there nothing that the self-improvement industry could not absorb?

ANDRÉ, DECEMBER 5

I was in my office, looking at all the piles of unloved books that sat around me, when the phone rang. It was Carl. He wanted us to talk about our story. About how it had all begun.

We were going far back in time. It was almost two years ago when we first talked about doing a book together. The initial plan was to use two semi-fictitious alter egos. I found the synopsis on my computer and started reading.

"This is how we described our respective characters," I said.

"Here's you: 'Carl's character will be a lofty philosopher. Carl experiments with smart drugs and digital implants, trying to find deeper meaning in his endeavors, describing them as moments of Heideggerian authenticity.'"

Carl began laughing. "I am not sure I've experienced moments of Heideggerian authenticity this year."

"And here's me: 'André's character is the opportunistic business school professor. He will wake up early in the morning, run ten kilometers, and post the details of his run on Facebook. Later in the day he'll do a presentation for an investment bank, telling them about the advantages of tracking the movements of their employees.'"

Carl was laughing again. "Sounds like what you tried to do, last month, when you wanted to become a self-help guru."

I said nothing.

Carl had stopped laughing now. "When did we decide to do it over the course of a whole year?"

"Don't you remember?"

"No."

"We were walking to the Portland Place tube station."

"Mm-hm."

"I said we should start the book with you waking up in Stockholm, on New Year's Day. It would be cold, dark, and depressing. And you would vow to change your life."

"Okay."

"And I would agree to do the same thing. Then we'd spend the whole year trying to do just that. And the final scene would be on New Year's Eve. Once again, it'd be cold, dark, and depressing. We had tried our best to improve our lives. But everything had gone to hell."

Carl was silent.

"Listen here." I had found a document on my hard drive. Title: book plan. Date: 20 November 2015. A long list of things we planned to do. I read out the challenges we planned each month: "January: Finish a book each. February: Carl: gym, André: marathon. March: Carl: French. André: coding. April: Mend our relationship. May: Get a modeling gig."

"Modeling gig?"

"This was before we decided to spend May on spirituality."

"And June?"

"There's just a big question mark next to the word sex."

Carl was laughing. I guess the question mark was still there.

I continued, "July: Hang out in Italy and increase happiness score. August: Mount art show, travel in California. September: Make as much money as possible by pitching best-selling thriller. October: Being good."

"I think that was my worst month."

"November: Become famous and gain loads of Twitter followers."

"I bought 10,000 followers on Instagram, and you had 10,000 people watch that video where you were naked on a train."

"December: There's another big question mark."

"That's what we have to figure out now."

CARL, DECEMBER 6

I had our US publisher, Colin, on the phone, hoping to gain some clarity from him.

"What would you say is the meaning of this project?" I asked.

"Well, you could read the project as a diagnosis of our time. We live in a society of stasis. We feel we can't change things around us, but we can still change ourselves," said Colin.

"True. Would you say the project is self-obsessed?" I asked.

"Yes, of course. Extremely self-centered."

I said nothing.

"But then you undercut that with failure. You seem to be wounding the ego more than boosting it," he said.

"Yes, that's right. It's been self-obsessive. But even more self-effacing."

Then I said: "Sometimes I wonder whether this project was sincere."

"Well, you never thought this would be successful, did you?"

"Probably not."

"It was a battle against impossible odds. You were doing it to prove it was not possible. But also, to investigate the process."

"True."

"And what about you and André?"

"What about us?"

"Your relationship far exceeds a professional one."

"I still have to work that out."

"Maybe it's a project about friendship?"

ANDRÉ, DECEMBER 7

Why hadn't I seen this before?

I was flicking through Gretchen Rubin's best-selling book, The Happiness Project, from 2011. A colleague had mentioned it about a month ago, saying it reminded him of our project, but it was not until now that I had actually checked it out. Looking through the table of contents, I was stunned. It looked identical to what we had done. Each month was dedicated to one aspect of her life. January was about energy, February marriage, March work, April parenthood. Reading on, I ticked off the many activities we had both undertaken. My heart was beginning to sink. I skyped Carl.

"Have you seen Rubin's book?" I asked.

"No. Who?"

"Gretchen Rubin. It's called *The Happiness Project*. Have a look," I said and sent a link.

"Got it." He was silent for a moment. Then I heard him sigh. "Fuck me!"

"I know. Have we wasted the year?" I asked. "Are we just rewriting a book that already exists?"

"I don't know. Let me call you back in two hours," Carl said, and hung up.

Waiting for Carl to Skype back I started looking for other books that might be similar to ours. As an academic, this was something I would normally do before starting a new research project. But this project was different. We were supposed to be clueless. But maybe not *this* clueless.

Within a few minutes I found a person called A. J. Jacobs. *Fuck!* His entire life seemed to be an experiment. There was one book where he tried to become the smartest man in the world, another one where he wanted to improve himself, and a third where he lived according to the Bible, which was exactly what I had been doing in May, albeit only for one week.

I kept looking, and I kept finding books that resembled ours. There was one called *Promise Land: My Journey Through America's Self-Help*

Culture by Jessica Lamb-Shapiro, which was described as a personal journey through the "eccentric and labyrinthine world of self-help." Then there was a book called *Living Oprah: My One-Year Experiment to Live as TV's Most Influential Guru Advises*. It was by a woman who spent a year doing everything that Oprah Winfrey recommended. If she was having relationship problems with her husband, she turned to *O* magazine for advice. If Oprah mentioned a new album on her TV show, she went out to buy it.

Two hours later, Carl was back on Skype.

"No need to worry," he said. "Our book is entirely different from Gretchen Rubin's."

"How?"

"Her aim was to actually become happier. It's very earnest. That wasn't really what we wanted."

"No?" I said. "What did we want, then?"

Carl was silent.

"Well, not that," he said eventually.

"Look, I found a few other books." I said, and read out the list of books I had just found.

"Never heard of them."

"Is this a problem?"

"I can't see how," he said. "It makes no difference now. We've done what we've done."

Carl's response was vacuous. Yet I found it strangely convincing. It reminded me of what I had learned at Landmark. *What is, is. What ain't, ain't.*

CARL, DECEMBER 7

What does your wife say about this?

Over the last year, I had been asked this question more times than I could count. I always responded in the same way: she's sick and tired of being asked that question.

But now we were in a restaurant, just the two of us, and I wanted to ask her precisely this question.

"It's been a lot of focus on you. Obviously."

"Has it been difficult?"

"The most difficult thing has been your relationship with André."

"How so?"

"One day, you're best buddies, and you're telling me what he's done. The next day, you hate him and say you want nothing to do with him. You're like two teenage girls."

I wanted to change the topic. I had spoken enough about my relationship with André already.

"Do you think I've become a better person?"

"Are you serious?"

"Yes. Some people have asked me this question. I still don't know how to respond. I'd be interested in your view."

"No. You've not become a better person. Well, maybe now, at least you know that you're not a good person."

It was a fair point. I had saved money to donate to charity and instead spent it on plastic surgery. After that, it'd be hard for me to claim that I was a good person.

We were talking about the year, which was now coming to an end. Despite my mood-swings and strange commitments, we agreed it had been a good year. Lots of things had happened. We were going to have another child. We were in love. And we were happy together.

"This project. Would you say it's been sincere?" I asked.

Sally laughed. I was waiting for a response. Instead she carried on laughing.

ANDRÉ, DECEMBER 8

The night was beginning to draw in as I walked into a familiar pub in Bethnal Green. Peter was sitting in his usual spot, hidden behind a pint of Polish lager and a copy of the *London Review of Books*. I had known Peter for nearly twenty years, and he was one of my closest friends. Since he attended my graduation from Landmark in January, I had kept him up to date with the project. If anyone could help me figure out the meaning of what we'd been up to, it was him.

"So you know I'm nearly at the end of this project now," I said.

"Thank god, I'm sick of hearing about it."

"Yeah, well, I want to ask you something. Seriously, what do you think this whole thing has been about?"

He took the last slug of his pint.

"It's really about two things."

I could tell he'd been thinking about this for a while.

"Number one: you guys are two frustrated professors who are trying to escape your narrow academic world."

I nodded.

"Number two: this whole thing is like a social science version of S&M."

"How's that?" I asked.

"Well, Carl seems to dole out all sorts of punishments."

"Like what?"

"Didn't he tell you to strip on the tube and then share the video? And what about you giving a speech about why you're an asshole at Speakers' Corner?"

"Yeah, but those were my ideas."

"But you spent the entire year complaining that you felt guilty because you weren't living up to Carl's expectations of you."

"I guess so."

"You know what I think? You wanted to feel guilty. You enjoyed your punishments. Just like some people enjoy getting whipped by a mistress in leather for being a naughty boy, you enjoy feeling guilt."

As I walked back home, it struck me that it wasn't just me feeling this way. The whole culture of self-improvement seemed to thrive on guilt. Even people who had done an Ironman felt guilty, as though they had not done enough.

And the flip-side to this seemed to be control. To get rid of the guilt, you tried to control your entire life: when to wake up, what to eat, who to talk with, how to move your body.

I was sick of waking up every new month knowing I had to change my life. And I was sick of feeling guilty all the time because my life wasn't changing.

CARL, DECEMBER 8

I was ill again, in bed, reading through my diaries. Back in July, I had learned from the book *How to Be Idle* that being ill was a "delightful way to recapture lost idling time."

As I read through the months, I was struck by the machine-like feel to this year. This was my new life, expressed in numbers. When working: five milligrams dexamphetamine, ten Pomodoros (twenty-five-minute bursts followed by five-minute breaks). When eating: 2,242 calories (100.6 grams carbs, 117.1 grams fat, 114.7 grams protein). When exercising: five days of lifting weights, two days of rest (three sets of six reps back squats on eighty kilograms alternated with twenty seconds on the rowing machine, followed by ten seconds of rest, repeated eight times). When sleeping: seven hours and six minutes (deep sleep: one hour, thirteen minutes; REM sleep: one hour fifty-eight minutes; light sleep: three hours, fifty-five minutes). When masturbating: minimum twenty minutes (use lubricants, avoid pornography). Searching for a job: make twenty phone calls in the morning. Improving your looks: seven milliliters of Restylane.

"How do we acquire the courage to live as a set of numbers?" Mark Greif asked in his book *Against Everything*. Counting yourself, he explained, produced an anxious freedom. "Here are numbers you can change." All you need is "willpower and sufficient discipline." Straighten yourself to a rule, and "you will be changed."

Was it this quantified willpower that made self-improvement so attractive to people? I'd be lying if I said that the year was just a meaningless experiment. All these apps and techniques had helped me achieve things I had previously thought impossible. Constantly pushing myself outside my comfort zone had paid off, whether I was memorizing digits, writing a thriller, or learning French. Looking back, my spontaneous feelings as I thought about the year were pride and surprise. I was proud that I had persevered and gone through with these things. And I was surprised that so many self-improvement techniques actually worked.

But I was not sure what was left of "me" here. Much of what had been achieved had come through renouncing my own self. Had I willingly turned myself into a machine, like André said that Murakami tried to do? He pushed himself to keep running and said to himself: *I'm not a human. I'm a piece of machinery. I don't need to feel a thing. Just forge on ahead.*

ANDRÉ, DECEMBER 10

It was past midnight, and I had unfinished business to attend to. His name was Lucian Luper. This dude was still hanging around, like a guest who'd outstayed his welcome. There was only one thing for it. Lucian had to die.

I had found the perfect place: a small convenience store that sold beer and vodka to passing drunks. Two bored Indian guys lurked behind the counter.

"Excuse me," I said to one of them. "I wonder if you could help me. What I would like to do is to lie down there." I pointed to a spot of worn floor next to a huge open refrigerator full of beer. "I'll pretend to be dead. All I want you to do is to film me."

He looked unimpressed.

"I can pay you," I added.

"Okay, I've got nothing better to do," he replied.

I handed him my phone, lay down on the floor and closed my eyes.

It felt serene down there. All I could hear was the hum of the fridge. I lay flat on my back for a minute or two. Was this the sense of tranquility that Epicurus had said we should strive for? The last time I had felt this relaxed was when sitting cross-legged on top of a mountain in Scotland.

Then my peace was interrupted.

"Mate. Mate! Mate!." A hand on my shoulder. "Mate!" I could hear the shopkeepers laughing. I stayed still. The shaking grew more violent.

"Mate, are you all right?" I opened my eyes and slowly drew my body up. Three young men dressed in tuxedos looked at me with horror and relief.

"Don't worry," I said. "I was just practicing being dead."

"Well, lucky you're all right," one said. "We're medical students. We thought we'd have to save you or something."

"Well, you did the right thing," I said, getting to my feet.

The shopkeeper handed me my phone.

"Thanks," I said. "Here's a fiver."

"No, keep it," he replied, "it was a funny prank."

Walking the rest of the way home, I started to ask myself whether this entire year had been one bad prank after another? Had it been nothing more than *Jackass* meets self-help?

CARL, DECEMBER 10

As much as I appreciated the techniques and apps, there was still something about the cult of self-improvement that rubbed me the wrong way. To understand why, I went back to some of the self-help classics.

"There are millions of people who believe themselves "doomed" to poverty and failure," Napoleon Hill wrote in *Think and Grow Rich*. This belief was delusional, he said. No one was doomed. We were all creators of our own lives. We could all be rich and successful.

This thought should be appealing to someone like myself. I was a white man in my mid-thirties living in a rich country. I had a house and a job and a family. I had savings and friends and traveled frequently. According to Napoleon Hill, I deserved it. My position was not a result of my circumstances. It was the result of my infinite thought power and unswerving belief in myself.

"We are what we are, because of the vibrations of thought which we pick up and register," Napoleon Hill wrote in the late 1930s. I was amazed that this kind of mumbo-jumbo was still in vogue. Rhonda Byrne, in her best-selling self-help book, *The Secret*, from 2006, made exactly the same point: "Your thoughts are the primary cause of everything." If you were poor it was your fault. If you were dying of cancer it was your fault. If you died in a natural catastrophe it was also your fault.

After the 2004 tsunami in the Indian Ocean, which killed close to 300,000 people, a journalist pushed Byrne on the issue, asking if these people were really victims of their own negative thoughts. Her reply: "they had to be on the same frequency as the event."

ANDRÉ, DECEMBER 11

Carl wanted some pictures for his PowerPoint presentation. I opened the photo folder on my phone. The first photo of the year I found was my face, in the light of a hotel room. I had a beard, tousled hair, and huge bags under my eyes. A failed human being. I swiped right. Up next was a picture of me at my computer keyboard. Me wearing running clothes. Me having my brain hacked. Me meditating on top of a mountain. Me trying to pick up women. Me eating meat. Me at the comedy club. Me trading. Me contemplating. Me in underwear on the tube.

Me. Me. Me.

There must be hundreds of selfies on my phone from this year. Some said the 1970s was the decade of me. Judging from my photo reel, 2016 was *my* year of me.

Or was it? I could not think of another year I spent more of my time doing things that were *not* me at all. It wasn't really me who tried to become a pick-up artist. It wasn't me who bought seats from commuters on the tube. It wasn't me who went on an all junk-food diet and then spent an entire week playing video games.

If it wasn't me, who was it then?

"What do you think the meaning of this project is?" I asked my Swedish publishers, Lawen and Richard, as we sat in a restaurant waiting to order.

"I don't know, what do you think?" Lawen replied. I began laying out my theory.

"When trying to make sense of this, I just end up in a series of paradoxes?"

"Such as?"

"Optimizing yourself seems like the most self-obsessive thing you could do."

"Right," she said.

"And at the same time, it seems to be completely self-effacing. I spent last month looking at pictures on Instagram. An endless series of full-body selfies from gyms. This seems like the pinnacle of narcissism."

"Right."

"But to get that body you need to work extremely hard, spend every day in the gym, and commit yourself to an extreme diet. It seems like the ultimate expression of masochism. Self-harm and self-adoration at the same time."

"But narcissism is both self-love and self-hate, isn't it?" Richard intervened.

"But I want to ask you. Why do you think we've done this? What's the point?" I took a bite of the fish, hoping to receive a long and elaborate theory. But instead Richard laughed. He was like a sly therapist, not offering any answers.

"Okay, so here's another paradox," I said. "It's all about the fantasy of transformation, right?"

"Right."

"You want to transform yourself into someone else. Someone better than yourself. But the transformation you're able to achieve is minimal."

"How so?"

"I gained fourteen kilos. Still, when taking pictures of my body, I looked the same as always."

My dining companions had finished their meals. My food was still practically untouched.

"I did everything to improve my looks. I dyed my hair, waxed my chest, bleached my teeth, spray-tanned myself, had plastic surgery. And when I was done, posting before-and-after pictures, someone said that I had gone from a 5 to a 6 on a scale from 1 to 10."

The waiter cleared the table and brought coffee.

"Sorry to keep asking, but what do you think the meaning of the project is?"

Richard took out his phone. He had taken notes.

"I think you've answered it yourself," he said and read out his notes, repeating the theories I had developed over the last hour instead of eating my food.

ANDRÉ, DECEMBER 14

"Thanks for coming along," I said, scanning the forty or so colleagues in front of me. "As some of you know, I have spent this entire year trying to optimize myself."

I took the audience through my experiences.

"And now it's December," I said. "And along with Carl, I'm trying to work out what it all means. I want to hear what you think."

A few hands shot up in the air.

"Were you really able to learn about these different worlds in such a short period of time?" a doctoral student asked.

I shuffled my papers. "Any anthropologist will tell you it takes at least a year to learn something meaningful about a culture. We spent a month on each area. But we spent an entire year studying the wider culture of self-improvement. It's the culture many middle-aged, middle-class people in the West inhabit today. It's a culture based around rituals of obsessive self-improvement. And the aim is the same as rituals in any other culture—to show that you are a good member of that community. The more time you spend on that ritual, the higher status you have in that community. So, running five kilometers makes you a self-improvement pleb. Running a half marathon is okay. A marathon shows you're trying. But if you spend the thousands of hours and thousands of dollars it takes to run a hundred kilometer ultramarathon, well, then you really are someone!"

"Yes," I said, pointing at another raised hand.

"Can you really get a good perspective on a culture if you only get a glimpse of it? Aren't you simply tourists?" she asked.

She was right, of course, but it seemed strange to say that we hadn't done enough when two of us had devoted our lives to the project for an entire year.

A senior professor in the department came to the rescue:

"You might have been a tourist, but this whole world of self-improvement is full of tourists."

· I nodded. "That's right. Most people seeking to improve themselves do many different activities at once and rarely fully commit to just one."

Another voice cut through: "Does your intention change what you found?"

"I guess our intention from the beginning was to write a book." I explained. "But I had genuinely hoped to achieve the goals I set for myself each month, and I felt devastated when I didn't live up to them. There were times when I completely lost sight of the fact that I was writing a book about this."

One of my doctoral students hesitantly raised her hand, and smiled.

"Isn't this a book about a midlife crisis," she said. "It could be sold to forty-year-olds so they can read about a midlife crisis instead of actually having one themselves."

"Or maybe it is a guidebook on how to have one," someone else added from the floor.

I was on the third floor of the Stockholm Culture House, on stage, facing an audience of over a hundred people. In the front row was an old friend I had not seen for ages. A few rows behind her was a group of my friends who had come there together. At the back of the room, I could see my parents, next to Sally and Esther and my mother-in-law.

I wanted the project to be taken seriously. I wanted it to seem sincere. I wanted the audience to understand that this was not an elaborate joke.

I talked through the months one by one, systematically, showing pictures and describing what we had done. I had worked on the script for days. The presentation contained more than one hundred pictures.

As I reached December, I said that this was where I was now at the present moment, and that I'd want to use the rest of the time to explore the meaning of the project.

Jenny, who had agreed to be the moderator, came up on stage and asked a series of questions. Then it was time for the audience to pose questions. I had been looking forward to this moment. Maybe they could help me figure out the meaning of this project.

"We have a question here." Jenny pointed at a man in the front row. He was given a microphone.

"I was wondering what you've continued over the year and what you've stopped doing?"

"I stopped using the wearables. I stopped using most of the apps. But I've kept using the Pomodoro technique, and I still use the smart drugs. And what else? Yes, I'm still doing CrossFit."

"And another question there," Jenny pointed to another man, farther back in the room.

"So, of all the stuff you've tried, what could you recommend?"

It was the same question again, but I tried to give a more elaborate answer this time, assessing and evaluating a range of methods and techniques.

"I have to intervene here," Jenny said and turned to me. "As you answer these questions, isn't there a danger you will become a self-help guru yourself?"

"Er, yes," I said.

The questions kept coming. But all I could think of was Jenny's remark. Had I spent a year exploring the world of self-improvement only to become another expert, a fairly mediocre one, telling people to download Pomodoro apps? Was this it?

ANDRÉ, DECEMBER 15

How much money have you spent on this project?

This was a question I had been asked on several occasions this year. Each time I had brushed it aside, since I preferred not to know. But now it was time to find out, so I sat down and totted up the cost of all those gadgets, courses, travel, books and subscriptions. The final figure was over £10,000. I sent off an email asking Carl what his figure was. About £10,000, he replied, adding that Tim Ferriss spent $100,000 dollars each year, testing new self-improvement products.

It was a lot of money. But we were not alone. According to one estimate, the self-improvement market in the US alone is worth nearly $10 billion a year. And this industry is a growing source of employment. Carl and I had met many people whose livelihood depended on self-improvement: life coaches, personal trainers, motivational speakers, doctors, researchers, psychics, yoga instructors, sex educators, plastic surgeons, personal brand managers, and other experts. They weren't all unscrupulous charlatans looking to exploit people's weaknesses. The vast majority were genuinely committed to using their expertise to help their clients.

I began to wonder what it would be like to work in the self-improvement industry. I found a new study of personal trainers in the UK which compared their working lives to serfs. Instead of being bonded to a landlord, they were bonded to a gym. The trainers could never be certain of their income, and they had to work hard just to break even. These trainers described how they looked forward to January each year, when people's New Year's resolutions brought them back to the gyms. As other sources of employment dried up, working in the gym was one of the few career options open. The personal trainer's parents had probably once worked in hard physical jobs, making things in factories. Now, their progeny continued to do hard physical work, but instead of making things, they shaped other people's bodies.

Then I came across another study about the future of employment by researchers at Oxford University. Many jobs were being automated out of existence, but not those in the self-improvement industry. They were expected to continue growing.

Had this year given us a peek into the workplace of the future? A workplace where people had highly insecure jobs trying to patch up the flagging self-worth of the guilt-ridden middle classes?

CARL, DECEMBER 16

It was late in the evening, and I was waiting for an incoming Skype call. I had scheduled a session with a life coach. His name was Tim.

I had never before thought of speaking to a life coach, but I was aware that the industry was huge, with 50,000 life coaches worldwide making $2 billion in annual revenue. It was designed to help people live "purposefully."

Tim was based in Florida. On his website, I learned that he was the author of seven books, had ten years of life coaching experience, and could help me if I was stuck. Stuck in my life. Stuck in my career. Stuck in finding clarity. I reckoned I needed help with all three.

Tim was in his study, wearing a t-shirt. It was a bright, warm day. I could see the sun sifting in through the window. Quite a contrast to Stockholm in the cold dark of December.

I asked Tim why he thought so many people spent so much time and money on self-improvement.

"The problem is that these people have not understood what is driving their behavior."

"What do you mean?"

"They're just looking for a quick fix. They feel their lives are shit. And they think it will all be fixed if they can locate the cause."

"You mean they invent the causes?"

"Yes. They think their life is shit because they're not productive enough, or because they don't have the right car, or whatever. And they think they have to get that, and then they'll get happy."

"This reminds me of last month," I said. "I was trying to optimize my looks and posted selfies on Instagram. I was struck by the sacrifices people went through to get the perfect body."

"It's an addiction."

"Addiction?"

"People get addicted to this stuff. They set a goal, and immediately after they meet that goal, they set another one. They want to gain five kilos of muscles. Then ten. Then twenty. And they get addicted to rewards. It's chemical."

"You know, I had plastic surgery last month. Immediately afterward I began to see other blemishes. I have this small wart on my forehead. I never thought of it before. Now I find it really annoying."

"This is what saddens me about my occupation. A lot of people come into this industry without knowing why. They get in touch with a life coach hoping to find a cure. They're suffering from bad self-confidence. Regrettably, many of my colleagues take advantage of that."

After we hung up, I continued thinking about the desire to improve oneself. Was it all driven by bad self-confidence? The inability to accept one's own limitations?

ANDRÉ, DECEMBER 17

Browsing through Twitter, I noticed a picture of a huge, muscular man in the pose of Rodin's thinker, pretending to read a book. I didn't know who he was, but I recognized the book. It was Tim Ferriss's brand new 700-page tome, *Tools for Titans*. The cover looked like a box for those muscle-building diet supplements that Carl took. I downloaded it immediately.

It turned out to be a twenty-first-century version of the Whole Earth Catalog for gym-going entrepreneurs. Instead of giving tips about how to build a composting toilet, it outlined how to do the perfect sit-up.

According to one report, 70 percent of self-help consumers are women. One way to grow the industry was to extend the appeal to men. And that was what Ferriss had done. His audience was 84 percent male. Maybe he was following Coke's marketing playbook. When the company realized that men would not drink Diet Coke because they thought it was too feminine, they put a similar product in a black can and called it Coke Zero. Only then did men start to drink it. Maybe Tim Ferriss was the Coke Zero of self-improvement?

Seeking to test out my new hypothesis, I dipped into the book. Ferriss described in the preface how he spent his mornings writing in his Parisian apartment and then headed out to the banks of the Seine in the afternoon, where he'd sit with creative writing students discussing their work. I couldn't help imagining that the students were all attractive young women. What Ferriss described was a classic middle-aged male fantasy. Wasn't it close to what Carl spent his summer doing?

As I read on, I came across many things that we had tried during the year: fasting, daily meditation, waking up before 5:00 a.m., not complaining for twenty-one days. But there were even more suggestions that we had not tried: taking ice baths, controlling the temperature of one's bed, doing a "real world MBA" with a $125,000 fund that you would invest in business ventures.

After flicking through hundreds of pages of interviews with people like Arnold Schwarzenegger and Rick Rubin, I closed the book. Had we just spent an entire year being a lamer version of Tim Ferriss? Was our whole project just one drawn-out, failed middle-aged male fantasy?

CARL, DECEMBER 19

It was another productive day. The last before the Christmas break. I had spent it with Jenny, at her place, taking dexamphetamine, working in bursts of Pomodoros, and listening to a playlist of ambient music called "deep focus."

To round the day off, we went to a bar for a glass of wine. When Jenny went to the bathroom, I checked my emails. There was one from the academic publisher to whom I had recently sent my book. Jenny came back, and sat down on the stool.

"You know that book I wrote in January?"

"Yes, the academic one. When we began taking the pills."

"Right. It was rejected by the publisher."

"I remember that."

"I sent it to another publisher a few weeks ago. They've responded."

"And?"

"They want it. They want to offer me a contract."

We clinked our glasses together and I drank, feeling happy for once, thinking that I had actually achieved something during the year.

ANDRÉ, DECEMBER 19

Was Carl Tyler? Was I Jack?

I had not seen *Fight Club* for more than ten years, but as it came on, the scenes were all so familiar. The self-help groups, the IKEA catalogue, the insomnia, the porn, the fighting, the ceaseless travel, the shaven-headed men, the locker-room challenges, the increasingly extreme behavior. But what I had not noticed before was how the fight club that Tyler set up had become a kind of model for masculinity more generally. His stoic speeches could have come directly out of the mouth of Tim Ferriss. The fight club HQ Tyler set up in an abandoned building seemed to have been the inspiration for so many CrossFit gyms across the world. Didn't Tyler dress like a pick-up artist and have the same haircut as any number of stoic self-improvement gurus? If this year had been about anything, it was a journey into the world of *Fight Club* stoicism.

After flipping through *Tools for Titans*, I had learned that Tim Ferriss's favorite book was *Letters from a Stoic* by Seneca. He had given hundreds of copies of the book away to people. In these 124 letters, Seneca returned to the question of death again and again. For him, learning how to live was about coming to terms with death.

Based on one of Seneca's letters, Ferriss had developed his favorite thought exercise, which he called "fear setting." It was quite simple: imagine your personal worst-case scenario in detail. No food, no home, no money—that kind of thing. Then for a few days, try to live as if the worst-case had already happened. Go without food, sleep outdoors, live without money.

The tests of endurance that Ferriss described was exactly the kind of tests we both had spent the entire year putting ourselves through. The whole year was like one long personal worst-case scenario in which we both spent twelve months doing some of the things we had hated most: reading self-help books and then following their advice in practice.

Living like this for a year, I had come to appreciate the comforts of my regular life.

CARL, DECEMBER 21

I was having lunch with my old friend Örjan. We were talking about the meaning of the project. After two hours of discussion, we had three theories.

The first was transformation: the fantasy that, if only you tried hard enough, you could turn yourself into someone else. It was an easy motivation to understand. Didn't most people wish they were someone else? Didn't we all, to some degree, want to escape the limitations of who we were?

The second theory was about death. We're all afraid of death, and we're terrified of growing older. Perhaps self-improvement was an escape from death. Plastic surgery slows down aging. Sexual experimentation promises a youthful spirit. Creativity courses help to reinvigorate the mind. And CrossFit keeps the body young and strong.

The third theory was about market value: self-optimization made you fit for work. It promised to make you more productive and give you a competitive edge.

As I was walking back home, I felt I had found some answers. But what was my motivation? Did I nurture a dream about being someone else? Was I afraid of dying? Did I want to boost my market value?

ANDRÉ, DECEMBER 21

Just after midday, my son, Julian, was born. This was the best day of the whole year, and it had absolutely nothing to do with self-improvement.

CARL, DECEMBER 23

It was late in the evening when I skyped Oliver Burkeman. He was at home in New York.

Oliver had spent years investigating the cult of self-improvement, writing a weekly column about it for the *Guardian*. He, if anyone, should be able to help me understand why people would be spending their lives trying to become better, faster, and stronger.

"I think, deep inside, we all want to be Tim Ferriss," he said, half-jokingly. "I don't think this is just about our present culture. I think there's a deeper human impulse. And Tim Ferriss appeals to that."

"But there is something sad about Tim Ferriss." I said. "I listened to a conversation he had with another man. And this man was just talking about how wonderful he thought Tim Ferriss was, listing all the amazing stuff he had done: the books he had written, the languages he had learned, and the challenges he had overcome. And then this guy asked, what will you do next? And Ferriss said that he was planning to make films. It just felt really empty."

Oliver paused. Then he proposed his own theory.

"What's interesting with someone like Ferriss is that he cannot speak about relationships or love. It's all about learning things or mastering stuff. He's completely silent on the question of love."

ANDRÉ, DECEMBER 25

After our Christmas lunch was finished, we pushed our plates aside and opened a second bottle of wine.

I was talking with Robyn, my mother-in-law, who was visiting from Australia.

"I've been following all these things you have been doing this year as part of your project. Are you glad it's over?" she asked.

"Yeah. But I'm starting to wonder what the meaning of it all was."

Robyn usually took these questions seriously.

"You know, I've spent my whole life trying to improve myself," she said.

"Why is that?"

"To justify my existence," she said, and then paused for a second. "And to be accepted."

She took a sip of her wine: "You know, even now I ask myself what's the point of my existence."

"And have you gotten any answers?" I asked.

"I wrote something down the other morning: To live. To love. To work."

"I've spent the whole year trying to track my progress using all these new technologies," I said. "How do you keep track of your progress?"

"Self-reflection," she replied. "I agree with Socrates: the unexamined life is not worth living."

Later, as I cleared the dishes away, I wondered what serious self-examination I had done this year. During Landmark, I had learned that self-reflection is the enemy. An obstacle to action. But now, as we were trying to work out what this all meant, honest self-reflection seemed to be the most difficult task. It meant looking myself squarely in the eyes and asking why, despite all this time and effort, did I still feel like so little had changed.

CARL, DECEMBER 27

I was at André's place, in his new kitchen, admiring little Julian. He was so small and cute, wrapped in a blanket, sleeping in his grandmother's arms. André was roaming around, opening a bottle of champagne, talking loudly, entertaining the guests.

Hours later, when the guests had left and the bottles were empty, we sat down in the lounge.

"You know what I've learned this year?" André slurred.

"No."

"I've learned to appreciate pop music."

André was sipping on a beer, stretched out on his armchair, looking pleased with himself. I had left my family behind in the middle of the holidays to travel to London. Why? Because André had asked me to. We had not seen each other since the summer, when we had lived as hedonists in Italy, and he wanted us to meet one last time before the year was over, to get closure.

And now I was here, in André's living room, listening to him as he explained that, having spent one year trying to optimize every aspect of his life, all he had achieved was a new appreciation for pop music.

ANDRÉ, DECEMBER 28

We sat in a cramped café waiting for breakfast and discussing that pressing question: what the hell was this all about?

"You know, when I presented our project to my colleagues, one of them said it was a thinly disguised midlife crisis," I said, before taking a sip of coffee.

"Yeah, I've heard that before," Carl replied.

"It's easy to dismiss, but maybe there's something in it."

"What's that?"

"Well, according to Elliott Jacques, the guy who coined the term, the average midlife crisis kicks in at thirty-seven."

"Mm-hmm."

"You're thirty-six, I'm thirty-nine, right," I said, and took another hit of coffee. "Elliott Jacques thought that at our age, people have to face up to the fact that a good part of their life has passed them by."

"And face the fact that they'll die one day?" Carl said.

"Exactly."

"So you're saying that this whole project has been about us trying to come to terms with our own deaths?"

"Could be," I said. "But another way to look at it is to see it as a way of confronting what we haven't achieved in our lives. You know, the gap between the dreams we had when we were young and how things actually turned out—our disappointments."

"Okay."

"Yeah," I said, pulling out my phone. "Listen to this. It's Elliott Jacques describing one of his patients suffering a midlife crisis: *For the first time in his life he saw his future as circumscribed . . . he would not be able to accomplish in the span of a single lifetime everything he had desired to do. He could only achieve a finite amount. Much would have to remain unfinished and unrealized.*"

I put my phone down. "Is that us?"

"Maybe," Carl replied. "But isn't self-improvement all about trying to make your dreams into a reality?"

"I guess so. I mean, you got to live your dream of hanging around at the seaside, smoking cigarettes, drinking wine, and writing a thriller."

"Yeah, and you got to live your dream of stripping on the tube."

"Very funny," I said. "Seriously, I think all this self-improvement stuff offers people a way of keeping their illusions alive, despite their disappointing lives. That's why all self-help gurus say things like *hold on to your dreams.*"

CARL, DECEMBER 28

"The fantasy of transformation, the fear of death, and the impulse to improve one's market value," I said, before taking my first sip of a champagne cocktail. "Those are my three explanations of why people get involved in self-improvement."

Dishes were now arriving at our restaurant table.

"I would add one more," André said. "Escape."

"What do you mean?"

"When I was running, I realized this was the best way to escape home and work."

André paused.

"I can think of one more theory," he said.

"What's that?"

"This is what everyone does. Everyone seems to be engaged in this culture, in one way or another. It's also a way for people to connect."

Which was no doubt true. I was thinking about the CrossFit. It was a community. It was the same with the meditation and the new age center. These were places for people to meet, to hang out, to spend time together.

"Do you think we will ever do a project together again?" I asked.

André was eating his dessert, his main course barely touched.

"I don't know," he said.

He paused.

"Doesn't really matter what I think. You don't want to work with me again, anyway."

I was silent.

ANDRÉ, DECEMBER 29

It was lunchtime, and we were sitting in the Morgan Arms, both staring into our pints of beer, saying nothing. It seemed like the last opportunity we had to figure out what this entire year was all about.

"Are there some things that you wish you had done this year, but didn't do?" I asked.

Carl continued looking at his pint. "Not really. Maybe ayahuasca," he said. "I was keen to try it. But maybe it was good not to do it. I don't want the project to be too much about drugs."

He took a sip of his beer. "And you?"

"Plenty," I said.

I could see a frown on Carl's face.

"It seems that we've engaged with this project very differently," he replied.

"How do you mean?"

"For me, every time I've woken up to a new month, I've been thinking that I should use all my time on the project. And for you, it seems to have been about doing enough, just doing the bare minimum."

Now I was angry, too, but I tried to conceal it. Carl downed his beer and we said goodbye. The parting hug was awkward.

As I walked home, one of the final scenes from Tarkovsky's film *Stalker* came to mind. The Stalker, the writer, and the professor had returned from their strange and life-threatening journey to the mysterious Zone. They were standing at the bar where they had begun their journey, saying nothing. The only difference from the opening of the film was that they now had a black dog with them. Maybe the black dog that sat with us, back there in the Morgan Arms, was the resentful silence.

CARL, DECEMBER 30

I was back home in Stockholm, sitting in our kitchen, staring into my computer screen.

"What are you doing?" Sally called from the living room.

"Just writing a letter."

"To who?" Sally was coming into the kitchen. She was trying on a dress for tomorrow. She was stunning. The most beautiful woman I knew.

"To myself."

"Why?"

"André said he wanted me to do it. We will open it when the book comes out."

"What are you writing?"

"I don't know yet. I feel angry."

"Why?"

"I don't really know."

Over the course of the year, André and I had been through more tests than I could recount. We were old friends. Now our friendship was in danger. It was crazy. André had gone through considerable sacrifices: getting nude on the tube, talking at Speakers' Corner, and testing pick-up techniques in bars. Few people would have done these things. And yet I felt angry and disappointed with him.

But what if this was not about André? What if these feelings were the result of my own transformation? Had the year turned me into a self-help fundamentalist with no patience for other people's faults and weaknesses? The core belief of self-improvement is that nothing is impossible if only you try hard enough. Maybe I had fully adopted that mindset, and as a result, I had lost my sympathy for those who didn't think that way.

André often said he wanted to take a realistic approach. I didn't. When he suggested he should run a marathon, I said he should run an Ironman. Whatever he suggested, I always thought it was not enough. I said he could do more and better. No wonder he was feeling guilty.

It was time to think less about myself now. I had kept the world at bay for most of the year. Never before had I read so little news, read so few novels, seen so few films, and spent so little time with friends. When I had written the academic book in a single month, I hardly spoke to anyone. When I trained for my weight-lifting competition, I spent every day in the gym. It was time to open the door, time to let the world in again.

ANDRÉ, DECEMBER 30

My newborn son was wrapped up warmly in his stroller. I sat next to him on a park bench in the cold light of late December, thinking about the year that was just about over. Running through everything that had happened, I kept coming back to one person: Carl.

We had parted on a sour note yesterday. How could that be? We'd been through so much together. Throughout the year, I had been amazed by his consistent ability to keep on pushing himself—as well as me—beyond any reasonable limits. There was no one else I knew who could do that. Sure, I had been annoyed with Carl more times than I cared to remember. His relentless single-mindedness had often worn me down. His need for control had become a source of frustration. But I knew these things were part of the reason we had made it to the end. Alone, I probably would have given up.

As I continued mulling things over, it began to dawn on me that my frustrations were not really about him. Or me. They were actually frustrations with the wider culture of self-improvement. Wasn't this a culture built on the idea that by relentlessly controlling everything in your life, it was possible to become a healthier, wealthier, and smarter person? Didn't it work by constantly making people feel like the only reason they weren't healthier, richer, or more intelligent was that they had not tried enough? Maybe it was the culture of self-improvement I was fed up with. Not Carl.

Looking back at my sleeping son's face, I realized that next year would be quite different.

CARL, DECEMBER 31

We were in Uppsala, at my sister and her husband's place, eating a three-course dinner, celebrating the new year. They had invited two friends.

"Carl, you have to tell them about the project," my brother-in-law said.

"No," I responded, and quickly changed the subject.

Later in the evening, André sent me a text. "We made it," he wrote, "in one way or another."

I went out on the balcony, waiting for the fireworks. I was feeling happy now. I was feeling relieved.

I thought about the ending of *Fight Club*. Edward Norton was standing next to Marla, high up in a skyscraper, looking out the window as explosions went off and the surrounding banks blew up and collapsed.

The sky lit up. It was over now. I would wake up tomorrow, free. No more posting half-nude selfies on the internet. No more plastic surgery. No more fake kindness. No more career counseling. No more sex toys. No more screaming into pillows. No more therapy with André. No more force feeding. No more fasting. No more electric shocks. No more wearables.

It had been a very strange year.

ANDRÉ, DECEMBER 31

With the light slowly bleeding from the sky, I took out my notebook and started scribbling. After filling up a few pages, I noticed a letter poking out the back of my notebook. It was addressed to me. Unopened. The writing was mine. It was the letter I had written six months ago while I was at the man camp. Now was the moment to take a look.

I hesitated, then carefully opened it and began reading. I had written that this project was a once in a lifetime chance. I signed off with the following phrase, stolen from Rilke:

You must change your life.

BOOKS REFERRED TO

Aristotle, *Nicomachean Ethics*. Oxford University Press, 2002.

Asprey, Dave. *Head Strong: The Bulletproof Plan to Activate Untapped Brain Energy to Work Smarter and Think Faster – in Just Two Weeks*. Harper Wave, 2017.

Aurelius, Marcus. *Meditations*. Oxford University Press, 2013.

Bly, Robert. *Iron John: A Book about Men*. Da Capo Press, 2004.

Bolles, Richard Nelson. *What Color is Your Parachute?: A Practical Manual for Job-hunters and Career Changes*. Ten Speed Press, 1987.

Burnett, Dean. *The Idiot Brain: A Neuroscientist Explains* What Your Head Is Really Up To. Faber, 2016.

Byron, Thomas. *The Dhammapada: The Sayings of the Buddha*. Random House, 2010.

Cain, Susan. *Quiet: The Power of Introverts in a World That Can't Stop Talking*. Broadway Books, 2013.

Carnegie, Dale. *How to Win Friends and Influence People*. Simon and Schuster, 2010.

Chia, Mantak. *The Multi-Orgasmic Man: The Sexual Secrets That Every Man Should Know*. Harper Collins, 2001.

Conze, Edward, ed. *Buddhist Wisdom: Containing the Diamond Sutra and the Heart Sutra*. Vintage, 2001.

Currey, Mason, ed. *Daily Rituals: How Artists Work*. Knopf, 2013.

Deida, David. 'the Way of the Superior Man." *Boulder: Sounds True*, 1997.

Duhigg, Charles. *The Power of Habit: Why We Do What We Do in Life and Business*. Random House, 2012.

Dweck, Carol S. *Mindset: The New Psychology of Success*. Random House, 2006.

Epicurus. *Letter to Menoeceus*.

Ferriss, Timothy. *The 4-hour Work Week: Escape the 9-5, Live Anywhere and Join the New Rich*. Random House, 2011.

Ferriss, Timothy. *Tools for Titans: The Tactics, Routines, and Habits of Billionaires, Icons, and World-Class Performers*. Random House, 2016.

Foer, Joshua. *Moonwalking with Einstein: The Art and Science of Remembering Everything*. Penguin, 2011.

Gotaas, Thor. *Running: A Global History*. Reaktion Books, 2009.

Greif, Mark. *Against Everything: On Dishonest Times*. Verso, 2016.

Hill, Napoleon. *Think and Grow Rich*. Hachette UK, 2011.

Hodgkinson, Tom. *How to Be Idle*. Penguin, 2007.

James, Aaron. *Assholes: A Theory*. Anchor Books, 2014.

Kabat-Zinn, Jon. *Full Catastrophe Living: Using the Wisdom of Your Body and Mind to Face Stress, Pain, and Illness*. Delta, 2009.

Kahneman, Daniel. *Thinking, Fast and Slow*. Macmillan, 2011.

Kama Sutra

King, Stephen. *On Writing: A Memoir of the Craft*. Hachette, 2001.

Kondo, Marie. *The Life Changing Magic of Tidying Up*. Random House, 2014.

Lasch, Christopher. *The Culture of Narcissism*. W. W. Norton, 1979.

Lears, Jackson. *Something for Nothing: Luck in America*. Penguin, 2004.

Levitin, Daniel J. *The Organized Mind: Thinking Straight in the Age of Information Overload*. Penguin, 2014.

Linden, David J. *The Compass of Pleasure: How Our Brains Make Fatty Foods, Orgasm, Exercise, Marijuana, Generosity, Vodka, Learning, and Gambling Feel So Good*. Penguin, 2012.

Lucan, Medlar, et al. *The Decadent Cookbook*. Four Walls, Eight Windows, 1997.

MacAskill, William. *Doing Good Better: A Radical New Way to Make a Difference*. Faber, 2015.

MacFarquhar, Larissa. *Strangers Drowning: Voyages to the Brink of Moral Extremity*. Penguin, 2015.

Mooji. *White Fire: Spiritual Insights and Teachings of Advaita Zen Master Mooji*. Mooji Media Publications, 2014.

Noakes, Timothy. *Lore of Running*. Human Kinetics, 2003.

Palahniuk, Chuck. *Fight Club: a Novel*. WW Norton & Company, 2005.

Parkin, Simon. *Death by Video Games: Tales of Obsession from the Virtual Front Line*. Serpents Tail, 2015.

Pavitt, Neil. *Brainhack: Tips and Tricks to Unleash Your Brain's Full Potential*. John Wiley & Sons, 2016.

Peale, Norman Vincent. *The Power of Positive Thinking*. Random House, 2012.

Plimpton, George. *Shadow Box: An Amateur in the Ring*. Little, Brown, 2016.

Rubin, Jerry. *Growing (Up) at 37*. Rowman & Littlefield, 2014.

Sanders, Jeff. *The 5 AM Miracle: Dominate Your Day Before Breakfast*. Ulysses Press, 2015.

Seneca, *Letters from a Stoic*. Penguin, 2004.

Seibold, Steve. *How Rich People Think*. London House, 2010.

Sheehan, George. *Running & Being: The Total Experience*. Rodale, 2013.

Strauss, Neil. *The Game: Penetrating the Secret Society of Pick Up Artists.* Canongate, 2005.

Strauss, Neil. *The Truth: An Uncomfortable Book about Relationships.* Dey Street Books, 2015.

Tolle, Eckhart. *The Power of Now: A Guide to Spiritual Enlightenment.* New World Library, 2010.

Wacquant, Loïc. *Body & Soul: Notebooks of an Apprentice Boxer.* Oxford: Oxford University Press, 2004.

Whitt, Emily. *Future Sex: A New Kind of Free Love.* Faber, 2017.

ACKNOWLEDGEMENTS

We are grateful to our editor Colin Robinson at OR Books. Thanks to Roland Paulsen, Jenny Jägerfeld, Mikael Holmqvist, Richard Herold, Lawen Mohtadi, and Rhymer Rigby for reading the manuscript and offering helpful advice. Thanks also to the people who appear in the book, not least friends and family, who never asked to be part of this project, but stoically put up with us throughout the year.

ABOUT THE AUTHORS

CARL CEDERSTRÖM is Associate Professor at Stockholm Business School, Stockholm University and the co-author or co-editor of five books. His writing has appeared in *The New York Times, The Guardian, The Atlantic* and *Harvard Business Review*.

Photo © Eva Dahlin

ANDRÉ SPICER is Professor at Cass Business School, City University London and the co-author or co-editor of five books. His writing has appeared in *The Guardian, Financial Times, Times, Independent* and CNN.

Photo © Marc Schlossman

AVAILABLE AT GOOD BOOKSTORES EVERYWHERE
FROM OR BOOKS/COUNTERPOINT PRESS

Beautiful Trouble
A Toolbox for Revolution
ASSEMBLED BY ANDREW BOYD
WITH DAVE OSWALD MITCHELL

Bowie
SIMON CRITCHLEY

Extinction
A Radical History
ASHLEY DAWSON

Black Ops Advertising
Native Ads, Content Marketing, and
the Covert World of the Digital Sell
MARA EINSTEIN

Assuming Boycott
Resistance, Agency, and Cultural
Production
EDITED BY KAREEM ESTEFAN,
CARIN KUONI, AND LAURA
RAICOVICH

**Swords in the Hands of
Children**
Reflections of an American
Revolutionary
JONATHAN LERNER

Folding the Red into the Black
or Developing a Viable *Un*topia for
Human Survival in the 21st Century
WALTER MOSLEY

Inferno
(A Poet's Novel)
EILEEN MYLES

With Ash on Their Faces
Yezidi Women and the Islamic State
CATHY OTTEN

Pocket Piketty
A Handy Guide to *Capital in the
Twenty-first Century*
JESPER ROINE

Ours to Hack and to Own
The Rise of Platform Cooperativism,
A New Vision for the Future of Work
and a Fairer Internet
EDITED BY TREBOR SCHOLZ AND
NATHAN SCHNEIDER

What's Yours Is Mine
Against the Sharing Economy
TOM SLEE

Distributed to the trade by Publishers Group West